THE HISTORY OF STEEPLECHASING

THE HISTORY OF
Steeplechasing

MICHAEL SETH SMITH
PETER WILLETT
ROGER MORTIMER
JOHN LAWRENCE

LONDON
MICHAEL JOSEPH

First published in Great Britain by
MICHAEL JOSEPH LTD
26 Bloomsbury Street
London, W.C.1
1966

PART I: © 1966 *by Michael Seth-Smith*
PART II: © 1966 *by Peter Willett*
PART III: © 1966 *by Roger Mortimer*
PART IV: © 1966 *by John Lawrence*

Printed in Great Britain
by Ebenezer Baylis and Son Limited
the Trinity Press, Worcester, and London
and bound by James Burn, Esher

with her gracious permission
this book is dedicated to
HER MAJESTY QUEEN ELIZABETH
THE QUEEN MOTHER

Thanks are due to Messrs Weatherby
for their unfailingly helpful attitude
in checking information for this book.

Contents

Illustrations

Foreword

By COLONEL HON. E. H. WYNDHAM, M.C.

THIS BOOK commemorates the Centenary of the formation of the National Hunt Committee in 1866. All who are interested in National Hunt racing owe a debt of gratitude to the four authors who have done a great deal of research work in a remarkably short space of time. This story which they tell is gratifying to us of the present generation as it tells of steady progress. It is clear that before the formation of the National Hunt Committee steeple-chasing was a completely lawless sport. In its early days the Com-mittee had a hard struggle to establish its authority and it is perhaps true to say that it is only in the last twenty years or so that National Hunt racing has acquired the degree of prestige that it deserves. As to the improvement in the ethics of the sport today it is almost unknown for anyone to incur the extreme penalty of warning off; in the past it was much more common.

For myself I am grateful that being Chairman of the Centenary Sub-Committee has enabled me to repay in some measure the debt I owe for all the fun I had riding under National Hunt Rules more than half a century ago. My merits as a jockey were I think reasonably assessed in the report I got when I went through the course at The Cavalry School, Netheravon, which, as the elderly may remember, was the forerunner of The Army Equitation School which was at Weedon throughout the inter-war period. As far as I remember the gist of it was that I rode quite nicely on a good horse but was no earthly use on a bad one. In justice to myself I will say that I did once manage to win a small race on a mare who, while you could not call her bad, was not an easy ride, as I had found to my undoing in a previous contest. But I owed such success as I had to one outstanding horse, Another Delight, mentioned by Roger Mortimer in the text.

This brings me to the idea which I wish to put into the minds of all who bother to read this Foreword before tackling the book. Surely the golden essence of National Hunt racing is the happy and harmonious partnership between man and horse without which there can be no true success. I do not believe that any man, however good a horseman he may be, would be capable of getting a horse round a steeplechase course if the animal really disliked the job and was determined not to help in carrying it out. I have no doubt whatever that the horses enjoy the sport as much as we do. I am equally convinced that the experienced ones realize that the object of the exercise is to be first past the post and are pleased when they win and disappointed when they lose. I know that was true of my Another Delight and the completely unanswerable proof of it is Mandarin's amazing win at Auteuil, which only makes sense on the basis that he knew what was expected of him and was determined to carry it out in the face of completely unforeseen and unprecedented difficulties.

And what a wonderful job nature achieved in designing them for speed, endurance and patience to say nothing of designing their backs as such ideal resting places for the human form. No wonder they hold a special place in our hearts.

For myself I know that when, in tragic circumstances, I stood by when the humane killer was put to Another Delight's head I am not at all ashamed to say that I burst into tears.

E. H. WYNDHAM

Caversfield
Bicester
14th December 1965

PART I

Before 1870

By MICHAEL SETH-SMITH

I

ONLY the opening verses of the Book of Genesis have greater impact than the classic introduction 'Once upon a time'. There is nothing definitely established by these words. Much is left to the imagination. A history of steeplechasing ought to begin in this fashion since its birthplace is Ireland. The sport originated from the 'pounding matches' which the Irish gentry held, particularly in Clare, Galway and Roscommon, throughout the eighteenth century. In each contest the leader, decided by lot, would choose as stiff a course across country as he dared. His opponent had to follow or lose by default. Victory went to the one who first 'pounded' his adversary to a standstill. Invariably the race was haphazard and although the pace slow, there were appalling accidents to horse and rider. Eventually it became common practice to decide the matches over an agreed line of country with a tower or church steeple as a landmark to the winning post. In 1752 one of the earliest of these 'steeplechases' occurred when Mr O'Calloghan raced Mr Edmund Blake over a distance of four and a half miles from the church at Buttevant with the spire of St Leger church as the guide.

There were no similar contests in rural England, unsullied by the Industrial Revolution, where the stag and the hare were hunted in forest and woodland. The horses used for the hunt had little speed, but were adept in getting through heavy ground, were safe jumpers, and being capable of enduring fatigue, were soon fit for work even after the most arduous day. With the gradual disappearance of the forests the number of stags declined, and sportsmen discovered the excitement of hunting the fox whom they had been accustomed merely to dig out of his earth. To their surprise they found that the chase was far more exhilarating than stag hunting had ever been. Foxes ran fast in open country and the heavy slow-moving hunters proved inadequate for the needs of riders who now found it necessary to jump stone walls, ditches, hedges and fences. The need was for lighter horses with more speed and the ability to jump quickly. Consequently it became the practice to use thoroughbred sires for the breeding of hunters. It was only natural that the pride of ownership of these horses would lead to rivalry, especially in Leicestershire where the enclosures offered the finest galloping land in England and the fences were enough to daunt all but the bravest. As the preparation for the chase consisted of 'a good blazing fire at six a.m., a splendid buttock of beef, or a venison pasty, with chocolate, besides a jug of old October,' even those whose nerves would not harmonize with Bohea were catered for prior to the day's sport. In the evening, the exploits of their horses—often exaggerated over the dinner table—led to the making of many steeplechase matches by the followers of the Belvoir, the Quorn, the Cottesmore and the Pytchley.

During the last years of the eighteenth century, news of these matches began to be recorded. In March 1790 Mr Loraine Hardy matched his horse for 1,000 gns. against one of the Hon. Mr Willoughby's. The nine mile course was from Melton Mowbray to Dalby Wood. Mr Hardy's valet rode his master's horse and won easily. In the same year the first known contest with more than two competitors was arranged. Sir Gilbert Heathcote, Lord Forester and Mr Charles Meynell rode over an eight-mile Leicestershire course from Barkby Holt to Billesdon Coplow and back again for 100 gns. a side. There were no rules as to gates and roads. Each was to come as he could—in fact Lord Forester was told by Mr Needham of Hungerton, 'I'll save you 100 yards if you'll come through my garden and jump the gate into the road'. All to no avail—Mr Meynell won.

On the last Wednesday of November 1804, three gentlemen raced from Wornack's Lodge to Woodwell, a distance of eight miles. The significance of this race was that it was the first time on which steeplechase riders had worn colours. Mr Bullivant— orange, Mr Day—crimson and Mr Frisby—sky blue. Another match which also took place in 1804 was between two officers of the 5th Light Dragoons, Captains Prescott and Tucker. The race was held near Newcastle-upon-Tyne and is the first military steeplechase. The Midnight Steeplechase reputed to have taken place at Nacton near Ipswich in 1803, so vividly described in the *Sporting Magazine* and illustrated by Henry Alken, is almost certainly a complete hoax, although as late as April 1865 a letter appeared in *Bell's Life* from a gentleman in Suffolk claiming authenticity of the race and stating that the proprietor of the Vine Inn at Wickham Market knew all about it.

During this era the Napoleonic wars were in full fight, and the glamour of becoming dashing cavalry officers appealed to many young gentlemen who might otherwise have spent their life hunting and making steeplechase matches. However, in 1810 at Bedford the first steeplechase over a deliberately constructed three mile course was held. There were eight fences each 4 ft 6 in high with a strong bar at the top. The race was run in heats, but although there were eleven subscribers, only two of them competed. All entries had to produce certificates to the effect that they had been in at the death of three foxes in Leicestershire. It has been claimed that 40,000 spectators watched the race, but since the runners were genuine hunters, it was not strictly the first organized steeplechase race-meeting.

A great number of other matches were recorded prior to 1826. In 1818 for example, two Oxford undergraduates steeplechased twenty-five miles from Chinery Court to Nettlebed. Two years later a race from Hartford Bridge to Mortimer necessitated skirting the Duke of Wellington's Park at Stratfieldsaye. One competitor elected to go round the park one way, whilst his rival went the other. They did not meet for over an hour. The first race in the Beaufort country took place in 1822 between Mr Codrington and Mr Evans. On April Fool's Day the same year an impromptu race was run near Rochester. Various members of the hunt including some officers of the Coldstream Guards met at six a.m. and only when hounds did not appear did they realize the date. Rather than go home befooled they got up a sweepstake and raced across the fields to the village of Chalk. An offer of 300 gns. for the winning horse, Ranter, was refused immediately after the race. Steeplechases of this nature caused much excitement, but there was little enthusiasm for hurdle races, the first of which was held at Durdham Down, Bristol on 2nd April, 1821. It was run in three heats of one mile with five hurdles in each heat. Also in April 1821 was run an astonishing race over a ten-mile course from Sturton Church near Horncastle to Wickenby Church. The country was very heavy and there were 120 jumps. The winner—a mare ridden by Mr Cartwright—completed the distance in forty-five minutes.

All these events were, however, of little importance in the eyes of any except possibly the contestants. The real business of the day was foxhunting. This was of all-absorbing importance. Napoleon, the politics of the day, and other vital issues were ignored. The world centred around Melton Mowbray. The leading figures were Squire Osbaldeston, and Thomas Assheton Smith. Osbaldeston was an almost legendary figure in the world of sport. Born in 1787, he was educated at Eton and Brasenose College, Oxford. Whilst an undergraduate he bought a pack of hounds from the Earl of Jersey. Yet he was no dilettante. His prowess as a cricketer, boxer, athlete and oarsman was exceptional. As a shot he was unrivalled—one of his most phenomenal achievements being to bring down 100 pheasants with 100 shots. From 1817–28 he hunted the Quorn six days a week, before he moved to the Pytchley country. His deeds with horse and hound brought him everlasting fame. He was an enthusiastic racing man, and actively supported steeplechasing,

2

both as owner and rider, taking part in many notable matches. Assheton Smith on the other hand disliked steeplechasing intensely and considered it 'rough' riding. Nevertheless, he sold Radical to Lord Kennedy for 500 gns. for the purpose of the famous match against Captain Ross's Clinker in 1826, over the same course from Barkby Holt to Billesdon Coplow as Mr Meynell had won over in 1792. Assheton Smith remarked as he sold Radical, 'whoever rides him must be as strong as an elephant, as bold as a lion and as quiet as a mouse'. Captain Douglas was chosen. Lord Kennedy suggested to Captain Ross that 'as such an enormous sum was pending on the match, both between themselves and others, he thought it advisable that they should start with as few openings for a wrangle as possible; that in a flat race crossing or jostling was not allowed, but that in this match he thought it would be best that the riders should do just as they pleased'. Ross answered, 'In short, I understand that we may ride over each other and kill each other if we can.' 'Just so,' replied his lordship. Years later Captain Ross wrote to a friend, 'Odd enough, the first jump was a five-barred gate. I lay with Clinker's head about opposite to Douglas' knee. When within forty or fifty yards of the gate I saw clearly that Radical meant to refuse, so, recollecting the bargain, I held Clinker well in hand. Radical, as I expected, when close to the gate turned right across Clinker. I stuck the spurs in, knocked Douglas over the gate, and sent Radical heels over head but lying on this side of it. Douglas did not lose his horse, for the rein was fastened to his wrist, and he was soon mounted again, but it finished the match effectually. I turned round, jumped the corner of the fence, and gained such a lead that he never caught me again.' I suppose, in these days, killing a man in that way would be brought in as 'wilful murder'; not so in 1826, the verdict then would have been 'justifiable homicide'. Until this time no regular course, save at Bedford in 1810, had been laid out. This necessitated the match rider having intimate acquaintance with the country, as well as judgement, knowledge of pace and courage. With the exception of Dick Christian, about whom Captain Becher once said 'If I had Christian's nerve, I would give all I had in the world', there were no 'professionals' who were paid for their services, and in all contests the owners either rode themselves or put up their friends. Contemporary accounts imply that the times for the races were fast, but in reality there was probably little or no exactness in either times or distances. The one certainty is that to these earliest matches, made between fox-hunting men, to ride their best horses across country, steeplechasing owes its evolution.

II

Henry Wright, bookseller and publisher of 51 Haymarket, London, issued his first Steeplechase Calendar in 1845. It is described as a consecutive chronicle of the steeplechasing sport in Great Britain since 1826—the year of the great match over Leicestershire between Clinker and Radical. It lists the number of steeplechase courses used in each year, from the one of 1826, none in the subsequent two years, one again in 1829 and the three in 1830. This is the landmark year in the history of steeplechasing because it includes the inaugural year of the St Albans steeplechase organized by Thomas Coleman. Coleman as a young man worked first for Greathead, who was stud groom to Lord Arthur Wellesley—later Duke of Wellington, then for Wetherall, a Yorkshireman who trained hunters at Cherry Down Lodge, Ascot. The hunters each carrying twelve stone competed in flat race plates for prizes awarded by King George III —the condition being that they had been regularly hunted with His Majesty's hounds. It was Coleman's task to ride these horses in order that they qualified for the races. In 1815, with England rejoicing at Napoleon's downfall, Coleman started training on his own at Brocket Hall—home of Lord Melbourne. For the next five years he won small prizes all over the country before obtaining permission from Lord Verulam to train in the park at Gorhambury near St Albans, where he became a tenant of one of the farmhouses and stables. It is not difficult to believe that during these years Coleman lived much on his wits—and it is highly probable that, where villainy, skulduggery and sharp practice were concerned, he was no better or worse than many of his contemporaries. Certainly he was ambitious, enterprising, understood horses and was a very capable promoter. Not satisfied with his farm-house he next acquired the old Chequers Tavern in St Albans, knocked it down and rebuilt it as the Turf Hotel. The hotel was a great success. Coleman was as astute as a hotelier as he was as a trainer. He provided the best food and wine and in addition baths with hot and cold water—a great innovation in those days. Billiard matches for high stakes were regularly played and one week Squire Osbaldeston lost £3,000. There was stabling for thirty horses. His patrons included General Grosvenor, Mr John Gully, Colonel Charretie and Prince Esterhazy. He was found useful by Lord George Bentinck who from time to time sent him a horse. In return Coleman gave Lord George much valuable information regarding the racing 'underworld'.

In 1830, Coleman who had previously arranged flat races in the locality, stage-managed the first St Albans steeplechase. It has been suggested that the idea of the race came as a result of a dinner held at the Turf Hotel by officers of the 1st Life Guards. If this is so, then Coleman equally certainly would have been cunningly responsible for putting the thoughts into the young soldiers' heads. Naturally the race was enormously popular with the local trades-people who saw it as an opportunity for much profit. At one tavern, the Woolpack, they took £87 in a day. There was such a rush upon all the public houses that many of them had to draw the beer in pails and dip the pots in to serve the people fast enough. A guinea a night was charged for sleeping. Coleman had to satisfy the farmers for running over their land by sending them dozens of wines and spirits. On the morning of the race, Coleman dressed in blue coat and kersey breeches, had a bugle sounded— at which moment the sixteen runners saddled in the paddock of the Turf Hotel, and then proceeded into the street to march up the town three deep in cavalry fashion. The start of the four-mile race—Coleman's idea was two miles out and two miles back—was from Hartlington Church to the obelisk in Wrest Park, Silsoe. The line was on a bend, so that Coleman could start the race, and then cut across to judge the finish. It was his idea that until the last moment none of the riders should know the 'line'. For this reason he concealed men in ditches with flags and only a few moments before the race started were the flags raised to mark the course. The winner of this very successful venture was Lord Ranelagh's grey horse, Wonder, ridden by a Guards officer, Captain MacDowall. Second was Nailer, an Irish horse, ridden by Lord Clanricarde, son-in-law of Canning, and at one time his private secretary. Long before the first St Albans steeplechase Lord Clanricarde had made a name for himself in the steeplechasing world of Ireland. He loved the sport and was an exceptionally good horseman. At a later date, when Parliament was sitting, he was invited to ride in a steeplechase at Bedford. He accepted the invitation, hacked down from London, rode, hacked home and was at Westminster that same evening.

The 1831 meeting was much better organized. The entries were brought to Gorhambury Park the previous week where they did their final training. The conditions of the race were:

'Ten sovereigns each, free for any horse carrying 11 st. 7 lbs., four miles across a line of country within twenty-eight miles of London to be rode by gentlemen, and no person to ride more than 100 yards on any road or lane in the race. The last horse to pay the second horse's stakes. The winner to be sold for 500 sovereigns if demanded within three hours after the race. The stakes on 17th February, and the starting point will be named on the morning of the race. Mr Coleman of the Turf Hotel, St Albans has the entire management of the affair. Mr G. W. Heathcote has consented to act as umpire.'

Moonraker, one of the greatest horses in the early history of steeplechasing, was an easy winner from eleven others. He had caused excitement by a prodigious leap across a lane whilst training for the race, and his victory was not unexpected. Owned by Mr Beardsworth—a prosperous livery stable keeper at Birmingham—his jockey sported the same jacket as had Mr Beardsworth's Birmingham when he won the 1830 St Leger. He had originally been bought with his sinews calloused from working in a water-cart for £35, then sold into the Warwickshire country for £80 and then again for £150. He was described as 'a good galloper, an extraordinary fencer who has been a good deal knocked about and fired, but is still a dangerous horse to bet against'. One of the horses to finish behind Moonraker was Wildboar ridden by young Captain Becher. In accordance with the customs of the day, Wildboar was bled so severely before being taken back to his stables that he died the next day. Another casualty was a Mr Stretfield, badly hurt when his mount fell whilst jumping a gate. One contemporary account claims that he too died the following day, others that he lingered for over a year before finally expiring.

The great drawback to these early steeplechases—many of which were still reported in the local press as 'Flag' races—from the spectator's viewpoint was that unless they were mounted and prepared to dash hither and thither, often jumping the fences themselves, they could see little of the race. This did not matter to the poor inhabitants of St Albans and the surrounding villages for whom the excitement of a day out, seeing the congregated aristocrats and squires, was amply sufficient, irrespective of the result of the race. They cheered every horse and rider, whether he finished first or last. However, from other quarters there was a certain amount of indignation arising against the sport. A sixty-five-year-old fox-hunting man wrote, 'In the chase the little checks that occur give relief to the animal and afford him the opportunity of recovering his wind. Not so in the steeplechase. There a distance of four or five miles is selected, over which the poor beast is ridden at the top of his speed and without a chance of regaining his wind, except by happening to fail at a leap over which his distressed condition was not equal to carry him. A dunghill bred one will give in before he arrives at this state, but the good one, true to his blood, scorns to yield and consequently falls a victim to a heartless and unsportsmanlike barbarity. It is not saying too much to assert that a chase of this description takes more out of a horse than hunting of a whole season. It is a bastard amusement which no true sportsman who values his horse would countenance and the sooner it is out of fashion the better.'

By 1832, the year that Parliament was busy passing the Reform Bill, the St Albans steeplechase was established. The conditions were similar to the previous year, except that the winner was to be sold for £400 and not £500. There were nineteen runners and Squire Osbaldeston was the Umpire. Coleman requested the Squire just before the 'off': 'Do face them for me, Squire. Hold up your head like a colonel and be very decisive.' This was odd advice to give the Squire, famous for his courage and the daring of his many achievements. His chivalry too should not be overlooked. Once prior to the Lincoln country ball he met at dinner the lovely Miss Burton—later Lady Sutton. It so happened that a rival beauty had a nosegay in which was an orchid of exceeding rarity. This attracted general admiration. Miss Burton admired it and was snubbed. Pleading an excuse after dinner, Osbaldeston rode twenty-five miles to the conservatory where the orchid had been grown and brought back another even more exotic specimen for Miss Burton to wear at the supper table. In all he rode for four hours to achieve this gallantry.

The scene on 8th March, the day of the race, is described by Pierce Egan—one of the earliest sporting columnists—in his *Book of Sports*. There should have been nineteen runners, but at the last moment Mr Anderson of Piccadilly was allowed to enter his grey horse. Moonraker, now owned by Mr Elmore, was again the winner. It was a desperately close race, and many, including Squire Osbaldeston, thought that the second, Grimaldi, should have won. In fact assertions were made that Moonraker had gone on the wrong side of one of the flag trees, but the objections were soon withdrawn. So confident was the Squire that he persuaded Mr Elmore to match Moonraker against Grimaldi for 500 sovereigns over Mr Elmore's farm at Harrow five days later— plus fifty sovereigns for making the match! Many onlookers agreed that, conditional to the Squire himself riding Grimaldi, then Moonraker would be beaten. It should be added that the Squire first had to persuade Grimaldi's owner to sell him the horse! On the day of the race, much time was spent arguing over the course—the Squire claiming that Mr Seffert, rider of the hard-pulling Moonraker, knew the line and he did not—and contrary to all steeplechase precedent they and their entourage set off over the course on their hacks. Eventually the race started at four p.m. Osbaldeston chaffed as they went to the start, 'It will be strange if the best man and the best horse in England together should be beaten.' Grimaldi won comfortably but the objections for crossing and counter objections continued for another twenty-four hours until a final ruling that the result should stand was given by a Colonel Anson at Tattersalls. The Elmore family over whose land the race had been run were the best known horse dealers in England. William Elmore who lived in Hampshire was described by the 'Druid' as 'a big man, sensitive and particular upon the subject of dressing—and equally so upon having a beefsteak pudding always ready for him on his return from hunting'. His eldest son, George, was a quiet man who hated steeplechasing. John and Adam, the brothers of George, excelled at buying and selling hunters. For choice the Elmores liked to buy five-and six-year-olds which, having been bred in Yorkshire, had been in the care of Leicestershire and Northamptonshire farmers for about two years.

After George Elmore's death in 1845, Adam maintained part of the family business in Edgware Road, whilst John moved to near Harrow, where he became so obsessed with every aspect of steeplechasing that he rapidly lost interest in everything except the negotiations connected with the purchase and sale of hunters suitable for steeplechasing. In this sphere he had no equal and—although a friend once said, 'If John had done me out of £10,000 I could not have found it in my heart to blame him'—he was immensely popular with the farmers and other dealers. His enthusiasm, like that of Coleman, provided a great stimulus to the sport in its infancy.

The success of the St Albans steeplechase encouraged the spread of similar events. Between 1830 and 1838 the number of meetings increased from three to thirty-nine, even though by 1838 the St Albans steeplechase itself had completely lost all public appeal. The first Vale of Aylesbury steeplechase took place in 1835 at the instigation of a party of hunting men after a Crockford's dinner. It was considered that the wide and deep brooks which intersected the Vale were eminently suitable for a race. A four-mile course was agreed upon between Waddesdon windmill and Aylesbury church. A cup valued at £50 was added to a sweepstake of 20 gns each. The second to save his stake.

Typical of the fixture list is that for March 1838:

Bath (home)	March 1	Grantham	March 14
Bath (open)	,, 4	Haverfordwest	,, 14
Maidstone	,, 6	Burton-on-Trent	,, 18
At Jacksons	,, 7	Trim	,, 18
Pickering	,, 7	Aylesbury	,, 20
Blackburn	,, 8	Long Sutton	,, 21
Banbury	,, 8	Leamington	,, 22
Wexford	,, 11	High Wycombe	,, 26
Nottingham	,, 11	Ashby de la Zouche	,, 26
Norfolk and Suffolk	,, 12	Warwickshire	,, 27
Chatham Garrison	,, 13	Cheltenham	April 4
Burton Constable	,, 13	Abergavenny	,, 4
Northampton	,, 13	Daventry	,, 4

In 1842 there were as many as sixty-six meetings recorded as having taken place throughout the year. Races were highlighted by the fame of horses such as Moonraker, Grimaldi and The Poet —but even more so by the fame of some of the riders—and in particular by Captain Becher. More than any other person, he is the connecting thread between the earliest days of steeplechasing and the emergence of Liverpool as the greatest steeplechase course in the country. His father had retired from the Army in 1791— he held a commission in Her Majesty's 31st Regiment—and began farming in Norfolk. As a boy Becher was taught to ride all kinds of ponies and horses, but was never allowed up on a donkey—his father arguing that if he rode a donkey well he would never be able to manage anything else! On leaving school he got an appointment in the Store-keeping General's department and in that capacity was stationed in Brussels at the time of Waterloo. Later he returned to Norfolk, broke and trained many horses and rode at all local race meetings. He served as a commissioned officer in the Buckinghamshire Yeomanry (the Duke was a distant relative), and did duty near Westminster Abbey at the coronation of King George IV—for which he received a medal. He was given his first mount by Coleman—on a horse called Reuben Butler. For years he made Coleman's Turf Hotel his headquarters, and rode most of Coleman's horses in the famous colours of 'white, red sleeves, black cap'. By 1829 he was riding all over England— sometimes travelling 700 miles in a fortnight. He was equally as brilliant a performer in the evenings at social gatherings as he was throughout the day in the saddle, his favourite tricks being to run

Moonraker with Mr Jesset up. *Painting by G. H. Lapore, 1831. Reproduced by kind permission of Lord Westbury*

PLATE ONE

Liverpool Great National Steeplechase, 1839

PLATE TWO

PLATE THREE

Engraved by J. Harris after F. C. Turner
Reproduced by kind permission of Arthur Ackermann & Son Ltd.

PLATE FOUR

Vanguard with Tom Oliver up. *Painted by Harry Hall, 1839. Reproduced by kind permission of Arthur Ackermann & Son Ltd.*

around a room on the wainscoting without touching the floor, kicking the ceiling, and most amazing of all, imitating the noises of almost every known animal.

In 1834 he won the Northamptonshire steeplechase on a very good horse of Captain Lamb's, named Vivian. The next year, riding Vivian, he won the first Aylesbury steeplechase. Vivian was by an Irish stallion, and had originally been bought in Dublin for 16 gns. On the same horse he once defeated the Marquis of Waterford in a 1,000 gns. match over the Market Harborough country. The Marquis was dissatisfied with the result; Becher promptly retorted, 'I am a poor man but your Lordship shall change horses, and I'll have you back again to where we started, for the same money.'

When he won the 1836 St Albans steeplechase on Grimaldi, the horse dropped dead soon after passing the post. As a souvenir Becher obtained one of the forelegs of the horse which ever afterwards he showed with affection to his friends. His last public ride was at Doncaster in 1847 when he fell off in Cantley fields beyond the hill. His worst accident occurred in his old age after he had given up riding. He was sitting on an old mare who caught her eye in her bridle as she put her head down to feed. Frightened, she reared up and threw Becher who broke his thigh in two places. Almost as a sinecure he was appointed Inspector of Sacks to the Great Northern Railway at Boston in Lincolnshire. He died aged sixty-seven on 11th October 1864. In later life he was described as 'thick-set, a sturdy man with bushy beard and thick grey locks— a shrewd, kindly, rugged face, enlivened by small but bright penetrating eyes. Something very resolute and vigorous about his bearing even in old age.' He used to wear a narrow brimmed hat set rather back on his head. After his death his effects were sold by auction in St Martin's Lane: his lathe, tool chest, fish can, grindstone and his scarlet hunting coat and three velvet caps, his driving whips, his racing saddle and his seven silk jackets. 'These seven,' said the auctioneer, 'have seen many a flourishing day'— whereat a sympathetic broker said "ear, 'ear' and finally got the lot for a crown.

III

As early as 1576 there had been race meetings in the Liverpool area. Every Ascension Day for several years races were held near Crosby over a four-mile course for a silver bell valued at £6.13.4. Two hundred years later racing was re-established in the area but was discontinued for lack of support in 1786. There were no more meetings until 1827 when John Formby, a local landowner, held races at Maghull. Mr Lynn, who owned the Waterloo hotel in Liverpool, and was a leading figure in founding the Waterloo Cup, had an interest at Maghull, renting the grandstand for £40 a year. However, there soon seems to have been collusion between some of the organizers to abandon the Maghull course and hold the meeting on a new site at Aintree. Details of this scheme are set out by John Formby in his booklet *An account of the Liverpool races established in the year 1827 with observations on the conduct of the committee formed in July, 1828*. Formby was furious at the thought that he was going to lose his meeting and felt that he had been let down by Lord Sefton of whom he said 'on the score of disinterestedness and liberality both in mind and matter, no man living ranked higher'. Despite the indignant protests of Formby, Mr Lynn went ahead with his plans to lay out a new course. Securing the lease of land at Aintree, he built a grandstand. The first flat-race meeting was held on 7th July 1829. However, it was not until 1836 that Mr Lynn felt confident enough to advertise:

'A sweepstake of £10 each with £80 added for horses of all denominations 12 st. each, gentlemen riders. Second horse to receive back his stake. Winner to be sold for £200 if demanded. Twenty fences in each of two circuits. Two flights of hurdles in the straight.' There were ten runners, victory going to Mr Sirdefield's The Duke ridden by Captain Becher. On the same day another three-mile steeplechase, a sweepstake of £5 each, £20 added, was run. Captain Becher finished second. It is claimed that Becher only lost the race because his spiteful groom maliciously attached the curb-rein to the bit in such a fashion that Becher had little control over the horse. The next year the conditions were altered. £100 was added by the town of Liverpool and the weights were changed. Four years—11 st., five years—11 st. 7 lbs., six years and over—12 st. Other conditions were that the umpire should choose the course, and that the ground should be shown to the riders on the morning of the race. There were only four runners and The Duke won again, ridden by a twenty-seven-year-old Cheshire man, Mr Pott. He stated afterwards that 'he was a bit ashamed of himself because he rode unknown to his parents. However there was some excuse because the horse belonged to a great friend and at the last moment the jockey who was to have ridden became ill.' It seems very likely that Captain Becher was the indisposed jockey. He had ridden The Duke in 1836 and again in 1838. In 1837 he had no mount.

By 1839 Mr Lynn's health was failing and he was not able to

'continue the unremitting exertions he had hitherto devoted to the Liverpool races'. His finances were also failing, and a sidelight on his difficulties is a letter that he wrote to John Ferneley, the sporting artist who had visited Aintree and painted two pictures of the races as a speculation. Three years later he negotiated to sell them. Mr Lynn had been approached, and replied, '. . . I must apologize for having neglected answering your letter received in December last. The fact is I have been so full of trouble I have not had the heart to do anything. I have now I trust got over my difficulties but I shall have to go through the Gazette to get quite out of the Race-course concern. It has been a most unlucky speculation for me. I should have been worth at least £30,000 if I had never had anything to do with it. Now I have to begin the World all over again after thirty years' industry.'

Consequently a syndicate was formed of whom the Trustees were Lord Stanley, Sir Thomas Massey Stanley, and Messrs Aspinall, Earle and Blundell. The race committee were the Earls of Derby, Sefton, Eglinton and Wilton. Lords George Bentinck, Stanley and Robert Grosvenor; Sirs John Gerard, Thomas Massey Stanley, and R. W. Bulkeley; the Hon. E. M. Lloyd Mostyn and Mr E. G. Hornby. The new syndicate obviously gave the race a stimulus. There were fifty-three entries for a sweepstake of £20 each, £5 forfeit, with 100 sovereigns added, 12 st. gentlemen riders. Four miles across country, the second to save his stake, the winner to pay ten sovereigns towards expenses, no rider to open a gate or ride through a gateway or more than 100 yards along any road, footpath or driftway. From the moment that the entries were published on 6th January, there was tremendous public interest in the race. The popular Irish owner, Mr Ferguson, entered four of his horses, one of whom, Rust, shared favouritism with Lord MacDonald's The Nun in the list of the more substantial bookmakers who operated an ante-post market from the Talbot hotel prior to the day of the race. The great day was Tuesday, 26th February.

'The morning,' wrote a contemporary, 'broke calm, bright and beautiful. As early as nine o'clock the road leading to Aintree was crowded with pedestrians of the usual class, including pie-men, chimney sweeps, cigar sellers, thimble riggers and all the small fry of gaming table keepers . . .

'. . . Not a vehicle of any description that could by any means be made to go was left in the town, not a coach or a cab was to be had for love or money by any save those who had engaged them

or secured places beforehand. All the omnibuses plying to places
in the neighbourhood, were put into requisition including many
that came under the denomination of "wrecked goods".

'For places in the omnibuses the original price of which was
2s. 6d. from half a guinea was offered and refused. The cost of
the Grandstand admission was 7s. for a single ticket or 10s. for
the two days. The Grandstand had not accommodation for
more than threequarters of the people who presented themselves and not an attainable point about the building, even to
the very summit of the chimneys, but was occupied. All the
minor stands even those which at ordinary race meetings are
all but empty, were likewise crowded to suffocation and in
addition to the vast numbers dispersed about the course,
masses of individuals were seen here and there far over the
country congregated at the points where the most dangerous
leaps were to be taken . . . We fancy there could have been
not fewer than forty to fifty thousand persons on the ground.'

Liverpool authority refused to allow the use of police, but a
body of special constables were enrolled. The race was due to
begin at one p.m. It started two hours late, and until the horses
paraded, the crowd did not know how many of the original entries
were intending to start. In fact seventeen did compete. There
were twenty-nine jumps, one horse—Dictator—was killed, and
Lottery, ridden by Jem Mason, was the winner. Early in the race,
after crossing a large field which was half grass and half plough,
the runners came to a jump which consisted of some very stout
posts and rails three feet high but inclined forward to lessen this
height, and placed about a yard from the bank on the take-off
side; then came the brook and a field adjoining which was considerably lower than that from which the leap was taken. The
whole was about twenty-three feet. Captain Becher was making
the early running when his mount Conrad fell at this obstacle.
Becher crept into the brook to shelter until the others had jumped.
He then remounted, little thinking that his action had immortal-
ized both himself and the brook, forever afterwards known as
Becher's Brook.

The day after the race the Editorial in the *Liverpool Mercury*
made especial reference to the great event of the previous day.
'Our readers who have paid particular attention to the observations which we have frequently made on the subject of popular
recreations will not be surprised that we do not on this occasion
partake of the enthusiasm with which the great steeplechase, as

it is styled, seems to have inspired our townspeople. It was no
doubt a very exciting spectacle, but we can no more be reconciled
to it on that account than we are to cockfighting, bullbaiting, or
any other popular pastime which is attended with the infliction
of wanton torture to any living being. That these steeplechases
are of this nature will hardly be denied even by those who are
most ardently attached to such sport.

'All the objections which may be urged against hunting the hare
or fox apply with still more force to such scenes as those which
were witnessed in our neighbourhood on Tuesday. In ordinary
hunting the sportsman can choose his ground and avoid those
perilous leaps which might endanger his own life and that of his
horse, but in these steeplechases the most formidable obstacles are
artificially placed in the course which the horse must necessarily
take and the almost certain result is the death of some of the
noble animals thus wantonly urged on to their own destruction.

'We have no taste for what is styled "sporting intelligence" and
we are not ashamed therefore to own that we never read the
writings of Nimrod who figures in the pages of the *Sporting Magazine*
but we have been told that even he—the champion of the turf
recreations—deprecates steeplechasing as equally cruel and
perilous, and with such authority on our side we are justified in
denouncing such practice.

'With these views of the subject we need scarcely add that we
have heard with alarm and regret that it is in contemplation to
establish steeplechasing annually or periodically in this neighbourhood. If any such design is seriously entertained we trust that
some means will be adopted to defeat it. Now if we were invested
with despotic power we most assuredly would inflict summary
punishment on those who permit their horses to run in these
steeplechases. We would not decapitate them but we would
compel them, whether rich or poor, titled or untitled, to go
through the purgatory of a steeplechase with sturdy drivers at
their heels to urge them over hedge and ditch, until they reached
the goal, and when they arrived at the end of the steeplechase,
they should do penance in white sheets or horse clothes in the
church until they confessed their iniquities and promised to be
more merciful to their animals.'

Notwithstanding this broadside against the first Grand National
a sporting note appeared in the paper the following week. 'We
learn that upward of fifty gentlemen have already subscribed to
another steeplechase next year, that forty subscriptions are fully
expected and that it is anticipated that the chase will be one of

the most splendid ever witnessed whether as regards the patronage
it will receive or the number of horses that will be entered.'

Strictly the race did not become known as the Grand National
until 1847. Originally entitled Grand Liverpool Steeplechase, it
changed to Liverpool and National Steeplechase in 1843.

Lottery, winner of this first Grand National, was described as
'mealy brown in colour, with narrow and short quarters, deep in
the girth, light in his middle and back ribs, with a perfect snaffle
mouth and fine head—yet a horse who could trot faster than most
others could gallop.' He was a half-bred, or 'cocktail'. Foaled in
1830 and initially named Chance, he was bred by a Mr Jackson
of Thirsk. As a four year old he ran twice at the Holderness Hunt
meeting, being successful in a minor flat race. Later he was sent
to Horncastle Fair where he was bought by Mr Elmore for
120 gns. His first steeplechase appearance was at Finchley in
December 1836 when, ridden by young Mr Henry Elmore, he
turned a complete somersault. He ran third in the 1837 St Albans
steeplechase and then won at many meetings including Barnet,
Daventry, Maidstone, Cheltenham and Stratford. Mrs Elmore
used to say 'she was quite ashamed at going about the country
and winning so much, and at every place'. Visitors to the Elmores'
house—if they arrived at a suitable time—would be astonished
to see Lottery perform his party trick. This consisted of cantering
slowly up to the luncheon table and jumping it—table, soup
tureens, glasses and all—with the greatest possible ease. The conditions of one steeplechase were 'open to all horses—Lottery
excepted'. The unusual conditions of a race at Finchley in October
1842 were—'All horses to carry 12 st., but Lottery's entry fee £40,
others £10 or £5 for horses that have never won.' He was trained
at Epsom by George Dockeray when he won the Grand National.
In 1840 he fell at the stone wall, and in 1841 and 1842 he was
pulled up. He ran again the subsequent year but made no show
under his huge weight. This proved to be his last appearance
at Aintree.

Jem Mason who rode Lottery was born at Stilton where his
father, who bred hunters and dealt in them, also had an interest—
which ultimately proved disastrous—in the local coaching stage.
The failure of his coaching business necessitated a move to Pinner.
For his son, this departure was a marvellous stroke of fortune, for
at Dove House Farm, Pinner lived Mr Tilbury, one of the most
famous dealers in England, who kept upward of two hundred
hunters. Soon Jem, whose 'good looks, mild but larkish dispo-
sition and slender form, made him a favourite with his father's

customers, was schooling young horses every day of his life, and impressing not only Mr Tilbury by his ability in the saddle, but everyone else who saw him. His first major success was on The Poet in the 1834 St Albans steeplechase. This victory appeared even more outstanding when it was learned that young Jem, who wore a jacket made for him when he was a little boy, had put up four stone deadweight. Later Mr Elmore who lived four miles from Pinner persuaded him to take over from the ageing Dan Seffert, now the worse from over-indulgence in gin and water, and become the stable jockey. There were few first-class professional riders at the time, and the wise Mr Elmore never had any doubts as to Mason's prowess as a jockey. It must be assumed that he approved of Mason in other ways too as, shortly after becoming his jockey, Mason became his son-in-law.

Although the names of Lottery and Jem Mason will always be linked, the extraordinary fact is that Lottery savagely disliked seeing Mason and invariably showed animosity whenever the jockey approached him. Once Mason was mounted, however, the horse behaved perfectly. As a combination their fame was national. In 1840 when they raced at Dunchurch, Dr Arnold dispensed with 'calling over' and allowed the boys of Rugby to go to the steeplechase in order to see the famous pair. The school-boys returned so enthusiastic that they raised £15 which was doubled by the townspeople of Rugby to sponsor a local race. Their illustrious headmaster was mortified when he compared this £15 to the pennies placed in the school chapel alms box. Lottery's last race was at Windsor in April 1844. It is sad to remember that after a brilliant career which made him the most famous steeplechaser in England, he should have ended his life, not in honourable retirement, but pulling the plough.

The 1840 Liverpool steeplechase had £150 given as added stake money, £30 to the second, third to save his stake, weights 12 st. each. Lord Sefton was begged to make a stone wall one of the obstacles to encourage the Irish owners to send over their horses. He agreed, but insisted on adding an ox-fence for the benefit of the Leicestershire entries. There were eleven runners. Tom Oliver broke his collar-bone at Valentine's Brook (named after an Irish horse), and the winner was Jerry, a good horse who had changed hands frequently and at one time had belonged to Mr Elmore. The next year a further innovation was that the winner of the newly formed Cheltenham steeplechase should carry an 18 lb. penalty. Lottery, therefore, had to carry 13 st. 4 lbs. at Aintree.

The general public were now taking great interest in steeple-chasing—not from a betting point of view, but rather as a spectacle. However, the antagonists of the sport were legion and they found their champion in Charles Apperley—better known as Nimrod. For nearly forty years, Apperley (1778–1843) was in a class of his own as an essayist and correspondent depicting the fox-hunting scene—even though he was accused of always being at pains to find six words to do the work of two. Nimrod stated that in 1839 he wrote letters expressing his views on steeplechasing to both *The Times* and *The Standard*, choosing these two papers deliberately because of their non-sporting character, in the hope that his sentiments would attract more notice than if they appeared in the sporting press. He claims that they never appeared as the person who took them to London disapproved of his views and consequently burnt the letters! Before his death in 1843 Nimrod wrote:

'Let us look at steeplechasing in all its bearings and all its repulsive forms. In the first place its cruelty. We can have no right or authority to call upon an animal to perform for us more than his natural powers, assisted by what is called higher bodily condition, enable him to do, without extreme danger to his life or at least great temporary suffering . . . The celebrated surgeon —Dr Wardrop—obtained the heart of one of the steeplechase victims in the well-known and victorious Grimaldi, who died from a rupture of it, after passing the winning post. "It was of uncommon dimensions," said he to me, "larger than that of Eclipse but it could not stand steeplechasing. It burst in the moment of victory." ' Nimrod continued, 'Is it possible that this barbarous pursuit can long continue to be a reproach to the character of Great Britain and Ireland . . . Hurdle races, al-though childish and silly exhibitions, cannot perhaps come under the denomination of cruel, but they serve to show the cruelty of steeple-races by the numerous falls of the horses that contend them . . . I do not think that walls should form part of steeple-chase fences, because in eight out of ten hunting countries walls are not met with, and consequently horses are not upon an equality.'

The death of Grimaldi also inspired the following letter written in 1839.

'Sir, I wish to record my sentiments at the painful exhibition I have this day, for the second time, witnessed—the Northamp-tonshire steeplechase. The opinions I formed on seeing the death of my old acquaintance Grimaldi at St Albans in 1835, I have this day seen reason to strengthen, and I do hope that as I have lived to see the commencement of this mad pursuit— I will not call it sport—so I may live to see its termination, as I boldly affirm that it is no criterion of the best horse, but a mere game of chance and gambling transaction. From many quiet and observant farmers I heard the following remark, "This is a cruel exhibition, with not one feature to recommend it . . . and if the good sense of Englishmen does not put it down, I hope the Legislature will." I will quote from a work now before me, language bearing entirely upon that point, "The steeplechase is the relic of ancient foolhardiness and cruelty. It is ridden at the evident hazard of the life of the rider and likewise that of the life and enjoyment of the horse." Nimrod, my early acquaintance, has done honour to his head and his heart in the decided way he has expressed himself upon it, and it is the duty of every man who values the most generous of all animals, the horse, to raise his voice against it.

> "Woe worth the chase, woe worth the day,
>   That cost thy life, my gallant grey." '

A postscript to the letter added: 'Notwithstanding the high-bred pleasantry of Lord Chesterfield I believe the majority of the spectators were disappointed with their day's recreation, many disgusted. The third impediment to the horse was the river Nem 27 ft wide and requiring an exertion of ten yards to clear. This reduced the field from twelve to two who struggled in the tortuous course, Mason arriving at the terminus first, at a pace a fast jack-ass could have kept.' Before the race Mr O'Seson, who was riding his own horse, Greyling, for whom he had given 400 sovereigns, declared that if he was killed, he left ten sovereigns apiece to all the jockeys and his horse to Mr Coleman.

Races confined to amateurs were also being criticized— especially some of the conditions regarding weight allowances. The suggestion that gentlemen in cocked-hats should be allowed 7 lbs. brought forth a letter, 'If absurdity be the object there ought to have been a tariff as follows:—Gentlemen tattooing their faces after the fashion of the Esquimeux Indians allowed 9 lbs. Gentlemen who between heats will grin through a horse collar for ten minutes, eat hot hasty pudding, climb up a greased pole or dip four pennies in a jar of treacle—10 lbs'!

Notwithstanding these criticisms, steeplechasing flourished and

3

the *Sporting Magazine* account of the 1843 National—when the race was a handicap for the first time—gives a fascinating description of the day.

'The entry for this "grand event" included a string of horses never congregated together in the palmiest days of steeplechasing. Lottery, Peter Simple, The Returned and Consul were of themselves sufficient to draw a host of admirers of the sport: but when to these were added numerous other horses "well-known to fame" the large concourse of spectators assembled at Aintree course was not to be wondered at. The cards of the day presented on one side the names of the horses with the colours of their riders, and on the other a map of the country, with the fences, artificial hurdles, walls, lanes and brooks to be encountered, which varied but little from the previous occasions. One of the most formidable was a strong post and rail fence, of considerable height, placed before an awful looking yawner just before arriving at Becher's Brook which was strongly objected to by some jockeys who felt pretty certain that if they once got IN they would not very speedily get OUT. The objection was however not deemed valid and fortunately no casualties occurred there. Becher's Brook and fence were as before. The stone wall at the distance post, within the training ground, was four feet high lapped with turf, and opposite the winning chair was the artificial brook, but widened from twelve to thirteen feet more than last year. On the previous evening the betting in the Rooms was very languid, but on the course just previous to the start it became animated, closing as follows:—3–1 Peter Simple: 4–1 Lottery: 4–1 The Returned: 8–1 Redwing and long prices about the others.

'The Stewards were the Earls of Sefton and Chesterfield and G. Payne, Esq. Mr Lynn, proprietor of the Waterloo Hotel, was indefatigable in his exertions to keep order, clear the course and the enclosures in front of the Grandstand—no very easy task. The Stands were nearly all filled, and the jockeys drew up in their party-coloured jackets in front of the Stand at three o'clock, presenting a splendid sight. The course was the usual two-mile circuit, twice round, and every field thronged with pedestrians.

'At twelve minutes past three, without a single false start, off they went at the signal given by Lord Sefton.'

The race was won by Lord Chesterfield's Vanguard ridden by

Tom Oliver, who had also ridden the winner—Gaylad—the
previous year.

IV

Tom Oliver was one of the great characters of nineteenth century
steeplechasing. He once described the law as 'being like a country
dance. You get led up and down by your coquettish partner, your
Attorney, till you were tired but never satisfied'. He was born in
Angmering, Sussex, where his father was a respected flockmaster.
His mother produced sixteen children. There is every likelihood
that there was Spanish or Gypsy blood in his veins, and that some
of his ancestors were Spanish smugglers who had landed on the
Sussex coast. As a young man, Tom sneaked off from home
whilst his family were at a fête celebrating the coming-of-age of
Mr Gratwicke—the son of a local squire—and went to his uncle
Mr Page, the Epsom trainer. His total worldly wealth was 14s. 6d.
and he could hardly read or write. To his credit his uncle soon got
him a job riding the light weights for Lord Mountcharles. His
first success was on Icarius for General Grosvenor in 1828. Next
he worked in Liverpool for Mr Farrell, the Irish coper. He was
riding with great confidence, was strong, arrogant and much in
demand as a steeplechase jockey. Although for most of his mounts
he was paid a sovereign, he was always in debt and frequently had
clashes with the law. Sent to Northampton gaol for a month, his
stay was made more pleasant by 'goodies' sent in to him by the
officers of the 12th Lancers. Before a local magistrate he once
said: 'Look here, your honour, you must excuse me if my answers
don't meet with your approval, but off the pigskin, I'm the biggest
fool in England.' He became landlord of the Star at Leamington
before he moved to Prestbury near Cheltenham. He won the
Grand National three times, on Gaylad—1842, Vanguard—1843
and Peter Simple—1853. He also finished second three times and
third once. After Vanguard's death he covered a sofa with the
skin of this favourite horse. He was considered a great man in the
village of Prestbury. Once he asked the baker to go for a walk
with him. The baker was elated and called out, 'Wife, bring me
my top-hat. I am going for a walk with Mr Oliver.' Whilst at
Prestbury he taught both George Stevens (winner of five Grand
Nationals), and the amateur Mr Pickering, to ride. What is less
generally known is the tremendous influence he had over a famous
young Cheltenham schoolboy. 'There now, you young devil,
you've rode a race at last,' said Oliver as the boy dismounted
after riding trials on the racecourse. Oliver used to get the boy to

come to his house of an evening. He loved hearing him recite. In return Oliver became the boy's complete and utter hero and in later life he was to show his hero-worship in many of his poems. The boy—Adam Lindsay Gordon.

> Here's a health to every sportsman, be he stableman or lord,
> If his heart be true I care not what his pocket may afford,
> And may he ever pleasantly each gallant sport pursue,
> If he takes his liquor fairly, and his fences fairly too.
> He cares not for the troubles of Fortune's fickle tide,
> Who like Bendigo can battle, and *like Oliver can ride*.
> He laughs at those who caution, at those who chide he'll frown,
> As he clears a five foot paling or he knocks a peeler down.

Despite the tirades of Dean Swift, despite the burning down of the Cleeve Hill grandstand in 1830, racing had flourished in the Cheltenham area ever since the end of the Napoleonic wars, when not only had the Duke of Wellington and some of his officers visited the Spa, but the Duke of Gloucester had attended the first meeting on Cleeve Hill and subscribed 100 gns to the race fund. In 1834 the Cheltenham Grand Annual steeplechase was inaugurated at a meeting held in the Vale of Prestbury. Vivian ridden by Captain Becher won in 1837, Lottery won in both 1839 and 1840. Early in the 1840s the steeplechases moved to a course near Andoversford, but it proved unsatisfactory, and in 1847 another move was made back to Prestbury. The basis of 'How we beat the Favourite' was this Cheltenham Grand Annual in 1847, won by Mr Holman on Stanmore. The race started at Perry Hill Farm near Prestbury, through the lane to Knoverton House, to the right of the latter, over a stone wall into Mr Turner's orchard, over a brook with gorse plants on the take-off side, through Mr Gyngell's meadows to Hewletts Hill. The turning flag was between Queen's Wood and Cleeve. Daddy Long Legs, ridden by W. Archer (father of Fred Archer), was beaten by a head. The Holmans, the Archers, Mr Christopher Capel, who was to own two National winners, Tom Pickernell, 'Fogo' Rowlands and George Stevens made Cheltenham a great and happy steeplechasing centre. Bonfires were lit on Cleeve Hill to celebrate news of each of Stevens's National victories. He was born in Cheltenham in 1833—the same year as Adam Lindsay Gordon, who was not only a life-long friend, but shared with him the distinction of having been taught the art of riding by Tom Oliver.

Stevens's first major success was in the Grand Annual at Wolverhampton in 1851. The following year he rode in the National, but fell. At his next attempt—four years later—he won on Free Trader, whose delighted owner gave him a present of £500. Although he was only twenty-two years old, his style of riding caused considerable comment. He never bustled his mount near a fence, and at times lay so far out of his ground that his chance of winning seemed remote to his supporters. However his judgement of pace was so accurate that on countless occasions his challenge, delivered at the last possible moment, swept him past his tiring rivals. He always insisted that more steeplechases were lost through horses being interfered with than by falling of their own accord. At Aintree he invariably dropped his horse out in the early stages of the race, being content to remain at the rear of the field and thus avoid much of the scrimmaging and jostling on the first circuit. Proof of the wisdom of these tactics is his unequalled Grand National record. After his victory on Free Trader in 1856, he rode in the next four Nationals without any success. In 1861 when Jealousy won he did not have a ride, being compelled to watch the race from the grandstand. The reason was that he had refused thirteen offers of rides in order to partner Jealousy whom he thought certain to win. At the last moment an owner holding a retainer put in a veto—much to his chagrin. 1862 brought him no better fortune. In 1863 he won on Lord Coventry's Emblem and the next year won on Emblematic— Emblem's sister—also owned by Lord Coventry. Emblematic was third to Alcibiade the following year, and Stevens was criticized for delaying his challenge too late even by his own standards. Four years after this slight contretemps he again won—this time on The Colonel, whose second victory the next year, running in the name of Mr M. Evans whose niece Stevens was married to, gave him his fifth Grand National triumph. This is one of the great achievements in steeplechasing history. Tragically, within three months of finishing fourth to The Lamb in the 1871 National, again riding The Colonel, George Stevens was dead. One June morning he was riding near his home, named Emblem Cottage, which was on the top of Cleeve Hill. A gust of wind blew off his hat and as a boy handed it back to him his horse shied, before careering down the hill. Stevens was thrown, fractured his skull and died without regaining consciousness a few days later. He was only thirty-eight years old.

Yet none of these personalities match up to Tom Oliver who, incidentally, was best man when William Archer married the daughter of the licensee of the King's Arms, Prestbury. Towards the end of his life when he was training at Wroughton he was asked by a fussy owner of a bad steeplechaser if his horse would win a particular steeplechase. 'Honoured Sir—Your horse can stay 4 miles but takes a h .. l of a long time to do it—yours obediently—Tom Oliver,' was the reply! A friend writing about him in his old age described him as, 'A small wiry man with a fringe of iron-grey hair round the face which made him look rather like a marmoset monkey, the effect being further heightened by a sallow complexion and by his extremely bright, black twinkling eyes.'

Inevitably there must be comparison between Oliver and Jem Mason. They dominated the professional jockey stage completely whilst they were riding. Mason was always a dandy, whilst 'Black Tom' Oliver was a much rougher diamond. Mason who usually rode in white kid gloves and who is reputed to have had his top boots made by two makers—the legs being worked by Batley's of Oxford Street, the feet by Wren of Knightsbridge— had his coats made by Poole. He once jumped a new 5 ft 6 in gate rather than a penetrable bullfinch, saying he intended to go to the opera that night and did not want to scratch his face. He then added that there was not a man in England would dare to follow him! Whether he was sitting on the strawberry-leaved drag of a Duke or the dog cart of a dealer, he was always the same, taking no liberties with anyone nor permitting any to be taken with himself. There can be no question that Mason was the more skilful when it came to putting his horse at a fence. He always rode with a long easy seat and light hand. He seldom had a fall or a bad accident. He hated to be on a second-rater which required nursing. On the other hand horses frequently refused when ridden by Oliver, yet he was far stronger than Mason and if the two landed together over the last fence it was odds on Oliver winning. When someone complained to Oliver that he had ridden a difficult horse, Oliver smilingly explained, 'You will not know what real misery is on horseback until you ride a hard-bucking, ewe-necked horse, downhill, in a snaffle bridle, with a fly in your eye, and one foot out of the stirrup.' Mason once rode a horse named Trust-me-Not belonging to Oliver at a time when the latter was in his usual financial difficulties. Before mounting, Mason took off the very severe bit used by Oliver and substituted an ordinary double-reined snaffle. He won the race. Afterwards Oliver declared 'that he would fight for Jem up to his knees in blood'. Later, again riding Trust-me-Not, Mason had a crashing fall which resulted in a broken leg. Oliver himself paid Mason the greatest compliment of all when he wrote, 'I have ridden hundreds of miles across country with Jem Mason, not only in steeplechases but in trials of recent purchases bought into the stable by his father-in-law, Mr Elmore. I can say without fear of contradiction that he was the finest horseman in England—I have never ridden with him without envying the perfection of his style.

Mason died of cancer of the throat in 1866—the year too of Squire Osbaldeston's death. He had been ill for a long time and towards the end of his life began to fret about the finance of his family. He need not have worried. There were many living who felt honoured to contribute to the 'Jem Mason' subscription got up by Tattersalls, although he was never told of this generous action.

Oliver outlived his friend and rival for eight years, dying on 7th January 1874. His last public outing was to Worcester races. Six months after his death, a horse he had trained at Wroughton—George Frederick—won the Derby at Epsom.

V

During the years 1844–60 the history of steeplechasing, and particularly of the Liverpool Grand National is comparatively uneventful. In 1844 the National was won by a horse called Discount; he had started life as Magnum Bonum but negotiations for his sale to a Mr Quartermaine were so protracted as the would-be purchaser kept on offering less and less money that on completion he was renamed Discount. The next year the meeting was badly affected by frost and Lord Sefton allowed the owners to decide whether or not they would prefer to race, or postpone the meeting. They agreed to race and Cure-All—a complete outsider unquoted by the bookmakers—won. In 1847 the race was won for the first time by an Irish horse, Mathew. Proof that some horses ran better at Aintree than anywhere else was that Jerry, the 1840 winner, was third to Mathew; Pioneer, the 1846 winner, was fourth; and Culverthorpe was fifth, having previously finished second to Pioneer.

The following year Captain Little won the National on The Chandler. At the time of his triumph, Captain Little was twenty-seven years old and, as a race-rider, limited in experience. He had held a commission in the King's Dragoon Guards but unluckily the Bank in which he had deposited all his wealth failed. This financial disaster necessitated his changing to the 81st Regiment of Foot. The Chandler as a young horse had been bought by Mr Robert Garnett of Moor Hall, Sutton Coldfield, from the keeper

of a chandler's shop; hence the name. It has often been stated
that Mr Garnett frequently drove him in his gig to the meeting
of the Bonehill Harriers, although to the day of his death in 1892
his owner denied this, as did his stud-groom, the last-named in
exceedingly emphatic language. One morning a horse which
Captain Peel, a friend of Mr Garnett, was due to ride, became
lame at the last moment. The Chandler was substituted rather
than spoil Captain Peel's day. He went so well that he was immediately bought by the Captain for £20 plus his lame horse. For the
next three seasons The Chandler carried Captain Peel brilliantly
to hounds. As a ten-year-old he was sent to Bradley at Hednesford
to be trained as a steeplechaser. On his second appearance on a
race-course, at Warwick, he did a prodigious leap which is still
considered one of the biggest on record. It is claimed to be thirty-
seven feet, although it must be pointed out that the jump was not
measured until some time after the race, when the imprint of the
horses' hooves had been badly spoiled by several other horsemen
and spectators who had come to marvel at the distance of the leap.
Certainly the length was not gauged with 'the same nicety that
a shopman measures out a couple of yards of Genoa velvet'. The
facts were that during the Hunt Cup steeplechase two of the
leading horses fell into a brook which was part of the river Avon,
and was guarded by a low scrub fence, of which the landing side
was somewhat lower than the take-off. The Chandler, coming up
behind the fallers, cleared the brook, horses and riders. Later
Captain Peel sold a half-share in The Chandler to his friend
Captain Little. Captain Little had learnt much about the art
of steeplechasing from Tom Oliver: it is ironic that Tom should
have finished second to him in the Grand National. Oliver's
horse, The Curate, was one of three horses killed in the National
the next year. The obstacles at which the three deaths occurred
were very low banks of dark earth—insignificant in size by comparison to Becher's Brook—yet it is claimed that since they were
formed of the same substance as the rest of the field the horses
never saw them in time.

Abd-el-Kadar, owned by Mr J. Osborne, who was an early
contributor to *Bell's Life*, won in both 1850 and 1851—his latter
victory being by the unusual distance of 'half-a-neck'. Abd-el-
Kadar was ridden by Mr Green, who also won in 1859 on Half-
Caste, whom he trained. Later he became trainer to Lord Poulett
at Droxford and was responsible for training The Lamb for his
second Grand National success in 1871. In 1852 there were
rumours that the water jump was dangerous. These rumours

Steeplechase Cracks. Painted by J. F. Herring. Reproduced by kind permission of Messrs. Fores Ltd.

Steeplechase paintings by 'Old Henry Alken', *c.* 1850. Neither the date
nor the place can be ascertained but the four pictures convey clearly

the picture of early steeplechasing. *Reproduced by kind permission of
Lt.-Col. John Thomson*

TOP : The Leamington, 1840; Marquis of Waterford leads on Columbine at the start. BOTTOM: The Leamington, 1840; Mr Jem Mason on Lottery beating Mr Powell on Seventy-Four by a head coming in. *Reproduced by kind permission of Arthur Ackermann & Son Ltd.*

were scotched the week after the race when Lord Sefton wrote the following letter to the Editor of *Bell's Life*.

'Sir—In the account of the Liverpool Steeplechase given in your paper of last Sunday, it is stated that the water jump opposite the Grandstand had been altered by my instructions, and that it was thus made a large and dangerous leap. This is not at all correct. In the constant preparation of this artificial fence the workmen have gradually diminished the depth of the ditch till it had become a mere splash of water, and I desired that it might be restored to its former dimensions in every respect. This was done and no more. The water is 13 ft 6 in in breadth and no more than 4 ft deep. The rail is about 3 ft high, strongly made and leaning towards the water. It is a very large but perfectly fair leap, and I do not remember any serious accident befalling a horse, except in one instance when a fine Irish horse broke his back, but this happened as a consequence of the frost.'

In 1853 Peter Simple who had won in 1849 won again, ridden by Tom Oliver and owned by Captain Little. Although victories such as this were immensely popular, towards the middle of the 1850s steeplechasing itself began to decline in general appeal. The reasons are not easy to determine. One of them was that clerks of courses were becoming 'gate money' conscious. They needed good entries for their races, and in consequence frequently advertised 'All over grass and no ditches'. The meetings near London at the Notting Hill Hippodrome and at Paddy Jacksons' hunting grounds at Kensal New Town, although enjoyed by the general public, had done nothing for the sport. The tracks were too small for any steeplechaser worthy of the name to be successful. Fences were reduced to a minimum in size. It is also possible that there were too many meetings—many of them very badly organized. For example, in March 1857 there were fifteen fixtures at:

Henley-in-Arden	Warwick
Liverpool	Hereford
Ludlow	Gullane
Doncaster	Birmingham
Market Rasen	Driffield
Thame	Coventry
Grand Military (Brixworth)	Moreton-in-the-Marsh
Beverley	

Another factor could be that the Crimean War and the Indian Mutiny offered many young officers excitement and action in such places as Balaclava and Lucknow, instead of in the hunting field and on the racecourse. In *Fifty Years of My Life* Sir John Astley described a steeplechase meeting held in the Crimea: 'We, the stewards, had hard work to get the course clear of stones and to make the fences, as the ground was five miles from our camp. We were very lucky in the day and all agreed the sport was first rate . . . We got up a flat race for the Frenchmen, which was clipping fun, they objected to the obstacles, so we found them a flat half-mile, and the winner flogged his horse long after he had passed the post . . . We had a large dinner afterwards at a French restaurant in the rear of the Third Division'. When peace was proclaimed the Sultan of Turkey gave three gold cups to be competed for by Army officers in steeplechases. Some time later a correspondent wrote in *Bell's Life* '. . . Why do the cavalry officers in England and France encourage steeplechasing amongst their subordinates? Because it excites that courage, presence of mind, and skill in horsemanship without which their glorious achievements at Balaclava and Inkermann would never have been recorded. It also checks riotous living and its worst accessory, the use of the gaming table . . .'

In January 1857 the *Sporting Review* stated: 'It is really humiliating to glance over the steeplechase records for the month. Windsor had a promising bill of fare out of which Marmaduke got some good pickings but as usual there was some odd work.

'Only five horses attended the Cambridge Hunt. The Aylesbury Aristocratic was sadly feeble, nearly everything tumbled in the principal Ipswich chase. The Great Melton steeplechase result is still veiled in painful mystery and at Waltham Abbey there were neither Stewards nor a properly defined course, and as a matter of course a sad wrangling at the last.'

Two months later, the *Sporting Review* took up the cudgels again: 'The Liverpool steeplechase weights are sillier than ever, running from 11 st. 2 lbs. to 8 st. 10 lbs. In fact, Oliver and the leading steeplechase jockeys have hardly a chance of a mount, and the struggle is left to some wretched ex-racers ridden by ex-jockeys and some light grooms. Alas! that Liverpool—which has seen Lottery carry his 12 st. over its walls—should have sunk so low! Well may gentlemen refuse to send anything like a weight carrying hunter to be beaten in a run in for speed by such 30lb. betting office trash who could not live two miles under 11 st. 7 lbs.!'

The 1858 National was postponed for three days because of

snow. When the race was run the attendance was poor, and the ground half-covered with melting snow. One of the conditions of the race was that the winner would be penalized thirty sovereigns towards expenses! This honour fell to Little Charlie ridden by W. Archer who at one time had gone to Russia with a retainer from the Czar who paid him £100 per annum with board, residence and all found.

There were still constant outcries against steeplechasing. In the *Sporting Review* appeared an article which began: 'The steeplechase is a mode of racing which I do not recommend. It is attended by a vast amount of danger, calls too much on the energies of the horse, and causes the death of many a valuable animal . . . To gallop a horse at racing pace over a heavy and unequal country with awkward fences to surmount and probably at the finish, when he is well nigh exhausted, to cram him at a hurdle (a favourite arrangement, especially at the minor meetings, is to have a hurdle at the run in), is an unjustifiable abuse of the animal.

'No fair bet can be made on a steeplechase owing to the number of accidents which take place, but it offers ample employment for the sharper and such as have no vast amount of character to stand upon. It is to be hoped that it will not become a lasting amusement of the people of England. Already it has begun to decline in popularity . . .'

Aintree was temporarily to deteriorate until by 1863 a contemporary wrote: 'It almost requires a microscope to discover the fences in walking over the ground, and with the exception of the three brooks and the made fence at the distance, the spectators on the stand would not know that any jumping was going on if they were not so informed by a reference to the backs of their cards.'

Again, 'A post and rail was put up in front of Becher's and Valentine's Brooks but all the other fences were mere narrow ditches of the most contemptible description and practicable for a schoolboy of ten years old and his pony. The thorn fence at the distance and the water jump were of the ordinary size and those were the only two, save that of Valentine's Brook, which required any doing.' Yet one of the worst National accidents occurred in 1862 when James Wynne, the rider of O'Connell, was killed. It was an unlucky accident in that first round at the hedge fence, some 5 ft 6 in height, which preceded the water jump in front of the stands, one of the leaders came down on his head. Neither he nor his jockey were injured, but the two horses which followed cannoned in mid-air. Wynne and his mount turned a complete somersault, with disastrous results. The jockey's breastbone was completely staved in, and he died within a few hours. His father had ridden Mathew to win in 1847.

Describing the 1864 Grand National an eye-witness wrote: 'The line was full of ploughed fields and in the back stretch by the canal there seemed to be nothing else. "Won't you stop and see the hunt," said the pedestrian to the canal boatmen—but they only shook their heads and smoked their pipes and sailed on their silent highway.

'The line began with wheat but with the Mark Lane quotations at 40s. 8d. there was not a case for heavy damages against the lessee. Becher's Brook had been cleared out and cut sharp and sloping. The nastiest jump was out of a ploughed field near the canal, over a rail, ditch and hedge with a bad take-off. The jump at the distance post seemed like a wattle of gorse and scotch fir and the hedge at the water jump was of the same texture with canvas on the inside. The water jump was not an unmerciful one, and the attendants kept throwing ashes occasionally to make the lighting ground safer . . . It is remarkable that three out of the first five should have been by St Leger or Derby winners, and the second by the horse who was a great steeplechaser in his day and winner of the Royal Society's Prize at Worcester.'

The years 1860–70 were exceptionally important in the history of steeplechasing. At the commencement of this decade there was a distinct possibility that the sport would decline into oblivion. Ten years later it was more firmly established than ever before. In the late 1850s there had been desultory attempts to revive various race-meetings, but they met with little success—partly due to the incompetence and dishonesty of the organizers, and partly due to the fact that so many people who could support steeplechasing were not prepared to do so. To many fox-hunting men it was still anathema, whilst the Jockey Club and the followers of flat-racing gave it no recognition. Early in 1860 an article in *Baily's Magazine* began, 'The attempts to revive steeplechasing appeared likely at one time to meet with satisfactory results and attract patronage of many leading members of the Turf, but the unfortunate wrangle at Croydon served to disgust all the aristocratic patrons of the sport, and later meetings at Reading and Slough proved anything but advantageous to the respective lessees . . . The race for the principal event was worthy of Liverpool, but the attendance was meagre in the extreme, and confined chiefly to the members of the ring.' Another factor was that

although there was never a dearth of runners, there were frequently betting coups on light-weights who had little or no
pretensions to class. To the genuine lover of a really good steeplechaser, to the man who revered the names of Lottery and Grimaldi,
this was outrageous. It was his hope that something should be done
about it . . .

The man most responsible for the revival was Mr Fothergill
Rowlands. He was born and bred in Monmouthshire, where his
father had a large medical practice amongst the miners. It seemed
natural that son should carry on father's business and for some
years this was done. However, in 1844, Fogo, as he was affection-
ately known to all, found that his love of horses was too strong to
allow him to continue when his heart was not in his work as a
doctor. A brilliant horseman with perfect hands, he was soon
making a great reputation as a gentleman rider. He often rode
for Lord Strathmore—and is seen on Lord Strathmore's The
Switcher in Herring's well-known painting 'Steeplechase Cracks,'
1847.* He invariably wore white kid gloves when race-riding, as
had Jem Mason. His greatest success was riding his own horse
Medora to win the Grand Steeplechase at Baden-Baden. He also
rode Medora in the 1863 Grand National. Later he kept a few
horses in training with Tom Oliver at Wroughton, before he
moved to Prestbury and began training on his own account. He
also trained for the Duke of Hamilton, Sir John Astley, Mr Reginald Herbert and Lord Marcus Beresford. When he moved to
Pitt Place at Epsom his head lad was John Jones whose father had
once been Fogo's gardener and whose son Herbert was to ride
Diamond Jubilee and Minoru to victory in the Derby. Fogo loved
making epigrams; 'Bad luck is good luck if you'll make it so' was
one of his favourites. Another was: 'Experience is worth nothing
unless you pay for it, but the less you pay for it the better'. Once
after dinner he matched himself to carry Mr Reginald Herbert
fifty yards up Monnow Street, Monmouth, quicker than a fat man
who had also been dining could run 100 yards. He won his bet!

An unsuccessful attempt was made by Rowlands in 1859 to
stage a hunt steeplechase at Market Harborough. The idea was
to provide a race for genuine steeplechasing hunters over a suitable course. It was hoped that the riders would be farmers and
hunting men, and that all local hunts would both subscribe
towards a liberal prize to the winner and also support the race.
Surprisingly and disappointingly only two hunts—the Vale of the
White Horse and the Old Berkeley contributed. The next year,

---

* Lord Strathmore's colours are now those of H.M. the Queen Mother.

however, the entire scheme appeared better managed. Conditions of the race were 'Grand National Hunt Steeplechase of £10 each, with £500 added. For horses which have never won before the day of starting. 12 st. each. 4 miles.' Twelve hunts subscribed towards the cost of the race:

> Duke of Beaufort
> Lord Fitzwilliam
> Lord Stamford (Quorn)
> Lord Dacres
> Lord Tredegar
> Mr T. T. Drakes (Bicester)
> Monmouthshire
> Warwickshire
> North Warwickshire
> Cambridgeshire
> Oakley
> Heythrop.

The race was a wonderful success. There were thirty-one runners, and the favourite, Bridegroom, owned by Mr B. J. Angell and ridden by Mr E. C. Burton, won in a canter by about twenty lengths. In the course of the afternoon, whilst celebrations to mark Bridegroom's victory were still progressing, a fearless and thoroughly competent horsewoman known to all as Skittles, jumped the brook in cold blood much to the admiration of everyone—especially as it had been claimed that the course was so stiff and the fences so large that some riders needed a considerable amount of 'jumping powder' to induce them to compete. The fame of Skittles was such that many wives, totally disinterested in fox-hunting, insisted on accompanying their husbands to Melton Mowbray for the season!

Mr E. C. Burton, the winning rider, was described by Sir John Astley as 'the best all round sportsman I have ever met.' He went to Christchurch in 1845. The following year he rowed in the Boat Race, and the next year became President of the Oxford Boat Club. Equally accomplished as a runner, he once defeated the fastest sprinter in the Guards, much to the astonishment of all except his faithful Christchurch supporters. The crack sprinter of the Guards was none other than Sir John Astley, who afterwards admitted that he had completely underrated his opponent and added that the best man won.

Although the 1860 Market Harborough race was a triumph, there was some dissension amongst the promoters which resulted in there being two races the next year. Mr Rowlands decided to organize a race at Cheltenham, giving as his reason for deserting Market Harborough that the ridge and furrow of the course was too much in favour of the local horses who were accustomed to such going. Towards the costs of the Cheltenham race the Cotswold Hunt put up £100. The original idea was that the course should be on land belonging to Mr John Newman, but he asked £100 for the use of his fields, which the organizers considered far too high a price. Consequently three tenants of Lord Ellenborough were approached. They agreed that the course should be over their land provided that they were recompensed for any damage caused by the steeplechasers. This course was two and a half miles from Cheltenham in the direction of Cleeve Hill. There were nine runners and the winner was The Freshman, who had finished second to Bridegroom at Market Harborough in 1860. Proof of the toughness of some horses at that time is the fact that later the same afternoon The Freshman won a second race at the meeting. He was ridden by Mr George Ede who rode under the name of 'Mr Edwards'.

Typical of the many gentlemen riders of the era, George Ede after leaving Eton went to be taught steeplechase riding by Ben Land—one of the best cross-country jockeys and trainers of the day. He rode twenty winners in 1858, including a second in the Grand National. He also rode on the flat and once beat George Fordham by a head at Manchester, the next day scoring 122 runs in a cricket match in Hampshire. He won the Grand National on The Lamb in 1868. For many years he lived with Lord Poulett at Waterloo, assisting him with the mastership of the Hambledon Hunt. As soon as the 1870 Grand National was over, Ede had arranged to return to Hampshire for a day's hunting on the morrow. He was persuaded to remain at Aintree to ride in a steeplechase on the following day. His mount, Chippenham, fell, and Ede sustained terrible injuries. He never regained consciousness, dying on the Sunday evening. Amongst his obituary notices was an Ode signed Amphion from which the following is an extract:

> 'A horseman's gifts, the perfect hand
> and graceful seat of confidence.
> The head to reckon and command
> When danger dulls the coward's sense.

'The pluck, unshaken by mischance
and care, unlessened by success
and modest bearing to enhance
the natural charm of manliness.'

Chippenham was trained by Ben Land whose son once caused
great embarrassment to Queen Victoria. There was steeplechasing
at Windsor and Her Majesty, whilst out driving, had ordered her
carriage to be drawn up close to a fence so that she might watch
a race. Unfortunately Ben Land's son, not seeing the Queen, was
urging his horse towards the fence, 'in his loudest voice, with some
of the choicest expressions of which he was so great a master.'
The royal carriage left immediately.

A week after the Cheltenham race, the organizers ran the
Market Harborough Grand National Hunt steeplechase. It is of
interest that the *Sporting Calendar* makes no mention of the Cheltenham race and records the Market Harborough contest as the
third in the series. The conditions of the race varied slightly from
those at Cheltenham. 'Ten sovereigns each with 300 added, for
horses that have never won a steeplechase, hurdle or flat race, or
started in a handicap steeplechase. Four year olds, 11 st. 7 lb.,
five year olds, 12 st., all others 12 st. 7 lbs.' Queensferry owned by
Mr Angell and ridden by Mr Burton won by thirty lengths in a
field of seventeen starters.

In 1862 a new course was tried at Rugby and the locals put up
£400. Unfortunately the course had far too many sharp turns,
and on the day of the race was like a quagmire. A crowd estimated
at 12,000 came to watch, but their view was frequently impeded
by other mounted spectators who galloped freely about the course
getting in everyone's way. It was therefore decided to return to
Market Harborough in 1863. In the *Sporting Review* the course
was described as 'a good deal stronger than that at Rugby though
there was nothing in the line to stop a hunter. Commencing in a
large field where this year the stand and enclosure were placed,
the line lay past the stand, through the winning flags. When over
the first fences the horses turned to the left, going up the hill over
three or four stiffish fences, with a rail or a ditch attached to each,
then, bending again to the left, the line lay down the hill over
the lane whence they came at the brook, a regular clinker measuring some 18 ft clear of water, then going on past the stand they
turned to the right through some stiffish bullfinches and over some
heavy ridge and furrow up hill, then turning to the right they
encountered the same fences as previous to the brook, avoiding

which they jumped a hurdle into the winning field and finished
with a straight run of 300 yards . . .

'The large number of people who attended at Harborough set
all attempts at clearing the course at defiance. The horses were
started in the midst of the mob, and how they even faced the
water with the crowd round it on the landing side was a matter of
wonder to all.'

There were forty-three entries for the race, thirty-four acceptors,
yet disappointingly only five starters. The winner was ridden by
Mr Alec Goodman, yet another of the gentlemen riders who had
a nation-wide reputation as a horseman. He had ridden his first
steeplechase winner as a boy of eighteen. Weight was never a
difficulty and for much of his life he could ride at as little as
9 st. 4 lbs. In 1852 he won the Liverpool Grand National on
Miss Mowbray. Fourteen years later, when he was forty-four
years of age, he again rode the winner—Salamander. On his
return to the winners' enclosure, his expression was so glum that
many observers commented on the fact. The reason was that
Salamander had spent the night prior to the race in a barn which
had a hole in the roof and looked so miserable that Goodman
countermanded a commission to put £100 on him at 40–1 and
also dissuaded many of his friends from backing his mount. The
victory of this outsider did not deter various tipsters from claiming
in *Bell's Life* that they had known Salamander to be a certainty.

The enthusiasm of a large number of gentlemen riders and the
support that they gave to the various steeplechase meetings was
unquestionably standing the sport in good stead. It was suggested
in the *Sporting Review* that 'whatever is run off on Doncaster Moor
ought to be the best of its kind, and perhaps a good hunt meeting
of one day with a couple of steeplechases, a hurdle race and two
hunter chases, one of them round the St Leger course, for five-
year-old hunters which have not been in a training stable before
January 1st of that year ridden by the "crack" gentlemen riders
would draw quite as well if not better than the present programme.

'Steeplechasing has looked up of late and the victory of a mare
like Emblem with such a steadier as 12 st. and giving 13 lbs. away to
the Liverpool winner summons up the remembrance of the golden
days of the sport. The officers are after all the heart and soul of it.'

There can be no doubt of the truth of the last sentence. Reginald
Herbert, himself an outstanding amateur, who one mid-summer
night in full evening dress rode a cow bareback at Waldershore
Park for the amusement of the assembled ladies, confirms this.
He wrote: 'Thus we virtually lived and messed together, some

4

score of us, for three consecutive weeks, only broken by spasmodic visits to town in reserved saloon carriages or sometimes special trains. What difference did a "pony" more or less make when one was betting in "monkeys" and thousands. What friendships too were formed! Friendships that have lasted a lifetime only to be severed by death.'

The finances of some of these gentlemen riders were frequently at very low ebb. George Hodgman in his autobiography, *Sixty Years on the Turf*, tells an astonishing story regarding the last day of the Autumn meeting at Shrewsbury in 1862. He claims that Captain Townley, Captain Little and Mr George Ede admitted to him that they were all 'broke'. He arranged a new race for the next day 'Welter Handicap—gentlemen riders— jockeys 5 lbs. extra—half a mile.' There were five runners, the result was as anticipated—and the £2,500 winning bets divided amongst the delighted and very thankful 'swells'.

VI

Robert Surtees who died in 1864 was not as antagonistic to steeple- chasing as Charles Apperley (Nimrod), but he gave vent to his views in *Mr Sponge's Sporting Tour*. Describing how the Grand Aristocratic came off, he wrote: 'Steeplechases are generally crude, ill-arranged things. Few sportsmen will act as stewards a second time, while the victim to the popular delusion of patron- izing our "national sport" considers—like gentlemen who have served the office of sheriff or churchwarden—that once in a life- time is enough. Hence there is always the air of amateur actorship about them. There is always something wanting or forgotten. Either they forget the ropes, or they forget the scales, or they forget the weights, or they forget the bell or—more commonly still—some of the parties forget themselves. Farmers, too, are easily satisfied with the benefits of an irresponsible mob careering over their farms even though some of them are attired in the miscellaneous garb of hunting and racing costumes. Indeed it is just this mixture of the two sports that spoils both, steeplechasing being neither hunting nor racing. It has not the wild excitement of the one, nor the accurate calculating qualities of the other. The very horses have a peculiar air about them—neither hunters nor hacks nor yet exactly race-horses. Some of them doubtless are fine, good-looking, well conditioned animals, but the majority are lean, lathy, sunken-eyed, woebegone, iron-marked desper- ately abused brutes, lacking all the lively energy that characterizes

the movements of the up-to-the-mark hunter . . .' Surtees was
critical, observant and many of his remarks justified.

There were others, too, who realized the need to improve the
organization of steeplechasing. It was obvious to them that there
must be a governing body to adjudicate, to rule and to plan.
Racing under Jockey Club rules was a flourishing, well-organized
sport, guided by the firm strength of Admiral Rous, and it typified
all that the supporters of steeplechasing envied. In the past, many
owners of hunters and steeplechasers had utterly disregarded any
decisions made by local stewards, whose authority was limited.
Any suspension of jockeys for foul riding, or of owners or trainers
for flagrant abuse of the conditions of races, could only be
effective at the meetings under their own control. There was no
liaison between the various Clerks of Courses. At one meeting the
committee and officials still refused to disclose the whereabouts of
surplus funds six years after the steeplechasing meeting was held.
At another an unscrupulous owner paraded a broken down cart-
horse in the paddock, whilst his genuine entry was waiting at the
starting post. He obtained long odds to his money and was
insulted when there was an objection to his winner! Far more
important, the Jockey Club gave no recognition to steeplechasing.
It was immaterial whether or not a jockey, owner or trainer had
committed heinous offences in the sphere of steeplechasing. If he
had not been 'warned off' Newmarket Heath, he was acceptable
to the rulers of flat racing.

As early as 1845 when Henry Wright produced his first Steeplechase Calendar—the whole properly arranged and furnished
with copious index, list of winning horses, rules, colours of riders,
etc.—he wrote in the introduction, 'The aim, object, and practice
of steeplechasing correspond in the main features so exactly with
Racing that the same Rules and Regulations have generally been
found equally applicable to either sport. In some minor particulars, however, the Laws of the Steeplechase differ or go further
than such as have hitherto been deemed amply sufficient for flat
racing and the following SUGGESTIONS have consequently been
drawn together from the usual articles appended to Steeplechase
announcements, or from decisions given on disputed points.'
The problem of the enforcement of these or any other Rules still
remained, even allowing for the fact that two years later Henry
Wright stated, 'For the Rules and Regulations more particularly,
he (the Editor) can boast of the unqualified approval from the
very highest quarters—among others the stewards of the last
Windsor races, who decided the objection to the winner of the

Grand Handicap avowedly by the 8th Rule of the Calendar and thus established the whole as an authority . . .' In fact the 8th Rule is:—'The term gentleman rider is used solely, a custom that should be carefully avoided, to apply or allude only to persons generally received into Society as gentlemen. Members of the London leading Clubs, Fox-hunting or Racing Clubs, Officers in the Army or Navy, Barristers, Solicitors or Medical men or others so considered by position and profession, and who do not and never have been in the habit of receiving remuneration for riding either directly or in the form of travelling expenses or any other indirect manner.'

With the Crimean war over, the effort of men such as Fogo Rowlands to re-establish steeplechasing brought the problem of a governing body once again to the fore.

In November 1862 *Bell's Life* published in a leading article a suggested code of laws and regulations with regard to steeple-chasing. The next week an anonymous letter appeared in the same paper: 'Sir—it is with very great pleasure that I see you have at last seriously taken up steeplechasing reform. I enclose you a copy of some rules which have been shown to the principal racing and steeplechasing men of the day and have been much approved of. I call the rules mine because I first compiled them this Spring, but they have been revised by many competent people and shown to all good judges of the sport.' The anonymous author of this letter is almost certainly Mr B. J. Angell, aided and abetted by Mr W. G. Craven. Mr Angell, an Etonian, was the owner not only of Bridegroom but also of Alcibiade, winner of the 1865 Liverpool Grand National. A brilliant fencer, Alcibiade was only a five-year-old at the time and thus became the youngest horse ever to have won. He was ridden by Captain Henry Coventry. Cherry Angell had been a leading supporter of steeplechasing for many years. A fluent linguist, he much enjoyed Parisian society and was just as at home in Baden-Baden where he was a frequent visitor. Mr W. G. Craven was an equally influential supporter of steeplechasing, but more significantly he was a member of the Jockey Club.

In December there was further correspondence on the subject. of the rules and a long important letter from Admiral Rous:

13, Berkeley Square,
December, 1862.
Although it is out of my jurisdiction as a Steward of the Jockey Club to interfere with the Rules and Regulations of the Steeple-

chase to be adopted at Market Harborough, I think it would be beneficial to the supporters of this extraneous branch of horse racing to suggest a few alterations which would tend to their efficiency and would assist the Stewards in the event of the usual disputes.

The law-makers commence by stating that the rules concerning horse racing in general apply to all steeplechases. This is an error, because fourteen rules out of sixty-six have no application therewith. Then they omit Rule 42 which gives instructions to the starter. This is a very important article and with a slight modification of fines, is essentially necessary to secure a fair start, otherwise there is no law to restrain a careless or unprincipled starter. Then strange to say Rule 43 is abolished, which forbids crossing and jostling, and prescribes a distance of two lengths or more before one horse can cross another's tracks, under the penalty of disqualification. Now if there is one rule in the racing code which is imperatively necessary for the existence of steeplechasing it is Rule 43. Nineteen disputes out of every twenty in steeplechasing originate from foul riding for which there are more inducements to indulge in than in flat-racing. A gap in a fence, a hard trodden path, a broken rail are all baits to seduce a rider to take unfair advantage, but by publicly ignoring the only rule to go straight the new code offers every encouragement to run riot and to start unfairly. I am therefore at a loss to know how the Stewards are to decide disputes relative to starts and foul riding on their own responsibility when there is no law to ground a verdict of guilty in the event of one jockey riding over his neighbour, or of punishing a starter if he makes an unfair start.

Rule 2 has a most absurd termination 'there is no appeal whatever to a court of law'. This is an imaginary edict, which would be laughed at even if it came from the Crown. No conventional agreement, no code drawn up by private individuals, can prevent a man in this country applying to a court of law for redress. Any person fancying himself aggrieved by the Stewards of races, can and will appeal to a superior tribunal, although the printed racing programme states that 'the decision of the Steward is final', as I have discovered to my inconvenience . . .

All the other rules are well expressed and raising the standard weights to 12 st. 7 lbs. is a sensible improvement.

H. Rous.

In January, the *Sporting Review* stated: 'The appearance of the new steeplechase Rules in the Racing Calendar is a good earnest for the sport at last. That March week, in which the Market Harborough day separates the Northampton and Croxton Park meetings, is enough to keep one alive, by anticipation . . . but although, as Admiral Rous points out, it is foolish for them to say that the law shall not interfere, the framers of the steeplechase Rules have done well to retain the announcement that the decision of the Stewards shall be final. It may often stand them in good stead when an appeal is made to a higher court and disappointed men had better not make one on light grounds.'

In 1863, Mr Angell and Mr Craven co-opted Lord Grey de Wilton as a member of their so-called 'National Hunt Committee'. Within a year a case came before them as a result of an objection to the winner of the Grand National Hunt Steeplechase held at Melton Mowbray. (*En passant* it is amusing to note that during the race one of the riders—Mr Canney—lost control of his horse and almost knocked over Captain Henry Coventry's mount. For the rest of the race Captain Coventry shouted and abused Mr Canney with all his might—to no avail as the unfortunate recipient of this tirade was both deaf and dumb! Mr Canney was killed in 1866 whilst riding at Scariff steeplechases.)

After Cooksboro ridden by Mr Loton won by some five lengths from Game Chicken ridden by Captain (Doggie) Smith, Mr Behrens, the owner of Game Chicken, objected to the winner on the grounds that Mr Loton was not qualified to ride as he had on a previous occasion been paid his expenses and this contravened the conditions of the race. There appear to be certain discrepancies as to how this objection was dealt with. It is a fact that the local stewards refused to give a verdict on the day of the race and that eventually the objection was sustained. It is also a fact that the decision to disqualify the winner was agreed upon at Epsom and the notice declaring this was signed by Coventry, Beaufort, Hastings, Fitzwilliam, Craven and Angell. It has been claimed that these men—all of them except Angell were stewards of the Jockey Club—signed in their capacity as Jockey Club Stewards. However there is no record of any such decision in the Minutes of the Jockey Club. It is therefore more likely that they agreed upon their decision as self-elected members of the steeplechasing committee—even though they had no legal authority.

The next year, a far more complicated and involved objection occurred, when the Grand National Hunt was held at Wetherby.

There were forty-four fences, twenty-nine runners, Mr Craven acted as starter, and the winner—Emperor—was owned by Mr H. Chaplin, a young man of twenty-three who the previous year had been involved in a *cause célèbre* when his fiancée, Lady Florence Paget, eloped with the Marquess of Hastings a few days prior to the wedding. In 1867 his horse Hermit was to win the Derby. Emperor was bred in 1858 by Orpheus out of a half-bred mare. Bought by Mr James Hall, the Master of the Holderness, Emperor won his first race at Thirsk over two miles and a month later was second at York in a race for *bona fide* half-bred hunters. Before this race an objection was lodged against him on the grounds that there was insufficient pedigree on his dam's side. The stewards found the objection 'not proven' and at the end of the year Mr Chaplin bought him for 400 gns. Emperor was then entered for the Wetherby race, the conditions of which read, 'The Grand National Hunt Steeplechase of 10 sovereigns each with 250 sovereigns added, for regular hunters that have not been in a public training stable since January 1st 1865 and that have never won any steeplechase, hurdle race or flat race value 20 sovereigns . . .' There were 112 subscribers. Immediately after the race Mr Studd, the owner of Cooksboro, disqualified from first place in the Grand National Hunt Chase the previous year, and of Lord George who had finished second to Emperor, lodged an objection on the grounds that Emperor had been in the stable of a Mr Welfitt, a public trainer. The objection took the form of a letter addressed to the stewards of the Grand National at Wetherby.

Sirs—Several of my horse's backers have insisted on my objecting to the winner of the Grand National yesterday on the ground of his having been under a public trainer's management since the 1st January last. As this is contrary to the terms of the race, I beg to bring the matter before you for your decision.

Yours respectfully,

Edward Studd.

Hallaton Hall, Leicestershire.

Mr Studd wrote a further letter to Weatherby's:

Dear Sirs—Much against my wish I have been compelled by my horse's backers to make the foregoing communication to the stewards of the Grand National at Wetherby. I feel exceedingly sorry at being called on to do so, and would far rather that Mr Chaplin should be first consulted on the subject, and if he assures me that the horse has NOT been trained by Mr Wel-fitt, I am satisfied and wish the matter to rest in oblivion.

Yours truly,

Edward Studd.

Mr Chaplin replied to the charges in a letter to Mr Studd:

Dear Sir—Messrs Weatherby have forwarded me your letter touching the G.N.H. steeplechase. I can quite enter into your feelings as to the nuisance of an objection generally, but in racing these things cannot be considered. My horses certainly were trained by Mr Welfitt, but as I paid Mr Welfitt nothing either for their keep or their training, and as my own servants were with them it will of course remain for the other stewards to decide whether that constitutes a public stable. I shall lay your letter before them and I think this will be the most satis-factory thing to both of us, and to anyone who may have backed either of our horses for the race.

Believe me.

Yours truly,

Henry Chaplin.

Lord George, Mr Studd's horse, was joint favourite at 5–1 with Emperor at 20–1. At Northampton races the complicated objec-tion was considered by the Duke of Beaufort, Lord Coventry, Mr Craven, Captain Barclay and Mr Angell. It was disclosed that Mr Welfitt was a farmer, a horse-dealer and for many years had trained steeplechase horses. In evidence Mr Chaplin admitted sending his horse to Mr Welfitt to be trained, but again pointed out that he paid nothing either for his keep or training, and that he had no intention of ever paying him anything. On this note the stewards decided to overrule the objection, although Mr Studd reaffirmed that he understood that all horses running for the Grand National Hunters Race were to be trained and brought out from HOME as regular hunters.

Commenting on the case, the *Sporting Review* stated: 'It is certainly unfortunate that since the Grand National Hunt steeplechase has reached anything like importance, two such awk-ward objections should have occurred. Last year Mr Studd's own horse, Cooksboro, was disqualified from his rider having admitted to occasionally receiving his travelling expenses, when there were, no doubt, at least half a dozen others that rode in the same chase against whom such a protest would have been equally fatal. Then

again, surely the intention of the conditions of the Wetherby Chase
was that a horse should come straight from his own hunting stable
and to debar anything like a professional preparation. Of course
the Rules will require some further remodelling and we would
caution the stewards against going specially out of their way in
consideration of farmers. But if a farmer is desirous of a turn in
these National Hunt Chases, let him be treated to none of these
petty distinctions but try his hand at equal main and chance.'

The question of gentlemen riders calling themselves farmers had
long been a cause of dispute. Some unscrupulous men would take
an unfair advantage by acquiring a small farm in an area hunted
by several packs so that they might qualify for hunt races as
farmers. Notwithstanding the prestige of the steeplechasing committee, many cases connected with the sport which required
arbitration were still going to the one man in racing England
whose verdict was virtually law: Admiral Rous. As late as 1865 a
case arose out of the steeplechases held in the Isle of Wight. The
facts were that an owner wished to enter two of his horses—Flying
Spur and Goshawk—for the same race. His trainer swore that the
horses had both been entered by letter to the Hon. Secretary of
the meeting. The Secretary received the letter, did not notice that
both horses had been entered, entered Goshawk only, and then
lost the letter! On the day of the race the circumstances were
explained to the local stewards who allowed Flying Spur to run.
He won, an objection was lodged and later withdrawn: nevertheless the committee declined to hand over the stakes and public
money. Admiral Rous was asked to consider the matter. He
replied to the stewards of the meeting:

13, Berkeley Square,
16th May, 1865.

Gentlemen:

The Secretary by unfortunately losing the trainer's letter,
which he was in duty bound to preserve, is the author of this
controversy. The stewards by allowing Flying Spur to run
sanctioned the legality of the entry, which could only be invali-
dated by the production of the lost letter with Flying Spur
omitted in the entrance. My answers are: 'The stewards were
justified in allowing Flying Spur to run, and when the objection
to the horse was withdrawn, the dispute was at an end. Flying
Spur is clearly entitled to receive the stakes.'

I am, Gentlemen, yours,
H. Rous.

The year after the objection at Wetherby, the Grand National Hunt was held in the West Country near Crewkerne. The winner was a horse owned by Mr Studd! The course was twisty, the prices charged by the local inn-keepers extortionate and the celebrated Charing Cross Barmaid engaged at one house of entertainment! In 1867, when the race went to Bedford, coincidentally another horse of Mr Chaplin's was the victor! Contrary to the policy of the National Hunt Stewards, who intended that the race should take place on a different course each year, in 1868 Bedford was again chosen. In 1869 Wetherby was selected but the meeting was abandoned owing to the appalling disaster which occurred when Sir Charles Slingsby, master of the York and Ainsty Hunt, his hunts-man Charles Ovis and many others were drowned in the River Ure.

By the end of 1865, the year in which Abraham Lincoln had been assassinated, and Lord Palmerston had died, the energy that Mr B. J. Angell, Mr W. G. Craven and Lord Grey de Wilton had shown in their efforts to get a National Hunt Committee recog-nized were successful. Agreement was reached with the approval of the Jockey Club that a separate entity should be constituted to govern the affairs of steeplechasing. The original members of the committee established in 1866 were:

B. J. Angell, Esq.	Sir Frederick Johnstone
C. H. Carew, Esq.	Captain James Little
Viscount Chaplin	George Payne, Esq.
Lord Coventry	Lord Poulett
Captain Henry Coventry	Arthur Sumner, Esq.
W. G. Craven, Esq.	Lord Westmorland.
	Lord Grey de Wilton.

The Duke of Beaufort was co-opted in April 1866 and Viscount Suffolk and E. C. Burton, Esq. in December 1867.

These sixteen men virtually held the destiny of steeplechasing in their power. Most of them were already members of the Jockey Club and in 1866 Mr W. G. Craven was Senior Steward. Lord Poulett, who owned The Lamb, winner of the National in 1868 and 1870, had ridden countless winners in Ireland, including six races in one afternoon. George Payne on resigning mastership of the Pytchley in 1839 had been presented with a silver épergne weighing 600 ounces with the inscription ending: 'by upward of 600 farmers, tradesmen and others of Northampton, . . . as a testimonial of the high esteem for him, and their gratitude for his unceasing efforts to promote the manly and healthy sports of the county'. Captain Little and Captain Coventry had both ridden National winners. Mr Angell had owned one.

The first recorded meeting of members of the committee was held on 7th February 1866: those present were Mr Craven, Sir F. Johnstone, Mr Angell, Mr Sumner and Mr Carew. The business was merely to consider the eligibility of certain candidates as gentlemen riders, and to add various Clubs to the list. At the end of the year, after pages of rules in the Minute Book, there appeared: 'The decision of the Stewards, or whomsoever they may appoint, is final in everything connected with steeplechases, and there is no appeal whatever to a court of law.' This gives little countenance to Admiral Rous's letter of December 1862. Significantly this was followed by: 'Any alterations in, or additions to, the Rules of Racing shall, as far as applicable to steeplechasing, be at once incorporated in these Rules.'

The question of gentlemen riders was still causing discontent in certain quarters. The National Hunt Committee had a letter published in *Bell's Life* on 18th November 1865 which stated . . . 'In all steeplechases advertised for Gentlemen Riders the following qualifications will be necessary—that the riders should be members of one of the following Clubs—The Jockey Club, Bibury, Croxton Park, the New Rooms or Coffee Rooms at Newmarket, the Jockey Clubs of Paris, Berlin or Vienna, the Army and Navy, Arthur's, Arlington, Boodle's, Brooks's, Carlton, Junior Carlton, Guards, Pratt's, Egerton Pratt's, Reform, Travellers', United Service, Junior United Service, White's, Oriental, Kildare St or Sackville St in Dublin, New Club, Edinburgh, or that they should be officers on full pay in the Army or Navy, or persons holding commission under the Crown, or bearing titles in their own right, or by courtesy.

'Persons not qualified as above who wish to ride as gentlemen riders, may send in their names to Messrs. Weatherby's office, proposed and seconded by persons qualified as above, and a ballot will take place from time to time . . .'

There was considerable outcry at even this. An irate member of the Liverpool Hunt Club wrote a complaining letter resenting that this Club was not included. Another wrote, 'One would have thought that the first thing that the Committee of the G.N.H. would have taken into consideration would have been the already established hunt clubs in the Kingdom. In the list they have published I missed the names of the Tarporley Hunt, Royal Caledonian, and Liverpool Hunt . . . In the curious conglomeration in which they have printed their list of London Clubs, I should like to know why a member of the Reform is a gentleman and a member of the Conservative is NOT.'

At the Houghton Meeting in October 1867 the Jockey Club had resolved 'that in future Hurdle races shall NOT be considered as coming within the established Rules of Racing and shall not be reported in the Calendar with flat races.' The National Hunt Committee added to this at a meeting prior to Christmas when they decided that at race-meetings where Hurdle races were advertised to be run under the Grand National Steeplechase rules, the same rules should all be applicable to Hurdle Races. It has been claimed that hurdle races originated when the Prince Regent and his royal party amused themselves by racing over sheep hurdles on the Downs near Brighton.

The year 1868 saw the members of the Committee rapidly gaining in confidence of their authority. At a meeting in March at the Adelphi Hotel, Lord Poulett read a letter from the committee of Tattersalls, declining to adjudicate on any question of disputed bets on steeplechases. It was agreed that they should be asked to reconsider their decision. During the summer a weight for age scale was proposed by Mr Angell. From 1st January–30th June, in two-mile steeplechases four-year-olds should carry 10 st. 3 lbs., five-year-olds—11 st. 8 lbs., and six years and upwards—12 st. 3 lbs. For the last six months of the year these weights should be altered to:—

four years	11 st.
five years	11 st. 12 lbs.
six years and upwards	12 st. 3 lbs.

Proof that the Committee did not intend to permit 'villains' was that they approached the Secretary of the Steeplechase Society in France requesting that he prevent owners and horses from racing in France who had been disqualified in England and suggesting reciprocal arrangements. Later in 1868 a Mr Bower Talbot was struck off the list of gentlemen riders for running a horse at Grantham Steeplechases under a false description and a jockey was warned off for two years. A more unusual incident was brought to the Committee's notice by a Captain Grosvenor who complained that the winner of a selling race at the St Albans November meeting was not offered for sale by public auction according to the conditions of the race.

The clerk of the course's explanation, that darkness had fallen before the stewards had decided whether or not the horse could be sold and that most people had gone home, was not accepted and a letter was sent to Captain Grosvenor informing him that he was entitled to purchase the horse at the price for which he had been entered to be sold.

Although by the end of the 1860s the National Hunt Committee were accepted as the ruling body of steeplechasing, there were still frequent outcries against the sport. Lord William Lennox wrote, 'Steeplechasing is very popular in February, but we own that it is with regret that we find this break-neck pursuit so much in the ascendancy, for to our ideas it cannot come under the denomination of legitimate sport. If, during, or at the end of a hunting season, gentlemen like to try the merits of their respective horses over four or five miles of a fair country, there can be no possible objection to such a proceeding—on the contrary it is an amusing and harmless recreation. But when horses that have never followed a hound, ridden by professional jockeys, are brought out to gallop three or four miles over a racecourse with stiff stone walls, strong posts and rails, awfully large artificial brooks, hurdles, thick fences and broad ditches, the whole feature is destroyed. Instead of its being a test of the goodness of a hunter, it degenerates to a mere gambling racing transaction, in which the best horse seldom or never wins, for with a field of fifteen or sixteen, the chances are that the favourites are put hors de combat by the rush and pressing of the others.'

A fairer, yet impartial summary appeared in an article in *Bell's Life*. 'Truly gratifying to the lovers of steeplechasing is the present state and prospects of that all invigorating and glorious sport. Time was, and not long ago either, when steeplechasing was synonymous with robbers, and with no recognized laws to protect it, and with the demoralizing light-weight system in full force, got up for the most part as an instrument of fraud and barefaced swindling, it gradually but surely sunk into the lowest depths of degradation, and abuse was literally heaped upon it from all sides. Whilst, however, consistently exposing its abuses we have ever steadily upheld steeplechasing as a national sport and vindicated it as a pursuit calculated alike to test the mettle and merits of the horse and his rider. In the good work of endeavouring to bring about a better state of things, we were ably supported by a few "good men and true", and the result is a triumphant and gratifying one. With laws to protect it, countenanced by Royalty, and patronized by the leading sportsmen of the day, steeplechasing is no longer the "illegitimate" despised thing it was, but now ranks proudly side by side with other ennobling and manly pastimes.'

PART II

1871-1914

By PETER WILLETT

I

THE PROGRESS OF THE SPORT

THE Grand National Hunt Steeplechase Committee, to give
it its name in full, had had a difficult birth, and at times
the infant committee seemed to be ailing. For several years
it was touch-and-go whether it would survive to reach man's
estate and exercise full authority. There were plenty of dubious
characters who were only too ready to treat it as a usurper, and
the Committee's minutes contain more than one reference to
'defiance' of the Stewards. In at least one instance defiance was
aggravated by the use of 'disgusting and insulting language'.

There was certainly no lack of disciplinary cases on which the
Committee could try its teeth. During the eighteen seventies these
cases covered the entire gamut of racing offences, including
ringing, not trying, suspicious riding, foul riding, fraudulent entry
and forged hunters certificates. Three men were warned off for
ringing at Tarporley, the Committee finding that they were well
aware that The Rambler was in reality the horse known as The
Rogue; perhaps the malefactors had shown too little originality
in ringing the change of names. It is hard to withhold a grain of
admiration, for sheer audacity and persistence in crime, from
Mr Barnes who, within weeks of getting away with it at Sandown
because bad weather prevented the collection of evidence, was
warned off for life for suspicious riding in a hunters flat race at
Cheltenham. On the other hand every right-thinking amateur
should spare a blush for Mr. C. Fenwicke, who was sent before
the Committee after a meeting at Sutton Park; at the hearing the
Committee expressed their great regret that 'the riding of a
gentleman should have given rise to such grave suspicion'.

Apart from dealing with malpractices as they occurred, the
Committee was concerned with two main problems, which were
perfecting their own organization and extending their authority
to all steeplechase meetings. The first problem was the easier to
solve. In the early days all business had been transacted by the
whole Committee, but in 1873 a sub-committee of three was
appointed to deal with objections and transact all minor business.
In the following year these three—Lord Calthorpe, Mr T. E. Case-
Walker and Lord Queensberry—were appointed the first stewards
of the committee. In May 1874 the rules and orders for conducting
the meetings of the Grand National Hunt Steeplechase Committee
were published. There were to be three general meetings each

year, members were to be elected by ballot, and the three stewards were to continue in office until the annual meeting in April, when the Senior Steward was to retire and a new one be chosen. Two years later the number of stewards was increased to five and in 1890 to six, at which figure it remained until 1950. In 1877 the Steeplechase rules were revised extensively. In 1883 the committee was reconstituted through the resignation of all the members, and was re-formed immediately with most of the same members and a considerable stiffening of Jockey Club members besides. Nine of the twenty-nine members of the new Committee were members of the Jockey Club, and it was thought that in this way National Hunt racing would be in a much stronger position to hold its own against pressures from the Jockey Club on one hand and the Government, who were suspected of an intention to suppress steeplechasing, on the other hand. During the next few years the somewhat unwieldly title of the controlling body of steeplechasing was gradually pruned down until in 1889, on a second revision of the rules, it became simply the National Hunt Committee, which it has remained to the present day.

The move to extend the authority of the committee to all steeplechase meetings was made in two phases. In 1870 a rule was passed that no horse running at a meeting in Great Britain not advertised to be under the National Hunt rules would be allowed to run at any meeting where the Grand National rules were in force. It soon became obvious that this rule did not go far enough, and in July 1875 the Committee, under the Chairmanship of Captain Henry Coventry, who had won the Grand National on Alcibiade, carried a resolution to strengthen the Committee's control through the following new rule: 'Every meeting must be advertised in the Racing Calendar. The advertisement must state that the meeting is to be subject to the Grand National rules, and must state as soon as practicable the days on which the meeting is to begin and end and the names of two or more persons as Stewards, and of the Judge, Starter, Handicapper and Clerk of the Scales.' The enforcement of this rule gave the Committee a supreme power in the realm of steeplechasing comparable to that wielded by the Jockey Club in flat racing.

The new rule armed the National Hunt Committee with the necessary powers, but a long time was to pass before those powers were brought to bear effectively on all the abuses and anomalies that were prevalent in British steeplechasing. There was a great need for closer supervision of the administration of meetings. Owners were continually complaining that payments of prize money were being delayed or not paid at all. Several Clerks of the Course, among whom Messrs M. and J. C. Verrall were particularly culpable, had to be suspended from acting as officials until the amounts owed to owners were paid. Nor were the local Stewards by any means invariably conscientious in fulfilling their responsibilities. As late as 1895 a writer pointed out that the card for the December meeting at Wye included a formidable list of Stewards, not one of whom put in an appearance. The meeting itself was no better than a farce. Of the six races originally advertised, one did not fill, two resulted in walk-overs and the remaining three were contested by an aggregate of nine horses.

In the last quarter of the nineteenth century small steeple-chasing meetings proliferated all over the country. Most market towns had a meeting of some sort. A list of the National Hunt Meetings of the period included many names which have long since disappeared from the fixture list. A representative selection might embrace Aylesbury, Banbury, Bungay, Colchester, Croydon, Hall Green, Ipswich, Maiden Erlegh, Malton, Monmouth, Moreton-in-the-Marsh, Portsmouth Park, Rugby, Shorncliffe, Totnes and Bridgetown, Usk and Llangibby, Wenlock, Woodbridge and, last but not least, Keele Park, now the site of a services area on the M.6 Motorway. There was also an abundance of Hunt meetings which occupied an intermediate position between the well organized point-to-point meetings and the small National Hunt meetings of a later date. There were even a few private meetings, like the one held by Sir Claude Champion de Crespigny at his place in Essex. Sir Claude gave an account of the construction of the course in his *Memoirs*: 'In March 1881 we set to work to make a course at Champion Lodge, and in less than a week had it ship-shape. The expenses were inconsiderable, as the work was performed by men in my own employ. There were several suitable fields round my house, and practically all we had to do was to make the necessary jumps, and erect a stand or two.' It all sounds delightfully simple and, as far as costs are concerned, in marked contrast to the figure of millions of pounds quoted for building a new course some eighty years later.

Some of these meetings operated in the face of severe disadvantages. The course at Portsmouth Park, for example, was situated on the far side of the railway from the road and, as there was no bridge or level crossing, was inaccessible to carriages. The lay-out and construction of many of the courses were primitive in the extreme. There were no wings to the hurdles at Ipswich, so experienced jockeys made it a rule to ride at the middle of the

hurdles; and one distinguished rider who had accepted an engage-
ment at Totnes thought better of fulfilling it when he found that
the course crossed the River Dart twice, exclaiming: 'I came to
ride, but not to swim!' The Stewards of the National Hunt Committee, on being required to adjudicate on an objection for going
the wrong course at Cheltenham, had no option but to declare
the objection invalid when they discovered that there had been
no flags to mark where the fences were supposed to be jumped.

It is not surprising that falls were numerous in these circumstances and, as fields were generally small, races were often won
by horses that had fallen and been remounted, sometimes more
than once. On the other hand the country meetings were great
fun, at least for the privileged few. The so-called gentlemen riders
usually had a separate changing room, and at northern meetings
there was always a butler in attendance to serve champagne
before and after the race. In the absence of any prohibition of
stimulants, it was a common sight to see a trainer give his horse
a shilling bottle of port and half a bottle of brandy before a race,
'just to steady his nerves'. Many of the jockeys used to take the
same dose for the same purpose, and some wild riding was apt
to result.

Croydon was much the most important of the courses mentioned. It had a steep uphill finish and provided a stern test of
stamina. Several valuable races like the Grand National Hurdle,
the Grand International Hurdle and the Great Metropolitan
Chase were run there, and its loss was felt keenly when it closed
down in the eighteen nineties.

In the early days of the Committee there were no regulations
whatever about the types and numbers of obstacles that were to
be jumped in steeplechases and hurdle races. In 1882 the Committee, with Captain Coventry again in the chair, received the
report of a sub-committee which had been appointed to study
this problem. This sub-committee, of which Mr E. C. Burton was
Chairman and Lord Marcus Beresford was one of the ten members,
opened the report with a preamble stating that steeplechasing
had been in its most flourishing condition between 1863 and 1876,
but then a decline had set in. The principal cause of this decline
was said to be the diminution in the size, number and variety of
fences. The report added: 'Fences have been trimmed down,
ditches filled up, brushwood and gorse substituted for growers
and binders, while brooks have been converted into concealed
water splashes, till the accomplished chaser has no chance of
proving his superiority over the half-educated racehorse, hence

A Steeplechase in 1870; racing across a natural line of country. *Reproduced by permission of Radio Times Hulton Picture Library*

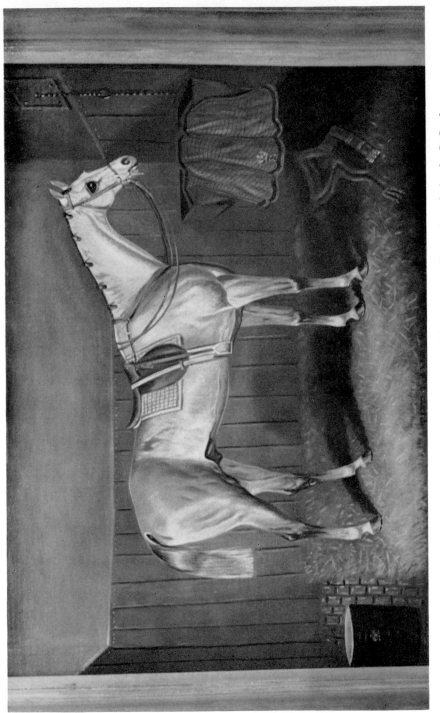

The Lamb, the Grand National winner of 1868 and 1871. *From the painting by S. Spode*

the almost entire withdrawal of the former from a sport which fifty years ago was all jumping, is now all galloping, but which nevertheless continues to be as attractive as ever to the race going public.'

In order to arrest the decline and restore the fortunes of steeple-chasing the sub-committee proposed that in each mile of a steeple-chase there should be at least one open ditch six feet wide and four feet deep on the taking off side, and the ditch should not be guarded in any way. In every steeplechase of two miles there should be at least twelve fences and in each succeeding mile at least six fences. In every steeplechase there should be a water jump at least twelve feet wide and two feet deep, and this jump should be left open, or guarded only by a single rail. To be eligible to run in a hunters race a horse must not have run on the flat since he was a two-year-old nor run in any race not confined to hunters in the previous twelve months. No horse should run in a hunters flat race unless he had jumped all the fences in a steeple-chase to the satisfaction of at least two of the stewards, and a certificate had been lodged with Weatherby's.

These recommendations were accepted unanimously by the Committee, and in July were incorporated in the rules, together with a rule that no hurdle race should be less than two miles nor over less than eight flights of hurdles. The height of the hurdles must not be less than three feet six inches from the bottom bar to the top bar.

It was one thing to accept the recommendations, quite another to ensure that they were implemented. Two years later the Com-mittee took the essential step of appointing the first Inspector of National Hunt Courses at the princely salary of £50 a year. The choice fell on Mr Thomas Pickernell, a retired amateur rider who had won three Grand Nationals and was the ideal man for the post.

Some regulations to ensure that the fences to be jumped in steeplechases were not only fair but more or less uniform through-out the country were long overdue. On the other hand both the preamble to the report and the recommendations indicated the split personality of steeplechasing at that period, simultaneously hankering after a carefree sporting past and striving to come to terms with the more sophisticated requirements of a growing entertainment business. There was a yearning to return to the natural obstacles of the hunting field from which steeplechasing had sprung. This yearning found even clearer expression in the steeplechase section of the Badminton Library volume on Racing.

In that section Arthur Coventry wrote: 'The primary idea of a steeplechase is a contest over so many miles of a fair hunting country, a course which differs in several important particulars from the made tracks at present in vogue.' He added that it was desirable that the course should include an open brook, a double, posts and rails and banks so that both horse and rider would be thoroughly tested. One of the advantages of a natural course, according to Coventry, was that it would eliminate cast-offs from the flat, who would be better employed between the shafts of a cab. This desire for a return to the past was in direct conflict with the needs of a properly organized sport, attracting large numbers of the public, staged on courses depending on gate money receipts for their survival and the satisfaction of their share holders, with horses specially trained for the job. In the long run progress could not be halted, and the wish to restore the primitive conditions of the hunting field was doomed to disappointment like all other attempts to stem the tide or put the clock back. Owners simply would not risk valuable horses, nor could the standard of steeplechasing be raised, unless the obstacles were made reasonably safe. By 1902 a number of modifications had been introduced of which the most important were the guarding of open ditches by a bank and rail not exceeding two feet in height and the placing of low fences in front of the water jumps.

Sir Claude de Crespigny was able to throw a good deal of light on the changes that had occurred in steeplechasing during his lifetime when he published his *Memoirs* in 1896. He stated that he had often been asked whether steeplechasing had degenerated, and gave his reply: 'On the whole, I am not prepared to say that it has. The horses are far finer creatures than they were a quarter of a century ago; no "cocktail", such as often used to win in those days, would have a chance in a big race now.' But Sir Claude felt that the sport had become rather a 'kid-glove' business in some respects. 'Many of the best and biggest courses are attended to almost like tennis lawns or cricket pitches', he wrote. 'The take-off and landing in particular are looked after with the greatest care. When a frost threatens, straw is usually put down to keep the ground from becoming too hard, and one even hears of the whole course being in some instances treated with the same tenderness.' Indeed Sir Claude's views provided a fair summing-up of the two aspects of the split personality of Steeplechasing.

Hurdle racing was regarded with good-humoured contempt by the old school of the steeplechasing fraternity. Arthur Coventry who, as we have seen, was a purist in his approach to cross-country racing, approved of hurdling because it had no affinity with the hunting field and no pretensions to be anything but a medium for gambling. He thought it answered this purpose admirably. There was no Champion Hurdle race, indeed there was no valuable weight-for-age race over hurdles, nor was there any handicap over hurdles that corresponded, even remotely, with the Grand National Steeplechase. Consequently no horse who could be schooled to jump fences with any degree of proficiency remained a hurdler for long. Thus Chandos, the best hurdler of his day, was hastened prematurely into the Grand National and paid the penalty; and Bellona, though only five years old and in her first season as a jumper, won the Grand International Hurdle at Croydon only three weeks before she ran in the 1887 Grand National, in which she fell at the second fence.

Wrack was probably the outstanding hurdler of the whole period. A member of one of Lord Rosebery's best thoroughbred families, he was a good miler on the flat and won the Newbury Spring Cup twice. He also possessed a natural talent for hurdling which was skilfully developed by his trainer Frank Hartigan. He was small, but broad for his height and very powerfully built. He was a hard puller and, ridden by George Duller, usually took his opponents off their legs in a manner which brought him victory in six of his seven races over hurdles. His most lucrative success was in the Gloucestershire Hurdle at Cheltenham in 1914, the race being worth £827 to the winner, or £2 more than the Imperial Cup and the Liverpool Hurdle, the two most valuable handicap hurdle races of the season. His last appearance under N.H. Rules was in the Shamrock Handicap Hurdle at Newbury in March 1915, when he carried top weight of 12 st 7 lbs to a comfortable victory. He won his second Spring Cup on the same course a month later and in the same year was sold to the United States, where he became a most successful stallion. He has an honourable place in the pedigree of Ragusa.

While artificial courses had come to stay and differed fundamentally from the natural conditions of the hunting field, the National Hunt Steeplechase and point to points became increasingly important as links between hunting and steeplechasing. The National Hunt Chase had been adopted by the Committee as a means of encouraging farmers to breed high quality horses suitable for both hunting and racing. The race was confined to maidens at starting and was made a movable feast in order to provide the right incentive in various parts of the country. This policy was followed so faithfully that the race, usually over four miles, was held on no fewer than twenty-two different courses after 1871 before it was given a permanent home at Cheltenham in 1911. The contribution from the National Hunt Committee was gradually raised, as the Committee's finances permitted, from £400 provided at Sandown Park in 1875 to £1,000 at Cheltenham in 1913. The number of high class horses who won the race during the period was limited. Why Not, successful in the National Hunt Chase at Malton in 1886, was the only one who went on to win a Grand National, but the 1879 winner Bellringer, the 1883 winner Satellite and the 1908 winner Rory O'Moore were above average performers.

Point to points, which began to be popular about the year 1880, were designed to perpetuate the ideal of a race across a fair hunting country. Originally the point to point was what its name suggests it should be, a race from one chosen point to another. Few guiding flags were used, perhaps none at all at the earliest meetings, but the competitors had to cross a natural country to some point usually four miles away in a straight line. It was not long before the increasing number of point to points aroused fears of encroachment on the country steeplechase meetings, but it proved possible in practice for these two forms of cross-country racing to exist side by side, to their mutual advantage, for many years. The authorities soon turned their attention to the new point to points, and as early as 1882 the National Hunt Committee gave their first ruling on the subject by stating that point to points need not be advertised, and horses having run in such races should not be disqualified from running at meetings under National Hunt rules, with the proviso that no part of a point to point course must be defined. In 1889 the committee ruled that each Master of Hounds should be allowed one point to point meeting a season with any number of races desired, but no two meetings should be held on the same course without permission. There must be no gate money, no prize greater than £20, and no race of less than three miles. Five years later rules 5 and 164 to 168 of the National Hunt rules were made applicable to point to points. These are the rules which empower the stewards of the National Hunt Committee to investigate and punish corrupt and fraudulent practices, and were essential for the proper control of point to point meetings. In 1908 the process of bringing order to point to points was completed by the regulation that no horse or person disqualified under any rules of racing or steeplechasing might take part, and that a horse registered must run under that name. Between the two world wars complaints were continually voiced against point to points which echoed the complaints made against steeplechasing in the eighteen eighties. It was said that point to point courses had lost all resemblance to the natural conditions of the hunting field. These complaints were disregarded for a similar reason, which was that point to points were assuming ever growing importance in hunt finances through parking charges and the sale of race cards. It was essential to provide spectators with value for money and to attract good horses.

Various problems of administration and legislation had preoccupied the National Hunt Committee during the thirty years before the appointment of Captain Stanley as a steward of the National Hunt Committee in 1910. During that time a good many offences of all kinds had been dealt with. In 1881 Mr Nicholson was reported to the Committee by the local stewards for his suspicious riding of Testerton in the Full Cry Steeplechase at the Lincoln Spring meeting. At the inquiry a Veterinary certificate was produced, signed by Mr Howse of Lincoln, stating: 'I hereby testify that on the 23rd ult I was requested to attend Testerton, the property of Mr Newell Melbourn, of Fillingham, near Lincoln. The horse was suffering from acute spasm, supervening influenza, and consequently the deranged condition of the horse's health rendered him incapable of performing severe exertion with impunity, and also prevented him from running in his true form.' As a result the stewards exonerated Mr Nicholson but severely censured Mr Melbourn for running a horse which he knew to be seriously amiss. Two years later Albert Nicholls was warned off for two years for wilfully riding Harebell out of the course in the Licensed Victuallers Steeplechase at Newton Abbot in order to prevent her from winning. Nicholson and Melbourn and Nicholls, and many others disciplined during this period, were small fry. Plenty of trainers and jockeys of higher standing, whose offences were no less grave and were certainly committed with greater regularity, used to get off scot-free. Captain Stanley, afterwards Brigadier-General Ferdinand Charles Stanley and a younger brother of the 17th Earl of Derby, was determined to end this situation. During his stewardship from 1910 to 1913 offenders were disciplined without fear or favour, and some of the leading figures in the sport found themselves in trouble. One of these was Mr George Gunter, who had been leading amateur in 1909 and was a prominent figure in Yorkshire sporting circles. In 1912 he was before the Stewards for his riding of Abelard in a National Hunt flat race at Wye, and the Stewards found that his riding was open to the gravest suspicion and cautioned him severely. In the same year Tom Coulthwaite was severely cautioned for the discrepancy in the form shown by Great Loss in the Grand National Trial at Newbury and the National Hunt Handicap Steeplechase at Cheltenham, and the following year he was warned off for two similar offences. Percy Woodland was sent before the Stewards of the National Hunt Committee to explain the discrepancy in the form shown by Wild Aster in hurdle races at the Hurst Park and Nottingham January Meetings. Woodland, who had won one Grand National on Drumcree and was to win another on Covertcoat, was then training in France and had sent over Wild Aster, who had dead-heated for the Grand Prix de Nice, to reap a rich harvest of victories in small National Hunt races in England. The stewards informed him that they were not at all satisfied with his explanation and that his riding was open to the gravest suspicion, but as a doubt existed they gave him the benefit of it and cautioned him severely as to his future riding.

The knowledge that great as well as small offenders were being brought within the net had a salutary effect on the morale of the steeplechasing community. If National Hunt sport was not cleaned up before the outbreak of the first world war, it was at least made to look a good deal more respectable than it had been a few years earlier.

II

THE GRAND NATIONAL

The Grand National is the thread upon which the history of Steeplechasing during the half century before the first world war is strung. By 1870 the race was a truly national sporting event and, although Steeplechasing as a whole came in for strong adverse criticism from various sources at times, the Grand National itself was always attended by large crowds and never lost its hold on the public imagination. The best horses had to run in it simply because there were no other races worthy of them. Other courses put on races with resounding titles like 'Grand Prize', 'Great Steeple Chase' and 'Grand International', but none of these were serious competitors with the Grand National in the long term. One or two of them carried large prize money for a year or two, but they did not last long and the Grand National remained supreme.

In consequence the Grand National fields were truly representative of the best jumpers. Some wholly unsuitable horses ran for lack of other opportunity. Chandos was a high class hurdler by vocation, yet he started favourite. The Midshipmite was a brilliant chaser up to three miles but had no pretentions whatsoever to stay the four and a half miles at Aintree, yet he ran repeatedly. On the other hand Cloister, Manifesto and Jerry M, who all carried 12 st. 7 lbs. to victory, proved their greatness to an extent that might have been impossible in a later period when the best chasers could win big money without going near Aintree at all and by taking part in weight-for-age races. Other chasers of almost equal merit never did get their due rewards. One of these was Congress, considered by Mr E. P. Wilson, who won the Grand National on Voluptuary and Roquefort, to be the best horse he ever rode. Congress had to be content with two seconds in the Grand National, for he was beaten by a neck by Regal in 1876 and was in the same place, carrying top weight of 12 st. 7 lbs., behind Austerlitz the next year.

While the exclusive position of the Grand National enabled the great horses to consolidate their reputations, the hazards of the race were as much in evidence as they have been in any other period, before or since. This aspect of the race stands out from the record of runners in the race owned by Lord Wavertree, who described his experiences, both fortunate and unfortunate, in his foreword to D. H. Munroe's *The Grand National*. Wavertree, who has a lasting place in British racing history through his gift of the National Stud to the Government during the first world war, had a close family connection with Liverpool. His father was Mayor of Liverpool, where he was also founder of the famous Walker Gallery which bears his name. Colonel Hall Walker, as he was before he was raised to the peerage, had a burning ambition to win the Grand National on his home course, and achieved it at the very first attempt with The Soarer in 1896. Thereafter nothing went right for him in the race. He had twenty-six other runners in the race, but never won it again.

The Grand National course began to take on its modern appearance during the last quarter of the nineteenth century. At the beginning of the period large parts of it were plough. Dick Marsh recorded that when he finished third on Thornfield in 1881 there were two long stretches of plough, the first extending from the second fence to Becher's Brook and the second being met soon after leaving Valentine's. It included a field of growing mangolds some of which had been pulled to provide a lane for the horses to pass through. Thornfield was so hopeless in the plough that he

pulled up to a trot at one point and it was not until he reached
the grass after Valentine's that he began to gallop properly at all.

About the same time many of the obstacles were very different
from what they were in 1966. During the eighteen seventies the
number of obstacles jumped in the two circuits of the course was
thirty, exactly the same as it is today, but no less than seven of
these were not fences at all, but flights of hurdles. The race
finished round the circumference of the 6 furlongs flat course
upon which were two, and sometimes three, flights of hurdles.
What is now the 'Chair', the biggest fence on the whole course,
was then known simply as the Brook in front of the stands, with
a small, trappy fence in front of it. It was the unfair nature of this
fence that was held responsible for the fatal fall of Mr George Ede,
the best amateur rider of his day, on Chippenham in a Steeplechase on the day after the Grand National in 1870.

During the next few years there was a growing volume of complaints about various aspects of the course. Dissatisfaction reached
such a pitch that in February 1874 a letter, signed by twenty-four
members of the N.H. Committee including Lords Poulett and
Calthorpe, was sent to Messrs Tophams, the organizers of the
race, demanding that improvements should be made. The letter
claimed that the principal causes of the casualties that were continually occurring in the Grand National were the crowds of
spectators closing in on the horses at the fences, and the increase
of the numbers of small, trappy fences. They requested
Tophams to rail off the course at every fence, to keep the fences up
to a proper standard, and to replace the fence in front of the stand
with a post and rail about four feet high. The letter was couched
in the strongest terms and Tophams meekly replied that they
would carry out the wishes of the signatories as far as possible.

Progress was somewhat slow. It was not until 1885, eleven
years after the vigorous protest of the National Hunt Committee,
that the whole course was railed in. It was in the same year that the
race was run entirely on turf for the first time, though patches of
plough reappeared on one or two occasions before the end of the
century. Three years later the course took on its final shape,
finishing over two small fences erected inside the flat race course
instead of finishing on the flat course itself. The new fences
probably robbed George Lambton of his finest opportunity to
win the race. Coming on to the racecourse the last time Savoyard
was four lengths clear and going so easily that Lambton, knowing
that the two new fences were particularly stiff, steadied the horse
in an attempt to make sure of getting over safely. The reverse

Mr Arthur Coventry. A great amateur rider and afterwards official starter to the Jockey Club.
Copyright W. W. Rouch & Co. Ltd.

Tom Coulthwaite, the trainer of three Grand National winners, Eremon, Jenkinstown and Grakle.
Copyright W. W. Rouch & Co. Ltd.

Arthur Yates—rider of 460 and trainer of 2,950 winners. *Copyright W. W. Rouch & Co. Ltd.*

Father O'Flynn, winner of the Grand National in 1892. *Copyright W. W. Rouch & Co. Ltd.*

happened, for Savoyard, put out of his stride, got too close to
the first of the two fences, brushed the top and turned over like
a shot rabbit on landing.

The best horses to win the Grand National in the period under
consideration were probably The Lamb, Cloister, Manifesto,
Jerry M and Eremon. It is convenient that one of these, The Lamb,
won the race in 1871, the opening year of the period. The Lamb
had several distinctions apart from his natural ability as a jumper.
He was the last grey horse to win the Grand National until
Nicolaus Silver exactly ninety years later, and he was the last
dual winner until Manifesto in 1897 and 1899.

In addition The Lamb was one of the smallest horses ever to
win the Grand National. At four years of age he was a pony
standing barely fifteen hands, though by the time he gained the
first of his Grand National victories as a six-year-old in 1868 he
had grown two inches taller. In 1868 he was ridden by the ill-
fated George Ede, but did not run in either of the following two
years, when victory went to The Colonel. On one of those occasions he had to miss the race because of a mistake on the entry
form, as he was entered under the wrong age. The Colonel, who
also earned lasting fame by winning the Grand National twice,
afterwards became a stallion in one of the German Imperial Studs,
where he enjoyed a fair measure of success in a completely different
role. Dreams and superstitions have played no unimportant part
in the Grand National story, but at no time has their impact been
more graphically illustrated than in the case of The Lamb's
second victory. His owner, Lord Poulett, a founder member of
the National Hunt Committee and for many years Master of the
Hambledon Hounds, had two dreams one night in December,
three months before the running of the race. Both dreams were
about The Lamb in the coming race. In the first The Lamb
finished last. In the second The Lamb won by four lengths and
was ridden by Mr Tommy Pickernell. He saw the horse, his own
cerise and blue colours, and Pickernell wearing them, with
extraordinary vividness. The very next day he wrote to Pickernell
and engaged him to ride. The power of superstition was seen
when a lamb jumped from a cattle truck in Liverpool Station
the day before the race and gambolled away between the railway
lines. The story spread and superstitious backers piled money on
The Lamb to such an extent that he started second favourite at
5–1.

Although he was so small, The Lamb was a model of what a
chaser ought to be. He was dark grey and tremendously thick set,

with great power everywhere. He had beautifully sloped shoulders, great depth through the body and perfectly shaped quarters, with a pronounced jumping bump. He hardly knew how to make a mistake and stayed forever. His agility was amazing. At the canal turn two horses fell in front of him and for an instant Pickernell saw disaster staring him in the face. He need not have worried, as The Lamb hopped neatly over his prostrate rivals without touching them, and went on unscathed. At the last fence he was as fresh as if he had just started and soared over it to win easily.

There was no more experienced Aintree rider than Pickernell, who rode under the assumed name of 'Mr Thomas'. He rode in seventeen Grand Nationals, had only two falls, and won the race on Anatis in 1860 and Pathfinder in 1875, besides on The Lamb. He always asserted that The Lamb was the best horse he ever rode. 'The finest fencer I was ever on in my life' was his tribute to this wonderful little horse.

In later years, Pickernell was apt to take a nip or two by way of jumping powder before riding in a race. He rather overdid it before riding Pathfinder and, on arriving at the start, was momentarily at a loss to know which way to go. Perhaps the horse was well named, because they set off in the right direction when the time came. Once the race had started Pickernell rode with his usual cool efficiency and rode one of his best finishes to beat Dainty by half a length.

The Lamb was bred by a farmer in County Limerick and was so undersized in his early days that he once changed hands for only £30. On the other hand his temperament was always delightful, hence the name he was given. Nor was there a lack of jumping ability in his pedigree, for his dam was by Arthur, who was second to Jerry in the Grand National in 1840. The Lamb soon showed the stuff of which he was made when he began to race, and Lord Poulett leased him for his racing career after he had won the Kildare Hunt Plate.

The racing careers of The Lamb and Thomas Pickernell ended rather sadly. The Lamb was sold to the German Baron Oppenheim, who started him for the Grand Steeplechase at Baden-Baden in September 1872. He was winning easily when he ran into a patch of boggy ground a hundred yards short of the winning post, and began to slow down. His rider, Count Nicholas Esterhazy, began to ride desperately but The Lamb, trying to accelerate in the mud, snapped a leg and had to be destroyed.

Tommy Pickernell's riding career came to an end when he had

a dreadful fall on the flat at Sandown Park in 1877, two years after his last Grand National victory. He had broken nearly every bone in his body in various falls, but on this occasion he lost the sight of one eye and damaged the other so severely that he was forced to retire, though he lived to a ripe old age.

The second victory of The Lamb was followed by the victory of a horse who was described at the time as one of the worst of all Grand National winners. This was Casse Tête, who was dismissed contemptuously as 'a varminty looking, washed-out chestnut mare'. She had been bought out of a selling race for 210 gns. and was carrying only 10 st. For her the road to victory at Aintree was paved with the misfortunes of better opponents. During most of the race the issue seemed to rest between Schiedam, who had won the National Hunt Chase, Harvester and Scarrington. Early on the second circuit Schiedam jumped on top of the fallen Primrose and, although he managed to keep on his feet, lost so much ground that he was virtually out of the race. Approaching the racecourse Harvester was going so well that Arthur Yates, who had made three previous unsuccessful attempts to win the Grand National, felt sure of his first success. There had been heavy rain during the previous week and Yates had fitted Harvester's shoes with studs so that the horse could get a surer foothold. As he landed over the last fence the studs of one of Harvester's hind shoes struck the heel of one of his forefeet, cutting him so badly that Yates had to pull him up. That left Scarrington in front of Casse Tête, and Bob I'Anson on Scarrington, having glanced round at Page, who was riding Casse Tête for all he was worth, realized that his own horse was going so much better that he called out: 'It's been a long time coming off, Jack, but I've done it this time.' So saying he set sail on Scarrington and came to the second last flight of hurdles nearly a dozen lengths clear. But I'Anson had spoken too soon. Scarrington hit the hurdle terribly hard and lamed himself so badly that he stopped almost to a walk. Casse Tête stayed on at her own pace to give Page, who had won the 1867 Grand National on Cortolvin, his second successful ride in the race. Casse Tête was certainly lucky in that her three most dangerous rivals all suffered mishaps, but she must have been a resolute stayer and it is hard to believe that she was not a good deal better than she looked or her contemporaries gave her credit for. Perhaps the real hero of that race was again The Lamb, who carried 12 st. 8 lbs. into fourth place, a marvellous feat for such a small horse in heavy going.

The victory of Casse Tête was followed by what may be called fairly 'The Machell Era'. Captain Henry Machell owned three of the next four Grand National winners (Disturbance in 1873, Reugny in 1874 and Regal in 1876). Disturbance and Reugny were both ridden by Mr J. M. Richardson, a wealthy man in his own right who trained them on his estate at Limber Magna in North Lincolnshire.

Maunsell Richardson had ridden Schiedam in the Grand National won by Casse Tête, and had learned from that experience that there is nothing more dangerous in a steeplechase than to ride at a fence directly in the tracks of another horse. He steered clear of his opponents, always going for the biggest and blackest parts of the fences, on Disturbance and Reugny, and reaped his reward.

Although Machell was one of the heaviest betters of the time and fancied Disturbance considerably, the horse was allowed to start at 20–1 because most people considered him too small a horse to carry 11 st. 11 lbs. successfully. Nor did Disturbance's chances look particularly bright when Rhyshworth came on to the racecourse well in front of him and apparently going well within himself. Rhyshworth had been a high-class horse on the flat, but Richardson had had him in his stable at one time and knew his weakness, which was that he had no stomach for a close struggle. He drove Disturbance alongside Rhyshworth at the last hurdle and, as they landed on the flat, glanced across to see Rhyshworth lay his ears back, and knew that he had won. Soon afterwards Rhyshworth cracked and Disturbance drew away to win by 6 lengths. The menu cards at the celebration dinner were headed 'Disturbance, but no row!', an admonition that was observed until, late in the evening, one of the guests fell into a tub full of ice-cold water intended for cooling champagne.

The next year Machell had three runners, these being Disturbance with the great weight of 12 st. 9 lbs., Defence and Reugny, who had only 10 st. 12 lbs. to carry. Reugny came best out of a trial between the three horses at Limber and Richardson made no mistake in selecting him as his Grand National mount. All the same it was touch-and-go in the last half-mile, because Richardson knew that Reugny was not a true stayer and dared not move on him. Chimney Sweep came on to the racecourse five lengths in front of him, but Jack Jones became nervous on Chimney Sweep half-way up the straight and gave him two strokes with his whip which made the tired horse go slower rather than faster. With Richardson still sitting still, Reugny sailed past to win by six lengths.

The Grand National, 1892 ; won by Father O'Flynn. *Reproduced by permission of Radio Times Hulten Picture Library*

William Dollery.
Copyright
W. W. Rouch & Co. Ltd.

Mr Charles Duff—
afterwards Sir Charles
Assheton-Smith—with
Cloister, the Grand
National winner of 1893.
Copyright
W. W. Rouch & Co. Ltd.

Manifesto, winner of the
Grand National in 1897
and 1899.
Copyright
W. W. Rouch & Co. Ltd.

The association of Machell and Richardson broke up after Reugny's victory. For the 1876 Grand National Machell's two runners, Regal and Chandos, were trained by the professional steeplechase jockey James Jewitt at Kentford near Newmarket. Regal was a superbly bred horse by the Goodwood Cup winner Saunterer out of Regalia, who won the Oaks. On the other hand he was a very moderate performer on the flat and Machell was able to buy him for only 360 gns. after he had won a selling race at Newmarket. Chandos was a greatly superior flat racer, for he was fourth in Doncaster's Derby in 1873 besides winning several races. He had become one of the best hurdlers of the century, but lacked the experience of Regal over fences. Regal had shown a natural flair for jumping fences and had been an easy winner of the Great Sandown Steeplechase over four miles.

During their Grand National preparation Regal and Chandos were put through their paces thoroughly at Kentford and in repeated four-mile gallops Chandos proved himself at least the equal of his stable companion. Machell came to the conclusion that Chandos was a certainty, with the single proviso that a jumper of so little experience might well be upset by the drop fences at Liverpool. As a result Chandos started a hot favourite at 100–30, but Machell was astute enough to have a good saving bet on Regal at 25–1 just in case the worst happened to Chandos.

On the second circuit of the course Regal and Chandos drew away from the rest of the field despite a bad mistake made by Chandos at the water jump in front of the stands. Chandos, ridden by his trainer, was still going easily, but his owner's misgivings were fulfilled at Valentine's, where the horse misjudged the drop and turned over on landing. Regal, ridden by Joe Cannon, was left in front and, although headed more than once in the later stages, fought back splendidly to beat Congress, ridden by Ted Wilson, by a neck.

Few Grand National winners have been as classically bred as Regal. Another in the same category was 'the beautiful, bold, dashing Empress, the only five-year-old mare that has ever won a Grand National'. It is a curious coincidence that Regal and Empress, whose Aintree victory came four years later, were exactly the same age, which is exceptionally young for a Grand National winner. Empress was out of a half sister of the Oaks winner Feu De Joie and had a stronger influence on future generations than any other Grand National winner of either sex. She was the fourth dam of Old Orkney, who won the Goodwood Cup and was Brown Jack's great rival, and was also the ancestress of

6

No Fiddling, a high-class miler of the early nineteen-sixties. She also passed on her jumping ability, for her son Red Prince II was not only a top class two-year-old on the flat in Ireland, but afterwards won the Lancashire Chase and became a leading sire of jumpers. Empress had things very much her own way in the 1880 Grand National. She had been thoroughly schooled by her experienced trainer, Linde of the Curragh, and would have given Mr Tommy Beasley an armchair ride if he had not had the misfortune to break a stirrup leather in the later stages of the race. Even so she beat the previous year's winner The Liberator comfortably enough by two lengths, and was so fresh that her jump at the last hurdle was measured as covering thirty feet from take-off to landing.

Empress became unsound afterwards and was never seen on the racecourse again. On the other hand her victory was only the beginning of the Aintree road for Tommy Beasley, who was generally considered the finest steeplechase rider, amateur or professional, of his day. Beasley, a member of a famous Irish racing and hunting family, won the next Grand National on Woodbrook and had a third success in the race on Frigate eight years later. The prowess of Tommy Beasley over all fences, and over the Aintree fences in particular, was remarkable, so it was a fine achievement by Lord Manners to beat him on his own horse Seaman in 1882. The oft repeated story that Lord Manners had never before ridden in a steeplechase is disputed, and as Master of the Quorn he certainly knew all about riding over fences in the hunting field. On the other hand he did not possess anything like Beasley's experience of race riding. In Seaman he had a first rate instrument for achieving his ambition of winning the Grand National. He bought the horse for a sum reputed to be £2,000 out of Linde's stable. Like Empress, Seaman was perfectly schooled to his job, and had previously won the Conyngham Cup at Punchestown, the Grand Hurdle at Auteuil and the first Liverpool Hunters Chase. Thus he was a completely equipped jumper and he would doubtless have beaten Beasley's mount Cyrus by a great deal more than the actual head if he had not broken down on landing over the last fence. Seaman was too badly injured ever to run in another race, but he served his owner, and his owner's children, for several years afterwards as a hack.

The 1883 Grand National resulted in another owner-ridden winner. This was the mare Zoedone, ridden by the Hungarian Count Charles Kinsky. As a young man attached to the Austro-Hungarian Embassy in London, Kinsky developed a strong taste for English field sports of all kinds and, as the son of one of the finest horsewomen in Hungary, had natural leanings towards hunting and racing. One of the most colourful personalities in the steeplechasing world of the late nineteenth century, he was brave, charming, utterly fearless and a polished horseman. He was also an intense admirer of England and the English and for him the outbreak of the first world war, which involved fighting against some of his best and oldest friends, was a great personal tragedy.

Zoedone was the safest of jumpers and had any amount of stamina. She had been third in the previous Grand National although, as she was the only other runner to get round without mishap except Seaman and Cyrus, this proved little except her ability to jump the fences. Kinsky did not buy her until after the Cesarewitch, on which he had a good win five months before his success at Aintree, and he was modest enough to realize that his lack of experience was a big handicap. One wise trainer of his acquaintance advised him to ride as if he were out hunting the first time round, then look about him and see how some of the others were going. He carried out this advice to the letter and, right to the end of the race, looked as if he was merely enjoying a fast run with hounds. Zoedone, never putting a foot wrong, did the rest. Two years later Zoedone started second favourite for the Grand National, her short price of 5–1 being accounted for by the fact that she was coupled with the Lincolnshire winner Bendigo in some big doubles. It was to a good many people's advantage to ensure that she did not win, and there is little doubt that she was got at before the race, though nothing could ever be proved. Kinsky felt that she was a dead horse as soon as he got on her and she fell heavily at the preliminary hurdle on the way to the start. Although she got half-way round the course she was never galloping and jumping properly and she ended up by giving her persevering owner-rider another heavy fall.

The Grand Nationals of 1884 and 1885 brought a change of luck at least to Mr E. P. Wilson, who had won the National Hunt Steeplechase no less than five times but had had nine unsuccessful rides in the Grand National. Voluptuary and Roquefort were the horses that enabled this tough, accomplished horseman, who was also an exceptionally shrewd judge of a potential jumper, to achieve his ambition at Aintree.

Voluptuary was trained by Ted Wilson's younger brother at Herrington in Warwickshire, and was one of the most extra-ordinary of all Grand National winners, for he had never run in a steeplechase before he went to Aintree. Originally owned by

Lord Rosebery, Voluptuary, by the Derby winner Cremorne, was a high-class colt on the flat as a three-year-old, when he won three races including the Dee Stakes at Chester and a Biennial at Ascot. Afterwards he lost all interest in flat racing and was weeded out of Rosebery's stable and bought by Mr Arthur Cooper for jumping. Having arrived at Wilson's stable he won hurdle races at Leicester and Manchester, but Wilson never divulged why he decided to give him his first race over fences in the testing circumstances of the Grand National. He did reveal to friends that Voluptuary had jumped practically every fence in Warwickshire in training, and he took him to have his final schooling gallop over fences at Upton, where Jenkins had one of the best strings of jumpers in the country. Both parties were determined to give as little away as possible but Ted Wilson, who rode Voluptuary on a wide outside throughout the gallop, declared himself perfectly satisfied by the result and asserted that Voluptuary would win the Grand National. Little could be seen of the running of the race because of thick mist, but in the closing stages Voluptuary appeared to have little trouble in fulfilling his rider's prediction and winning from Frigate and Roquefort.

Voluptuary was still only six years old when he won the Grand National, and his subsequent career was equally remarkable. He achieved little else as a chaser and, after being unplaced in two more Grand Nationals, he retired from racing for a career on the stage. He was bought by the actor Leonard Boyle, who rode him night after night in the Grand National scene of 'Prodigal Daughter' at Drury Lane, jumping a water jump which had been erected on the stage. Voluptuary always got a round of applause from the gallery for a leap as faultless as any he had made at Aintree, but even more rapturous applause was reserved for Boyle whose role was to fall off the horse's back and land in the water with a splash. For this the actor earned a supplementary fee of five shillings a night.

In spite of the mist on Grand National day in 1884, Ted Wilson had not failed to notice the extremely promising performance of Roquefort, a five-year-old gelding by Winslow out of Cream Cheese, a half brother of Miguel, who had been second in the St Leger. Wilson himself negotiated the purchase of Roquefort for Arthur Cooper before the next Grand National and his judgment was again vindicated. A beautiful short-legged horse, Roquefort had great ability, but was wilful and far from easy to ride. His chief fault, apart from pulling hard, was a tendency to run out of the course to the left. Wilson was confident that he could control him and his second Grand National victory was probably the finest feat of horsemanship of his riding career.

As things turned out, Roquefort came nearest to disaster in the 1885 Grand National not through trying to run out, but through hitting one of the early fences very hard. He was nearly down and for some way afterwards Wilson was hanging on desperately round his neck. Indeed he would probably not have got back into the saddle if Jack Childs, on Albert Cecil, had not stretched out a hand and hauled him back. 'Why the hell I did it I don't know, for I fancied my horse very much, and I ought to have been glad to see Ted on the floor', said Childs ruefully after the race. From that point Roquefort, whose impetuosity had been curbed by his mistake, jumped faultlessly and went on to beat Frigate, who was second again, in a canter.

Roquefort's erratic ways had been brought under temporary control, but not permanently cured. He was going well under 12 st. 8 lbs. in the Grand National two years later, having fallen in 1886, but took fright as the rider of Savoyard raised his whip on the second circuit of the course and made a sudden dart to the left, tried to jump the rails, and gave Wilson a heavy fall. Despite his flaws of temperament, Roquefort loved jumping and was a true Aintree specialist. His last appearance in the Grand National was in 1891, when he finished fourth to Come Away.

The winner in 1887 was Gamecock, who had been third to Old Joe and Too Good the previous year. Gamecock was level with Savoyard at the last hurdle but Gamecock, showing the courage for which he was afterwards famous, wore down his opponent in the run-in to win by five lengths.

Gamecock was indeed well named and his marvellous battling qualities made him the most popular chaser of his day. He became the idol of the racing crowds at courses round about London, and ran many of his best races at Windsor and Croydon. He continued to run until he was sixteen and took part in more than a hundred races altogether. In many of his races he looked hopelessly beaten and was trailing the field, but time after time, by sheer stamina and guts, he overtook less resolute opponents in the final stages to pluck victory out of defeat.

Frigate was second to Voluptuary and Roquefort, and was destined to be the runner-up once more, to Playfair in 1888, before her turn to win a Grand National finally arrived. She was unlucky not to win in Playfair's year, for she and Usna were a long way in front of the rest of the field when Usna fell at the canal turn and, in doing so, carried her so wide that she lost far more ground than the ten lengths by which she was beaten. Opportunity seldom knocks more than once in the Grand National so it was satisfactory that Frigate did at least get her reward in 1889, when her jumping ability, gameness and stamina gained her a richly deserved victory by a length from Why Not, who was to win the race five years later. Like Roquefort, Frigate was an Aintree specialist and, besides winning the Grand National, had a success in the Grand Sefton to her credit.

Why Not provided Arthur Nightingall, the outstanding professional steeplechase jockey of his day, with his second Grand National success. His other winners were Ilex in 1890 and Grudon in 1901. The victory of Ilex immediately preceded what may be called the Cloister and Manifesto era, because these two great horses more or less dominated the Grand National situation, or at least discussion of the race, from 1891 until Manifesto's last appearance in 1904. Unfortunately Cloister and Manifesto never met, for Manifesto first ran at Aintree in 1895, two years after the last Grand National appearance of Cloister. It is tempting to try and compare these horses, who were undoubtedly two of the best Grand National winners of all time and each carried 12 st 7 lbs successfully in the race. Comparisons of this kind were apt to be sterile and inconclusive, but in this case it seems fair to sum them up by stating that Cloister, at the peak of his form, was the more brilliant, whereas Manifesto had a tougher constitution and was able to maintain his form over a much longer period.

Manifesto ran in eight Grand Nationals, but Cloister's appearances in the race were confined to three. He was second to Come Away in 1891, occupied the same position behind Father O'Flynn the next year, and gained his unforgettable triumph in 1893. There is little doubt that he ought to have beaten Come Away, for his rider Roddy Owen made an error of judgment in trying to make his effort between Come Away and the inside rail after jumping the last fence. Owen hated to travel a yard further than was necessary in any race and snatched many victories he was not really entitled to by coming the shortest way, but on this occasion the experienced Harry Beasley on Come Away quite rightly cut him off and refused to let him through. The next day the *Daily Telegraph* carried this graphic description of the finish. 'Harry had the Captain in the same position as a man with a cork half-way in the neck of the bottle; one little push and it will go down.' The horses were locked together for the last two hundred yards and at the winning post Come Away had half a length to spare.

The quick-tempered Owen was breathing fire and slaughter as he dismounted, declaring that he proposed doing all sorts of things to Beasley. 'I don't think I should if I were you,' warned Cloister's trainer Dick Marsh, 'you might be second again, you know.' Owen contented himself with lodging an objection and, while the stewards were deliberating, was surrounded by a crowd of infuriated Irishmen, the supporters of Come Away, vowing that they would have Owen's blood if the objection were sustained. The stewards rightly overruled the objection, and all concerned were the best of friends by the next morning. The next year Owen was on Father O'Flynn, and that finest of all soldier riders had learnt from his previous mistake and took his mount to the front two fences from home. Cloister had made nearly all the running up to that point but was trying to give 26 lbs to Father O'Flynn, who profited from this big pull in the weights to draw right away for an easy victory.

After these two preliminary misfires Cloister's victory, when it came in 1893, made an indelible impression on the minds of all who witnessed it. The weather was exceptionally hot for March, and the ground was so dry that the dust was flying as the horses cantered to the post at Aintree. Cloister, ridden by the professional William Dollery, appreciated the conditions to such an extent that he won in a style that had never been seen in the race before and has never been seen again since. Although Cloister was carrying 12 st 7 lbs, 8 lbs more than the previous record weight carried successfully by Cortolvin in 1867, Dollery made practically no attempt to restrain him. Indeed Cloister took up the running after the first fence, was half a dozen lengths ahead of his nearest opponent on completing a circuit of the course, and made the race a procession on the second circuit to beat Aesop by forty lengths. In spite of the heat, he looked fresh enough to go round again as he passed the winning post. It would be easy to jump to the conclusion that the rest of the runners must have been of poor quality for Cloister to have won so easily with top weight, but it should be noted that a subsequent Grand National winner, Why Not, was beaten into third place, and a previous winner, Father O'Flynn, could finish only sixth. The inescapable conclusion is that Cloister was a super horse that day, and this conclusion is supported by the fact that his time of 9 minutes 32 2/5 seconds was easily the fastest recorded since the course had been altered in 1863. His performance set up three new records—record weight, record time and record winning distance.

Shortly afterwards Cloister was beaten in a minor race at Sandown Park. This defeat did not cause a great stir at the time because most people, including his trainer Arthur Yates, assumed that he had not fully recovered from his exertions at Aintree. The incident assumed greater significance in retrospect, for Cloister, who had been a hot favourite in the ante-post betting, went lame shortly before the next Grand National and was unable to run. In 1895 exactly the same thing happened as Cloister, having changed stables and won the Grand Sefton in the meantime, again went lame a few days before he was due to take part in the Grand National, and had to be scratched.

The mysterious and recurrent lameness of Cloister caused a tremendous sensation at the time. The aspect of the great chaser's misfortunes which worried many people was that on each of the occasions that he went lame the bookmakers appeared to know all about it, and lengthened the odds, before anyone else, even his owner and trainer. In those days the intelligence services of the bookmakers, which were to achieve such a remarkable degree of perfection in later years, were still not fully developed or appreciated by the public. Cries of 'treachery' arose on all sides and Cloister's owner, Mr Charles Duff, always a suspicious man, saw a potential nobbler behind every tree. From the moment that Cloister's troubles began he had the horse closely guarded by relays of plain clothes detectives. At one time the Plough Inn at Alresford, where Yates trained, was full of heavily built men passing themselves off as gentlemen's servants. This implausible tale mystified Yates's stablemen, until a uniformed policeman arrived at the Plough one day to pay the 'gentlemen's servants' their wages. Duff would never believe that there had not been foul play. Yates had a much simpler and more likely explanation. He always maintained that Cloister had suffered an internal strain, probably involving damage to his kidneys, when he gained his overwhelming triumph at Aintree. The injury manifested itself for the first time in the minor race at Sandown, and recurred whenever he was subjected to repeated long gallops in the later stages of his preparation for the Grand National.

Cloister has one further claim to a place in the annals of the Grand National, as one of the most curiously bred of all the chance-bred winners. Bred in Ireland by Lord Fingall, he was by Ascetic, who had been useless as a racehorse and was used for fetching the post from the village every day, out of a mare, Grace II, who was useless for both racing and hunting and was put to stud only as a last resort. From this unpromising mating

sprang one of the greatest chasers of all time. Cloister's excellence
revealed the merits of Ascetic, who then became the best sire of
jumpers of his time and got two more Grand National winners,
Drumcree in 1903 and Ascetic's Silver three years later. Cloister
was described by his first trainer, Marsh, as standing 16 hands
3 inches with beautiful shoulders, wide hips and a boldly defined
bump on his quarters. He was extremely well mannered and
intelligent. The only respect in which he could be faulted was
that he was a trifle long in the back.

Cloister gave an impression of rugged strength. Manifesto, on
the other hand, was one of the most bloodlike animals ever to
run in the Grand National. Emile Adam was asked to paint
Manifesto's portrait after his second Grand National victory,
but demurred at the request to waste his talent on a mere steeplechaser. Finally he was persuaded to accept the commission and,
as soon as he set eyes on Manifesto, stood back in amazement
and exclaimed: 'Why, this is a racehorse!' It is remarkable that
a horse of such quality should also have been tough enough
to stand repeated exertions in the most strenuous race in the
world.

The greatness of Manifesto may be conveyed most vividly by
a summary of his performances in the Grand National. He ran
in the race eight times, won twice, was third three times, fourth
once, sixth once and fell once. On his first appearance in 1895 he
was fourth behind Wild Man from Borneo in a field of nineteen,
of whom eleven completed the course. He fell when The Soarer
won from Father O'Flynn the next year and carried the moderate
weight of 11 st 3 lbs to his first victory in 1897. He missed the race
in 1898 and from then on had more than 12 st on his back each
time he ran. In 1899 he equalled Cloister's feat of winning under
12 st 7 lbs when, patiently ridden by the excellent professional
George Williamson, he beat Ford of Fyne rather more easily than
the margin of a length suggests. He was really second best in 1900,
for Williamson eased him up a few strides before the winning post
when he saw that he had no chance of beating Ambush II, and
was overtaken by Barsac for second place practically on the post.
Manifesto was carrying the enormous burden of 12 st 13 lbs and
giving 24 lbs to Ambush II, who was ridden by Algy Anthony
and carried the colours of the Prince of Wales. In this way
Ambush gave his owner a good start to a wonderful racing year
in which the Prince of Wales carried off the Triple Crown with
Diamond Jubilee.

Manifesto missed the Grand National again in 1901 and could

congratulate himself on his absence, because the race was run in a blinding snowstorm and the vilest conditions ever known for both horses and riders. In his book *The Grand National* D. H. Munroe appended the following note to his details of the race: 'Just what happened to the various horses in this race is very indefinite. Eight finished in the order indicated above; but the weather conditions were so impossible that neither spectators nor jockeys could get any detailed idea of the race.' Indeed the jockeys protested against the race being run at all before going to the start, but the stewards ruled that the show must go on. Grudon, with his feet packed with butter to prevent the snow balling in them, made nearly all the running to win from Drumcree, who was to have his hour of triumph two years later. Manifesto returned in 1902 to finish third, carrying 12 st 8 lbs and giving 35 lbs to the winner Shannon Lass. He was third again the next year, when only four of the twenty-three starters got round safely. He was carrying 12 st 3 lbs and giving a stone to the winner Drumcree, but he had reached the advanced age of fifteen and was showing unmistakable signs of old age, as he finished the better part of 100 yards behind the winner. On his final appearance in 1904 Manifesto again completed the course—by then he could surely have jumped around in his sleep—but he had not enough speed to threaten the slightest danger to the leaders. The winner was the New Zealand-bred Moifaa, an enormous horse standing more than seventeen hands who had won many races over fences in his native country before being brought over to England by Mr Spencer Gollan, a wealthy pioneer who was also a first rate all-round athlete.

The end of the Cloister-Manifesto era left a yawning gap in the ranks of chasers capable of capturing the imagination of the public. The next horse of more than ordinary ability to win the Grand National was Eremon, whose merit is not fairly reflected by the bare fact that he carried only 10 st 1 lb when he was successful in 1907. Eremon overcame exceptional difficulties on the way to his victory, for his rider Alf Newey broke a stirrup leather at the second fence and had to concentrate on remaining in the saddle rather than giving his horse assistance for the rest of the race. Moreover Eremon was persistently hampered by the attentions of the riderless Rathvale for a long way, and it was not until Newey was able to shake off the loose horse on the second circuit of the course that Eremon was able to gallop and jump freely. Eremon had taken up a lead of nearly fifty yards by the time he reached Valentine's the second time and, although Tom

West made up ground in the last half mile, Eremon still had 6 lengths to spare at the finish.

Newey's was one of the finest feats of horsemanship in the history of the race. Some idea of how easily Eremon might have won if Newey had been able to do more than just sit on and steer may be gleaned from the fact that he went to win the Lancashire Chase at Manchester with a 12 lb penalty a few days later, having then won four races in the space of twenty-four days. In that year the Grand National first prize had been raised to £2,400 from the £2,175 credited to Ascetic's Silver in 1906. As the Lancashire Chase was worth £1,725, Eremon reaped a rich harvest by the prize money standards of his day.

Eremon was owned by Mr Stanley Howard and trained by Tom Coulthwaite at Hednesford in Staffordshire, and the same combination of owner and trainer was successful with Jenkinstown at Aintree three years later. Coulthwaite, who trained a third Grand National winner, Grakle, in 1931, was one of the most remarkable men ever to train horses under National Hunt rules. He was said never to have sat on a horse in his life. He was an excellent athlete and began his training activities in charge of cross-country runners. He had a genius for developing the qualities of athletes whether human or equine, and it was generally conceded that he never had a superior in the art of preparing a horse for the Grand National. On the other hand his way of expressing his Lancashire opinions was blunt to the point of eccentricity, and inevitably he made some enemies. Nor was the running of his horses always as consistent and straightforward as it might have been. In 1913 he was reported to the stewards of the National Hunt committee for the running of Bloodstone and Jacobus at the February meetings at Hurst Park and Birmingham respectively. His explanation was not accepted, and he was warned off and not reinstated until 1930. Bloodstone and Jacobus were both high-class chasers, as Bloodstone was second to Jerry M in the 1912 Grand National and Jacobus was second to Ally Sloper in 1915, when the Grand National was run at Aintree for the last time until the end of the first world war.

Jenkinstown's victory was preceded by the victory of two foreign-bred horses, Rubio in 1908 and Lutteur III in 1909. Rubio was the first American-bred winner, though his sire Star Ruby had been bred in England and was a half-brother of Sceptre, the winner of four classic races. Rubio once changed hands for only £15 and was far from a sound horse, so it was a notable feat of training by Fred Withington to win a Grand

National with him. Withington also supplied the second in Rubio's Grand National, Mattie MacGregor, from his Stock-bridge stable.

Lutteur III was bred in France although, like Rubio, he was by an English-bred horse. His sire was St Damien, a son of St Simon. Trained at Lewes by Harry Escott but ridden by the French jockey Parfrement, Lutteur was a powerful if leggy horse and gave a fine performance to win at Aintree since he was only five years old, being the fourth and last horse of that age to win.

Lutteur was not the first French-bred horse to win the Grand National. That honour belonged to Alcibiade, who was successful in 1865. But Lutteur was the first French-bred horse to win after steeplechasing became fairly established in France with the opening of the Auteuil jumping course in Paris in 1874. In the meantime many English horses had crossed the channel to win both the Grand Steeplechase and the Grand Hurdle at Auteuil, these English winners including such famous horses as Too Good, Seaman, Congress, General Peace and Royal Meath, of whom the last-named was considered an even better horse than Cloister by his trainer Dick Marsh until he broke down during his prepar-ation for the 1891 Grand National. Gladiateur was called the avenger of Waterloo when he came from France to win the Triple Crown in 1865. What Gladiateur did for the reputation for French horses on the flat, Lutteur did for French chasers, and his victory at Aintree avenged the defeats of French by English horses at Auteuil over a period of nearly a quarter of a century.

One last great chaser was to adorn the English steeplechasing scene before the outbreak of the first world war. This was Jerry M, who finished second to Jenkinstown, to whom he was giving 30 lbs, in the 1910 Grand National. Jerry M was fortunate enough to miss the freak Grand National of 1911, when the race was run in appallingly muddy conditions and only Glenside of the field of thirty-three got round without falling and, to quote the words of a contemporary observer, 'staggered past the post like a drunken man'. Jerry M had been causing a great deal of worry to his trainer Bob Gore. He had gone over to win the Grand Steeple-chase at Auteuil after finishing second to Jenkinstown, but hurt himself in the process and was out of action for the whole of the following season. Indeed he had only one preliminary race before he reappeared at Aintree in March 1912, gaining a comfortable victory over Bloodstone in a race at Hurst Park a few weeks before the Liverpool meeting. Many of the critics were shaking their heads, saying that no horse came back to his best after breaking down, and certainly not to the extent of winning a Grand National with 12 st 7 lbs. But most of the criticism was silenced abruptly when Jerry M was led into the paddock at Aintree, for he looked the very model of a perfectly trained racehorse, full of muscle and bursting with energy. As a result he was backed down to start equal favourite with Rathnally at 4–1. The confidence of his admirers was completely justified. Rathnally fell, but Jerry M hardly made the vestige of a mistake throughout the four-and-a-half miles and won most convincingly by six lengths from Bloodstone, who must have grown weary from chasing such a brilliant opponent.

Jerry M never ran again. He was entered for the next Grand National and was allotted top weight of 12 st 10 lbs, but in January Bob Gore announced that he had become a roarer and was being scratched from the Grand National. Fortunately Gore had an adequate substitute, as Covertcoat took Jerry M's place in the Grand National field and won the race for the Findon stable for the second year running. If Covertcoat lacked the massive good looks and class of Jerry M he too was an above average Grand National winner.

Jerry M and Covertcoat were owned by Sir Charles Assheton-Smith who, under the name of Charles Duff, had won a previous Grand National with Cloister. Duff had inherited a baronetcy in the meantime and changed his name. Gore was one of the best trainers ever to specialize in jumpers. Born near Dublin in 1860, he rode on the Continent for a dozen years before settling down as a trainer in Sussex at the turn of the century. His exceptionally keen judgment of jumping material was well illustrated by his choice of Jerry M. Assheton-Smith had been reluctant to buy this thick-winded horse but Gore persuaded him that Jerry M was capable of doing great deeds before his wind infirmity became serious enough to curtail his racing activities.

III

SOME FAMOUS RIDERS AND TRAINERS

If any one man may be named as representative of Steeplechasing in the period from 1871 to the outbreak of the first world war, it is Arthur Yates. The career of Yates as amateur rider and trainer spanned the entire period. Although he was born as early

as 1841, he was still riding at the height of his form at the beginning of the period, and did not retire from training until 1913.

The bare statistics of his career reveal his fantastic successes in
both roles, since he rode 460 winners and trained 2,950 winners.
The year 1872, in which he was deprived of his best chance of
winning the Grand National on Harvester by sheer bad luck,
was a milestone in his career, as he rode his best total of sixty-
seven winners, including thirteen on the Continent, and at the
same time began to train for a few friends on his farm at Bishop's
Sutton near Alresford in Hampshire. Extreme toughness and
resolution were his main characteristics as a steeplechase rider.

On one occasion at Baden-Baden he fell early in the race and
broke his collar-bone but remounted and, with his useless arm
tucked into the front of his jacket, set off in pursuit of the leaders
and was beaten by only a neck. On another occasion at Croydon
he had a fall at the water and rose from the mud just in time to
see his mount Harold going off on his own. Running after the
horse, he seized him by the tail and, with amazing agility, scram-
bled back into the saddle. As his two opponents had also fallen he
proceeded to win the race. In honour of this achievement the
Sporting Life printed the following verse:

> 'In racing reports it is oftentimes said
> That a jockey has cleverly won by a head;
> But Yates has performed, when all other arts fail,
> A more wonderful feat—for he won by a tail!'

Yates became increasingly fat as the years went by, but ignored
all the pleas of his friends to give up riding until he was shamed
into retirement by the comment of a female acquaintance after
he had won a race on Settling Day at Kempton Park in December
1884. The lady called out to him as he rode into the unsaddling
enclosure: 'Well done Arthur! but the joint is rather too big for
the dish now, you know.' After retiring from race riding he
developed a rotund and jovial appearance suggestive of the 17th
Earl of Derby, the owner of Hyperion, at a later date.

Yates traced his ancestry to a Derbyshire squire who had fought
for Charles I in the Civil War, and considered it beneath his
dignity to be a professional trainer. For this reason his horses
usually appeared as trained by his head lad, John Swatton, who
has been credited with training Cloister when that great horse
won the Grand National. In fact Cloister was trained by Yates,
as were two other Grand National winners, Roquefort and Game-

cock. In this way Yates more than made up for his bad luck in not riding a winner of the Grand National.

There was no spit and polish about the Yates establishment at Bishop's Sutton. The horses, who often totalled upwards of eighty, were stabled in any old tumbledown barn that was available on the farm. They seldom carried much condition and usually looked pretty rough. On the other hand they were lean and fit to run for their lives. Yates often saddled two or three runners in a race. They were all doing their best, and Yates liked to have £2, his invariable bet, on the one he fancied most, which was not necessarily the one that came out best at the finish.

Yates always insisted that there was little to choose between the best professional and amateur riders of his time. Amateurs rode scores of winners for his stable, but he also had the good fortune to have the services of three first class professionals who were attached to the stable. They were Billy Sensier, the artist of the party, who was killed in a selling hurdle race at Plumpton when still in his prime; Jack Childs, whose unselfish act saved Ted Wilson from falling off Roquefort in the Grand National; and Bill Dollery, who had the precious knack of 'falling light', so that he never had a serious fall in his life. Dollery learned the inadvisability of dropping his reins to hold on his cap on the occasion of his very first mount in public, and afterwards won the Grand National on Cloister.

The latter part of Arthur Yates's riding career coincided with the golden age of amateur riders. Between 1871 and 1885 twelve of the fifteen Grand Nationals, or 80%, were won by amateurs. After 1885 there was a distinct falling off in the amateurs' ratio of success. For the whole period from 1871 to 1915 only twenty Grand Nationals, or 33%, were won by amateurs, and from 1897 to 1915 only three Grand Nationals, or 16%, were won by amateurs. Of the three amateur successes in the final period two went to Jack Anthony, who turned professional after winning his third Grand National on Troytown in 1920, and the other went to Aubrey Hastings, who was also the professional trainer of his winning mount, Ascetic's Silver.

In the golden age Mr J. M. Richardson and Mr E. P. Wilson each won the Grand National twice. The partnership of Captain Machell as owner and Maunsell Richardson as trainer and rider, which carried off the Grand National with Disturbance and Reugny, was one of the most successful, during its brief duration, but also one of the most ill-assorted in the history of steeplechasing. Machell and Richardson had little in common apart from their athleticism, their love of racing, and their almost uncanny judgment of young horses. Machell used to perform the spectacular after-dinner feat of jumping from the floor to the mantelpiece and he once won a £1,000 bet by beating England's leading professional walker in a match from Newmarket to London. Richardson, whose agility earned him the nickname of 'the Cat', played cricket for Harrow and Cambridge and was also a first class fencer, hurdler, footballer and racquets player. In other aspects the two men were poles apart. Whereas Richardson had little but contempt for heavy betting and the planning of coups Machell, who first made his mark in the racing world when he brought off a killing with Hermit in the 1867 Derby, was called by Dick Marsh 'something more than tepid', a phrase which was a masterpiece of understatement. Machell was deeply impressed when he saw Richardson, as an undergraduate, ride Schiedam to victory in the National Hunt Chase at Cottenham in 1870. Schiedam was owned by Mr Henry Chaplin, for whom Machell was racing manager. When Richardson went down from Cambridge, Machell decided to send him some jumpers to train. Soon afterwards Richardson bought Disturbance, Reugny and another splendid jumper, Defence, for £1,200 on Machell's behalf after he had won a seven furlong race on the flat at Ayr on Disturbance. It was a brilliantly judged purchase, and everything seemed to be working out well when Disturbance won the Grand National in 1873 and all three horses were doing well in their Grand National preparation the following year. Then the storm began to break. Reugny went much better than Disturbance in a searching gallop and Richardson, having informed Machell, proceeded to pass on the information to his Lincolnshire farmer friends. The result was that Machell, who was not as quick as usual in taking a good price, found that he had been forestalled in the market and was able to obtain only 5–1 about Reugny's chance. Furious recriminations followed, and Richardson was so sickened by the whole business that he decided to give up race riding after he had ridden Reugny safely to victory in 1874. 'I never regretted the step I took,' Richardson used to remark, 'because in reality I always preferred hunting to race riding.' He became Master of the Brocklesby Hounds, married Victoria Lady Yarborough, and won the former radical stronghold of Brigg for the Conservatives at a bye-election in 1894 and held the seat at the next general election.

Maunsell Richardson was probably the finest horseman among all the riders, amateur and professional, of his day. His coolness

The 1901 Grand National winner, Grudon, ridden by Arthur Nightingall. *Copyright W. W. Rouch & Co. Ltd.*

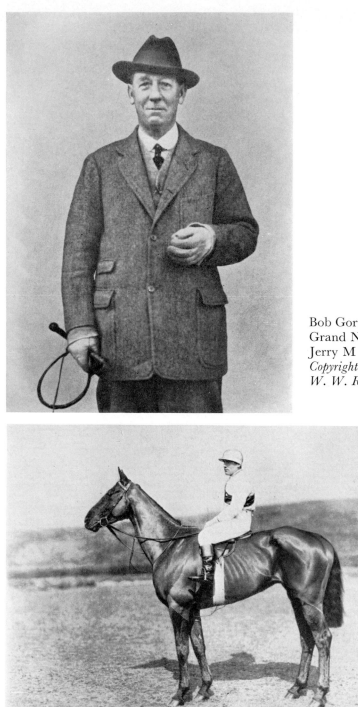

Bob Gore, trainer of two
Grand National winners,
Jerry M and Covertcoat.
Copyright
W. W. Rouch & Co. Ltd.

The Grand National winner of 1907—Eremon,
ridden by Alf Newey. *Copyright W. W. Rouch*
& Co. Ltd.

and judgment of pace were exceptional and were matched by his thoroughness, for he never rode on an unfamiliar course without walking round it at least once and often several times. In his best season, 1872, he won fifty-six races including four on the flat.

Ted Wilson was a man of a different type. He was distinctly short of funds many times during his career, and it was not until he brought off his boldly planned coup with Voluptuary that he really set himself up. He was a tremendously strong horseman and wonderfully brave, and his nerve never faltered although he broke almost every bone in his body at one time or another. Many of his contemporaries thought he had an ugly seat on a horse, for he pulled his stirrups up several holes shorter than was customary, but in this respect he foreshadowed the style of a later period. He was a bit of a rough diamond on the whole, but had a marked vein of generosity in his nature and a number of people who were indebted to his kindness, like the professional Tom Skelton who won the Grand National on Old Joe, were devoted to him.

Other leading amateurs of the late nineteenth century included Arthur Coventry, Roddy Owen, George Lambton, Reggie Ward, Charlie Cunningham, Dan Thirlwell and the three Irish Beasley brothers. Arthur Coventry was one of the very few among them who could hold his own with the best professionals not only over fences but on the flat. He never had the good fortune to win the Grand National, as his brother did on Alcibiade, but he won nearly every other important jumping race in the calendar. These included the National Hunt Chase on Bellringer and the Great Metropolitan Chase at Croydon on The Scot, besides the Grand Hurdle at Auteuil on Brutus.

Arthur Coventry used to call himself the ugliest man in England. On the other hand he had immense charm which enchanted his friends of both sexes, and he was extremely popular in all walks of the racing community. After he gave up riding he became a starter and in 1890 was appointed official starter to the Jockey Club. In this role he enjoyed the confidence and respect of the jockeys. He had a quiet and unobtrusive manner, but could adopt a parade ground tone and produce an impressive flow of invective when these were called for.

There was an aura of romance about the career of Roddy Owen. He might have been the hero of a G. A. Henty novel if Henty had ever written about racing, though Henty would surely have contrived a happier ending for his hero than to condemn him to die of cholera on the Dongola campaign. In his own time Owen was described as 'far in front of all soldier riders', and the same is

7

probably true of all other soldier riders of earlier and later periods. George Lambton, who rode against him many times, called him 'as good a steeplechase rider as I ever saw'.

Roddy Owen was a much more complex character than the vast majority of racing men. Two important formative influences in his character should not be overlooked. The first was the Celtic temperament which he inherited from his Welsh ancestors, and the second was the environment of his boyhood home at Cheltenham where cross-country sport, then as now, is in the atmosphere of the place. He was quick-tempered, as he showed after losing the Grand National on Cloister, but his bursts of anger passed as quickly as they came. No one could dislike him or resist his high spirits for long.

Roddy was commissioned in the 20th (East Devonshire) Regiment at the age of twenty in 1876, but his regiment became the Lancashire Fusiliers on the reorganization of the army five years later. Service in various foreign stations prevented him taking up race riding in earnest during his early years in the army and it was not until 1884, when he began a lengthy period of home service, that he was able at last to do so. From then until his triumph on Father O'Flynn in the 1892 Grand National he was able to indulge his love of racing to the full. Often he rode in as many as five races in a day, and then travelled practically all night to ride at another meeting in some distant part of the country the next day. Not surprisingly the calls of military duty tended to be thrust aside by the prior claims of race riding. On one occasion when he was stationed at Aldershot the Commander-in-Chief, General Sir Evelyn Wood, remarked to him coldly; 'Captain Owen, you have been here for two months and I have not yet had the pleasure of making your acquaintance.' Owen, as quick-witted as he was quick-tempered, replied without hesitation: 'My loss, General, not yours.' The reprimand which the General had intended dissolved in laughter.

Roddy Owen's qualities as a steeplechase rider were summed up in his own maxim: 'Keep on to the finish.' He never gave up a race as lost until the winner had passed the post, and he was successful many times by remounting and persevering on horses that had fallen. Another of his principles was never to give a yard away in a race. These tactics may have cost him the Grand National on Cloister, but they undoubtedly won him many other races. He was shameless in soliciting rides on horses that he fancied, and his charm soon appeased any feelings of antagonism that his predatory behaviour may have provoked. Between 1882, when he was stationed in Ireland for a time, and 1892 he had 812 mounts which yielded the astonishingly high total of 254 winners. In his best year, 1891, he won forty-nine races. His successes included most of the important races over fences and hurdles. He won the National Hunt Chase on Monkshood, the Grand Military Gold Cup on St Cross, the Aintree Hunt Chase on Tenby, the Sandown Grand Prize on Franciscan and the Grand Sandown Hurdle race on Maypole. Perhaps his finest achievement was to get the best out of the brilliant but ungenerous Kilworth, on whom he won the Sandown Great Chase twice and the Irish International Chase at Leopardstown.

His remarkable judgment of horses was illustrated by his choice of Father O'Flynn from six mounts that were offered to him in the 1892 Grand National. He rode the horse in a gallop at Gatwick some weeks before the race and promptly wrote home: 'I have settled to ride him and he will win the Liverpool'—'the Liverpool' being the colloquial name for the Grand National at that time.

There was a vein of seriousness in Owen's character for which few people gave him credit in his riding days. Despite his apparent preoccupation with steeplechasing, he always intended to give up the sport as soon as he had won the Grand National. 'To win the Grand National is the first of my ambitions,' he often said, using the word 'first' literally, whereas his friends interpreted his statement as conveying that winning the Grand National was the most important of his ambitions. None of them imagined for a moment that he would be as good as his word, but the day after he had won on Father O'Flynn he took a train to London, volunteered for foreign service, and four days later left England for West Africa. He took part in several minor campaigns in Africa and India before meeting his death, at the early age of forty, in Kitchener's Army in the Sudan.

The golden age of amateur riders was already approaching its close when Roddy Owen retired from racing. Various reasons were advanced for the decline of amateur race riding. Arthur Yates attributed the decline to the disruption of the Boer War and the deaths of a number of the most dashing young officers. George Lambton thought that the disappearance of hunters' flat races, which he regarded as perfect nurseries for young amateurs, was the principal cause. The truth was probably that numerous different causes were at work. A good many of the former amateurs had been amateurs merely in name, and would never have passed through the net spread by the National Hunt Committee in later times. Many of the so-called amateurs may have belonged to the qualifying clubs, or have been officers on full pay, or have borne titles in their own right or by courtesy, or have been proposed and seconded by persons so qualified, but they were in the game to make a living just as much as the professionals themselves. As National Hunt racing became further and further removed from the hunting field in which it had originated and became a highly organized sport of its own, so did the genuine amateur find it increasingly difficult to hold his own.

While the amateurs were declining a new generation of expert professional steeplechase jockeys was springing up. The foremost of these professionals was Arthur Nightingall, who became the greatest steeplechase jockey since the death of George Stevens. Born in 1868, Arthur Nightingall was one of the most distinguished members of the famous Epsom racing family. 'For coolness, judgment, nerve and power,' wrote a racing journalist of the time, 'Arthur Nightingall could stand comparison with any of his famous predecessors in the same popular branch of sport.' He won the Grand National three times—on Ilex in 1890, on Why Not four years later and on Grudon in the snow storm race in 1901.

Nightingall himself always declared that Ilex was the best horse he rode, but his first sight of the horse was far from encouraging. He had been engaged to ride the horse in a small race at Leicester, but on entering the parade ring he was horrified to see a mean-looking chestnut horse with little in the way of neck or shoulders, but a remarkable amount of belly. To his surprise Ilex gave him a perfect ride and won in a canter. A few weeks later he rode him again at Leopardstown and, after finishing third to Roddy Owen on Kilworth, realized that Ilex was a horse of exceptional possibilities. When Ilex came up for sale some time later he persuaded Mr George Mastermen to buy him and sent him to his father, John Nightingall, to be trained. Ilex gained his Grand National victory very easily by twelve lengths and went on to win the Lancashire Chase shortly afterwards.

Nightingall's Grand National record speaks for itself, for he rode a second and four thirds, besides his three winners, out of fifteen rides in the race altogether. In addition he won the Scottish Grand National on Leybourn and had many successes abroad, notably in Germany and Austria.

It is unlikely that many followers of modern steeplechasing are aware that the exaggerated backward seat over fences ever had any theoretical justification other than diminishing the risk of

PART III

1919-1939
By ROGER MORTIMER

I

THE inter-war period forms a link between the earlier days of steeplechasing with their happy-go-lucky, rather rough and ready atmosphere and the highly organized, strictly controlled sport with its many rich prizes that exists today. In the nineteen-twenties it was still a common jibe to speak of those who went jumping as 'the needy and greedy', while journalists liked to refer to National Hunt racing as 'the illegitimate sport'. The majority of the leading owners on the flat and most of the flat-racing 'regulars' never went jumping from one end of the year to another, except perhaps to Liverpool for the Grand National, or to the Grand Military Meeting at Sandown and the Household Brigade Meeting at Hawthorn Hill for purely social reasons. Jumping, in fact, was still very much the poor relation and was frequently reminded of its position. Any suggestion that jumping might one day take place at Ascot would have been regarded as too far-fetched to be even mildly amusing.

Rich owners were few and far between, and considering the paucity of good prizes to be won this was hardly surprising. Broadly speaking, jumping owners were inclined to be of two types; firstly, horse-lovers, who raced one or two horses which they had probably bred themselves, purely for sport and without hope of profit; secondly gamblers, who were only interested in the betting side and who were rarely hampered in the attainment of their objectives by the possession of moral scruples.

Gradually, however, the position began to change. A number of rich Americans began to take an interest in the sport, principally in the hope of winning the Grand National, and National Hunt racing derived nothing but benefit from the patronage of Mr J. H. Whitney, Mr and Mrs F. Ambrose Clark, and those fine riders the Bostwick brothers. Not long ago, when Mr Whitney took up his post as United States Ambassador to Great Britain, a once famous jockey, who had ridden many winners for him, had fallen on difficult days and was reduced to 'doing his two' at a Newmarket stable. 'It's the times we live in', he observed philosophically. 'Look at poor Mr Whitney, even he's had to get a job now.'

In addition to the Americans, there arrived on the scene that remarkable and unique personality, Miss Dorothy Paget, who took up ownership in a big way, spoke her mind, betted freely and gave the sport a considerable boost. Lord Bicester, who specialized in fine big horses of the so-called 'Grand National type', became another valued patron, though of course of a very different sort from Miss Paget, and so did the Lancashire miller, Mr J. V. Rank. In addition, the colours of leading flat-race owners such as Lord Rosebery and Lord Glanely began to be seen more frequently.

Slowly but surely the all-round quality of National Hunt racing began to improve. Fields tended to become larger, the sport more competitive, while the betting market took a far wider range than it had frequently done in the past. Those races in which only two horses were seriously backed while the remainder all too clearly were 'non-operational' began to disappear, and it became rare, even at the most 'jungly' minor meeting, to see a race the result of which had been clearly decided beforehand. The standard of competence and responsibility among stewards, at least at the major fixtures, started to show a marked improvement and from 1937 onwards the local stewards had the assistance of stewards' secretaries appointed by Weatherby's. The reputation of the sport began to improve and its popularity increased as the average punter came to realize that by and large he got as fair a run for his money as he did on the flat.

At this period the pattern of National Hunt racing was very different from that of the present day and considerably duller as well. Owing to the lack of any other races of comparable stature, the Grand National dominated the entire season and it was the Grand National horses that provided most of the interest. Sport was invariably slow and stodgy up till Christmas, most of the programmes being composed of very ordinary bread-and-butter events. In fact proceedings only really started to warm up with the publication of the Grand National weights, after which the leading competitors for that event began to show their paces in earnest. March was the climax of the season, with the National Hunt meeting at Cheltenham, the Grand Military Meeting at Sandown and the Liverpool Spring meeting following each other in swift succession.

There were then many more small meetings in the spring and summer than there are today. The standard of sport was not high and the *laissez-faire* attitude on the part of most of the authorities doubtless deplorable. However, despite the acts of cheerful villainy sometimes perpetrated and the not infrequent and totally inexplicable reversals of form, these meetings were fun. Attended chiefly by people who lived in the locality, they possessed an atmosphere both friendly and convivial that more than atoned for the primitive standard of comfort. Moreover these fixtures, where it was rare for a race to be worth £100 to the winner, provided welcome opportunities for the small trainer and the little-known rider who could seldom compete at the major meetings with more than a thin chance of success. 'I had my ideal race today', remarked the jovial trainer of half a dozen indifferent horses in the bar at Pershore one afternoon. 'Four runners, two I knew weren't trying, one was my own and the fourth the one I backed.' Alas, Pershore, where the Land of Plums Chase was a feature event, failed to survive the last war and so did other meetings that elderly racegoers remember with nostalgic affection such as Colwall Park, Rugby Hunt, Melton Hunt, Hawthorn Hill, Bungay, Tarporley, Brocklesby, Cardiff, Torquay, Quorn Hunt, Bridgnorth, Wenlock, Glamorgan Hunt, Oswestry and Hethersett.

Even allowing for the difference in the value of the pound, the general level of prize-money throughout the season was low. Take the season of 1929–30 for example. The one really big prize was the Grand National, which earned the winner £9,800. In the entire season there were only five other races worth £1,000 or more to the winner. These were the Champion Chase (£1,570), the Liverpool Hurdle (£1,270) and the Grand Sefton Chase (£1,255), all run at Aintree; the Lancashire Chase (£1,725) at Manchester and the National Hunt Chase (£1,266) at Cheltenham. The Gold Cup and the Champion Hurdle, both run on the first day of the National Hunt meeting, were worth £670 apiece to the winners. In fact in 1930 the eighteen winners at the National Hunt meeting earned a total of £8,076 as opposed to £41,159 amassed by the winners at that fixture in 1965.

Nearly every meeting started off with drab inevitability with a selling chase and a selling hurdle, the subsequent proceedings at the sale ring being in the nature of a farce with just occasionally a touch of corruption or intimidation thrown in. Bold indeed, even rash, was the bidder who kept on nodding after a hoarse whisper had apprised him that 'the guvnor wants 'im back'. Some of these old platers, such as Tim and Ned Carver in the nineteen twenties, had a great following among the racing public, while later on there was no more popular horse than Ferrans, who, in his plating days, was trained by George Beeby and who went on winning until he was seventeen years old. Captain Peter Herbert, who in due course became a most proficient amateur rider, established his reputation when a young officer by his many victories on a most consistent plater named Courtesy, trained by Jack Pendarves, who had a string of extremely moderate horses at Epsom. Even the National Hunt meeting at Cheltenham included four sellers in the nineteen thirties.

One of the more significant changes that occurred in jumping during this period was that the sport began to be speeded up in no uncertain fashion. It may be remembered that at the beginning of the century the so-called 'American Invasion' made a lasting impact on racing under Jockey Club Rules. One of the major results was that within the space of a few years the traditional English riding style had completely disappeared. American jockeys like Tod Sloan and the Reiff brothers made their English rivals look like policemen and English jockeys had no option but to shorten their leathers and crouch forward or get out of the game for good. As the sport tended to become far more stream-lined, inevitably the pace at which races were run increased. Forcing tactics became more common and long distance events ceased to be an elegant dawdle followed by a sprint. The strain imposed on horses became noticeably more severe and easy races were few and far between. The custom of running horses, even two-year-olds, twice or perhaps three times at meetings like Ascot and Goodwood more or less died out. In addition the Americans gave us some valuable lessons in stable hygiene and the plating of horses; one or two of the American trainers that came over knew a good deal about doping as well.

In due course the growing emphasis on speed had its effect on National Hunt racing, too. Methods of training, which not infre-quently had bordered on the primitive, became rather more scientific or at any rate less crude. The old-fashioned Grand National preparation that usually included a number of four-mile gallops nicely calculated to remove any vestige of speed the horse may once have possessed, gradually disappeared from the scene. Furthermore the traditional 'Grand National types', big Irish-bred horses that would have carried a fifteen stone man to hounds across Leicestershire, became very much rarer, being replaced by horses that were possibly not their equals for stamina or sheer power, but could make rings round them when it came to a question of speed. Hurdle races tended to be run at a true pace throughout and it ceased to be a paying proposition to put mere sprinters over hurdles, as with the new trend they had little or no hope of staying the distance.

Inevitably the style of riding altered, too. In the nineteen twenties the general style was a hang-over from the days when courses were much rougher and the fences stiff and straight. Riders, therefore, rode with longish leathers, sat well back—over hurdles as well as over fences—and gave their mounts plenty of rein with the laudable objective of remaining on board if the horse clouted the obstacle good and hard. It was not a pretty style even when executed by real experts and the less polished jockeys not only looked crude and awkward, but were undoubtedly hard on their horses' mouths. Photographs of a steeplechase during this era make the riders appear perhaps more inelegant than they really were and certainly the best of them were very difficult men to dislodge. The few advocates of a more forward seat based on the style generally in use on the continent, where the fences were admittedly easier, were ridiculed as impractical theorists and it was generally accepted that if a forward seat exponent rode in a chase and his horse over-jumped or made a mistake, he would be catapulted from the saddle and would probably never stop rolling.

With the growing emphasis on speed, it became the general custom on the majority of courses to give fences a more friendly slope and in general to render them less severe. The gulf between racing over hurdles and racing over fences perceptibly narrowed, while the gulf between Aintree and the average park track became wider than ever before. On park courses a horse could go round jumping off his forehand, whereas at Aintree he was still compelled to stand back and use his hocks. Jockeys adapted their methods to the new conditions. By the thirties stirrup leathers were shorter and the pronounced lean-back was already looking old-fashioned and slightly absurd, having been largely replaced by a rather upright position during the actual leap. The forward position of the body throughout the parabola of the jump, combined with even shorter leathers and reins as practised by some of the most skilful and successful riders of today, was still a little way off.

Taking the professionals first, two outstanding riders in the nineteen twenties were George Duller and F. B. (Dick) Rees. A short, strongly built man with features that can be politely described as homely, Duller rode almost entirely over hurdles and possessed little aptitude or fancy for fences although he did on one occasion accept a mount in the Grand National. It is arguable that he was the greatest hurdle-race rider in history; he certainly revolutionized the style of riding. When he began his career, most of his contemporaries sat well back; he himself adopted a crouching seat and a very firm one it was, too. He never shifted his position when the horse took off, and by having his weight well forward, he assisted his mount to recover the rhythm of its stride again on landing. His judgment of pace was uncanny and on dismounting he could be relied on to give a remarkably accurate estimate of the time in which the race had been run. This skill he derived from his early days under his father, who at one time trained trotters and was a great believer in the clock.

In Duller's heyday hurdle races were usually run at a considerably slower pace than they are today and his judgment of pace frequently enabled him to dictate the terms on which the race would be run. In particular he was a master of the difficult art of waiting in front. He could ride a strong finish but in that one respect he was perhaps a little inferior to Frank Wootton, who of course had been a leading rider on the flat until he became too heavy.

On five occasions Duller rode the winner of the Imperial Cup at Sandown, the most important hurdle race of the season until the inception of the Champion Hurdle at Cheltenham. He won three years running on the great hurdler Trespasser, who carried twelve stone the first time he won and 12 st 7 lbs on the other two. It was only fitting that Duller on Blaris should win the first race for the Champion Hurdle in 1927. He was attracted to speed in every form and apart from piloting his own aircraft, he frequently drove in car races at Brooklands. In his memory the George Duller Handicap Hurdle is now run at the Cheltenham National Hunt meeting.

Dick Rees was the son of a South Wales Veterinary Surgeon, who rode in point-to-points up to the age of sixty, and Dick and his brother, L. B. Rees, began riding at an early age for D. Harrison's Tenby stable with which the Anthony brothers had once been associated. Before the war, in which he served as an Observer in the Royal Flying Corps, Rees rode as an amateur, but in 1920 he became a professional and it was not long before he reached the top of the tree. Tall and strong, with a beautiful seat on a horse and the best of hands, he was the supreme stylist of his day and many of those who saw him in his prime reckon him superior even to Bryan Marshall and Fred Winter at their best. No one could put a horse at a fence better than he did, and his strength in a finish was demonstrated in a welter race at Brighton in 1919 when he beat the great Bernard Carslake by a head. He won the Grand National on Shaun Spadah, the Grand Steeplechase de Paris on Silvo, and the Gold Cup on Red Splash, Patron Saint and Easter Hero. No ascetic, he was troubled by increasing weight for some years before he finally gave up riding and in the days of his retirement at Lewes he became a very heavy man indeed.

Other very successful riders in the nineteen twenties were Jack Anthony and Ted Leader. Jack Anthony was the son of a Carmarthenshire farmer. He and two brothers, Owen and Ivor, found fame and fortune in the racing world; a third brother entered the army and ended up a Major-General.

As a boy Jack Anthony rode his father's horses in local shows and point-to-points and his first winner under National Hunt rules was at Ludlow in 1906 when he was only sixteen. Tough and completely fearless, he was good over hurdles, better still over fences and invariably at his best at Aintree. He did not turn professional until 1920 and as an amateur he won the Grand National on Glenside (1911), Ally Sloper (1915) and Troytown (1920). He was twice second in the National on Old Tay Bridge and third on Bright's Boy. Only a man as strong and as fit as he was could have coped with Troytown and even so there were moments when his strength seemed to be giving out. 'He wasn't a horse, he was a steam engine,' Anthony used to say. When Troytown took off too soon and made a dreadful mistake less than a mile from home, 'it felt,' Anthony said, 'as if this big, robust, dynamic horse had knocked the fence clean off the course'.

Anthony retired in 1927 and a year later began training at Letcombe Regis with Mr J. H. Whitney as his chief patron. Easter Hero, winner of two Gold Cups, and Thomond II were the two best horses he ever had under his care, while he also won the Champion Hurdle with Brown Tony. It was ironical that after surviving years of race riding without serious injury, he was lamed for life when he fractured a leg dismounting from a hack during a holiday in America in 1930.

Ted Leader, son of Newmarket's leading jumping trainer Tom Leader, was equally good over fences or hurdles. He combined strength and determination with a polished style and was masterly on big, powerful horses such as Sprig on whom he won the 1927 Grand National. It is impossible to imagine a finer piece of riding than when he won the Champion Chase at Aintree on Mount Etna, who did not fancy the course at all and would certainly have refused if Leader had given him half a chance to do so.

Ernest Piggott, who had won a pre-war National on the great Jerry M, was still going strong in the nineteen twenties and for a comparatively short time Eric Foster was very successful. His most fervent admirer could hardly have claimed him a stylist, but under his vigorous driving horses seemed to run on and he certainly rode a lot of winners. Fate, unfortunately, has not dealt kindly with him since he retired from the racing scene.

In the early nineteen thirties two of the best and most popular riders were Billy Stott and Billy Speck. Both were small men, brave and tough, but although the racing public were inclined to bracket them together, they were in fact entirely dissimilar in character. Speck, with his very short bow legs hardly appeared the ideal jockey for Aintree, but he was broad-chested, strong and immensely difficult to dislodge from the saddle. In the Becher Chase at Aintree in 1932 he was riding that good horse Thomond II, who was twice placed in the National and who won the Becher Chase three years running. At the fence before Becher's Speck lost an iron and at Becher's itself his saddle slipped. Undaunted, Speck pushed the saddle back and continued in the race bareback to win by half a length, an outstanding feat in which skill and courage both played their part. To the great regret of all who knew him he broke his back at Cheltenham in 1935 riding a bad horse in a selling race and died six days later. He left £19,000, a lot of money for a jumping jockey in those days.

Billy Stott died young, too. He had a bad car accident in 1933 from which he never really recovered and he died very suddenly three years later. Brave as a lion, he was six times champion jockey and in 1933 he won the Gold Cup on Golden Miller. To everyone's surprise he was not given the ride on Golden Miller in the National and instead had the mount on Pelorus Jack, who was just slightly ahead of Kellsboro' Jack when he fell at the very last fence.

The general standard of riding steadily improved in the nineteen thirties and there was certainly no lack of competent performers. Gerry Wilson's career is dealt with later on in the chapter that includes Golden Miller's National victory in 1934. It will suffice to say here that he was a popular and worthy champion. Staff Ingham, who as a boy had won the Royal Hunt Cup at Ascot on King George V's Weathervane, was an exceptionally polished and skilful rider over hurdles. Tall, quiet-voiced and cool-headed, he bore all the hallmarks of having served his apprenticeship with Stanley Wootton. French-born Georges Pellerin was another fine hurdle-race rider, while Jack Moloney and Gerry Hardy were both consummate horsemen whom it was both an education and a pleasure to watch. Sad to say, good fortune rarely shone on those three once they had given up riding.

Jack Fawcus turned professional after a successful spell as an amateur and for several years rode for Mr J. V. Rank. Quiet and patient in his methods, he could play the waiting game to perfection. Five years as a prisoner-of-war in Germany had a

damaging effect on his health which suffered further from two
serious car accidents but he has managed to conduct a small
'mixed' stable with a good deal of success and has borne the ups
and downs of life with pluck and good humour.

Billy Parvin and Eric Brown both rode stacks of winners,
mostly for Major 'Bay' Powell's stable, and Brown was in fact
champion for one season. Keith Piggott, father of Lester Piggott,
was consistently successful without quite reaching the front rank,
and though Danny Morgan never had the luck to ride a Grand
National winner for the Wroughton stable, he was probably a
better all round rider than Dudley Williams and Evan Williams
who both did. 'Frenchie' Nicholson, so called because he was
originally an apprentice in France where his father was a professional huntsman, was tremendously strong and without a
superior at driving a tired horse into the last fence. He is the father
of David Nicholson, one of the most successful and best-liked
riders of today.

Fred Rimell and George Archibald, whose careers were interrupted by the war, were both stylish and effective, particularly
the former who was very good indeed in his prime, while Bruce
Hobbs, who rode Battleship to victory in the Grand National at
the age of seventeen, looked like going to the top of the tree when
he had a bad fall and seriously injured his spine. Those paladins
of the Turf, Noel Murless and Paddy Prendergast, were both
professionals under National Hunt rules, but their prowess in
the saddle was in inverse proportion to the glittering success they
have achieved as trainers on the flat. Who could have guessed in
those days that Paddy Prendergast, riding for the most part
indifferent horses at second or third class meetings, would one
day turn out to be an outstanding figure in European racing?

In this era amateur riders—mostly genuine amateurs though
one or two were reputed more expensive than the leading professionals—still took a leading part in the sport. For instance in
the season 1926–27 over 150 amateurs rode winners. For ten years
after the war the outstanding amateur was Harry Atherton
Brown. Brought up in the heart of the Atherstone country, he
began owning horses as soon as he left Eton and rode his first
winner in 1907. Two years later he was the leading amateur rider.
After war service in the Household Cavalry he again rode with
consistent success and in one season he earned the distinction of
being champion jockey, the last amateur to achieve that feat.
He never won the Grand National but in 1921 he was second on
The Bore, gallantly remounting after falling and breaking his

8

collar-bone. For many years he trained as well as rode, one of the best horses he had being Dudley, a brilliant two-miler who held the record for the number of races won until this was beaten a few years ago by Crudwell. At one period Brown acted as a private trainer for Mr J. V. Rank and he also coached the Prince of Wales in cross-country riding.

Harry Brown was a man of wit and charm who spoke with an attractive drawl. He was also highly competitive and there were some who inferred that like Squire Osbaldeston, with whom he undoubtedly had certain traits in common, he was occasionally a trifle on the 'warm' side. However his charm and presence of mind could usually be guaranteed to extricate him more or less unscathed from unpromising situations. Apart from his brilliance as a race rider, he was one of the best shots in the country and an expert stalker and fisherman. One day he arrived at Hereford, where he was due to ride Dudley, an hour or two before racing, and disliking the prospect of hanging about aimlessly on the race-course, he backed himself firstly to catch the biggest salmon of the season on the Wye and then to ride a winner, within an hour. He caught a 44 lb salmon, the best of the season, but for once Dudley let him down, falling at the final fence when ten lengths clear.

Harry Brown died in 1961, but is assured of a permanent niche in English literature, being easily recognizable as 'Charlie Pepper-corn' in Siegfried Sassoon's *Memoirs of a Foxhunting Man*.

Another good amateur in the immediate post-war era was Captain 'Tuppy' Bennet, a vet. He won the 1923 Grand National on Sergeant Murphy, but died the following year after a bad fall at Wolverhampton. Others to shine in the nineteen twenties were Peter Roberts, Percy Whitaker, Pat Dennis and Stratford Dennis. Major J. P. Wilson and Bill Dutton both rode Grand National winners, while 'Ginger' Whitfield was killed at Hurst Park just when he looked like making a champion. Captain R. E. Sassoon, who was fatally injured when Clear Note fell at Lingfield, was not a great rider, being for one thing desperately short-sighted. He was, however, the bravest of the brave and immensely popular with the racing public. Quite rightly he was given a tremendous reception when he won a steeplechase at Aintree on his brilliant mare West Indies.

In the nineteen thirties the two best amateurs were Fred Thackray and 'Pete' Bostwick. Thackray was equally good over fences and hurdles. Quiet and modest, he never rode again after a terrible fall on Gregalach in the Grand National. Bostwick, a small, tough, rich American was good over fences and fully the equal of the best professionals over hurdles. One of his more important successes was to win the Imperial Cup on Flaming. Little behind these two was Alec Marsh, the present Jockey Club starter. The Fairlawne stable, where Harry Whiteman then held the licence, had three amateur riders, Anthony Mildmay, Edward Paget and Peter Cazalet. At this stage of his career Mildmay was rather weak and lacking in confidence and nothing like as effective as he became in the nineteen forties. Paget, second on Egremont in the 1932 Grand National, was sound and competent, while Cazalet, who had gone up to Oxford from Eton with a high reputation as a cricketer and racquets player, suddenly took up riding there and met with plenty of success until a bad fall at Sandown terminated his career. John Hislop firmly established his reputation in the seasons just before the outbreak of World War II. Neat and stylish, he could ride a more polished and effective finish than many of his professional contemporaries. Up in the north Reg Tweedie, more recently the owner of that good chaser, Freddie, enjoyed a record of consistent success.

At any rate until Hitler was firmly in power, soldiering between the wars afforded in general a pleasant and leisurely existence, the powers in Whitehall dispensing the convenient theory that another major conflict in Europe was highly unlikely. Although the number of cavalry regiments had been reduced and there were signs that others, if not all, would eventually be overtaken by mechanization, there was no lack of officers with the time, the money and the inclination to take up racing. Soldiers not only formed a sizeable proportion of riders at point-to-points, but provided a useful nucleus of proficient amateurs for racing under National Hunt rules. There is no doubt that the popular and well-organized 'bona fide' military meetings at Aldershot and Tidworth provided admirable training grounds for both horses and riders, while the races confined to infantry officers were apt to provide useful practice for army doctors as well. 'Bona fide' meetings have now ceased to exist, but roughly speaking they were point-to-points run under National Hunt rules and courses were permitted to make a charge for admission. At Aldershot any informality in dress on the part of the many officers who went there would have been considered in deplorable taste, and bowler hats, blue overcoats and stiff white collars could be observed there in rich profusion.

The pick of the soldier-riders, at any rate of those who remained in the army for the whole of their riding careers, were 'Perry'

Harding of the 5th Inniskilling Dragoon Guards and Peter Payne-Gallwey of the 11th Hussars. Neither could afford to own horses except on a very modest scale and both came up the hard way entirely on their merits. Harding is one of the only two amateurs to win the Champion Hurdle—Alan Lillingston is the other—a feat he accomplished on Our Hope in 1938. Payne-Gallwey rode nearly sixty winners between the season of 1931–32 and that of 1934–35. At one time he owned a very useful chaser called Backsight who was by no means an easy ride as he was always liable to pitch awkwardly on landing. Backsight, with Payne-Gallwey up, won the Grand Military Gold Cup despite a fearful blunder in the early stages of the race. Unkind persons were sometimes heard to suggest that it would be no bad thing if Messrs Harding and Payne-Gallwey devoted less time to racing and more to their military duties, but the war made that suggestion look rather stupid. Harding finished his military career as a Major-General with the D.S.O. and bar, while Payne-Gallwey, a dashing armoured leader, was awarded the D.S.O. and two bars. It is perhaps worth mentioning that General Sir Richard McCreery, who eventually commanded the 8th Army, and Lt-General Herbert Lumsden, who was killed in the Far East after commanding a Corps at El Alamein, were both admirable riders and both won the Grand Military Gold Cup.

Frank Furlong and Fulke Walwyn both served for some years in the 9th Lancers and followed the example of a former officer of that regiment, General Sir David Campbell, by winning the Grand National. Bobby Pennington of the 11th Hussars nearly achieved that distinction, too, being beaten a mere length in 1927 on his 100–1 outsider Bovril III. Cecil Brownhill of the Irish Guards won a lot of races, including the Scottish Grand National, on Drintyre. He was killed in a car crash in South Africa shortly before the war and in accordance with his wishes his ashes were brought home and scattered at Sandown. Reggie West, killed with the Grenadiers in 1940, rode a lot of winners and so did Peter Grant-Lawson of the Blues, Peter Herbert of the Life Guards and Bobby Petre of the Scots Guards. Petre's big triumph, of course, came after the war when he won the Grand National on Lovely Cottage. Mark Roddick of the 10th Hussars won the Grand Military three years running and other good riders from that regiment were 'Roscoe' Harvey, now the senior Stewards Secretary; Colin Davy, who wrote some entertaining books about racing; and Kim Muir who was killed in 1940. W. Filmer-Sankey of the Life Guards owned a top-class chaser in Ruddyglow

Lutteur III, the French-bred and owned winner of the 1909 Grand National. *Copyright W. W. Rouch & Co. Ltd.*

The 1912 Grand National winner Jerry M, ridden by Ernie Piggott. *Copyright W. W. Rouch & Co. Ltd.*

and from the 17th/21st Lancers came Lord Fingall and Major A. Gossage. 'Babe' Moseley, who transferred to the Royals from the Royal Navy, was another good rider and won the Grand Military on his own horse Slieve Grien. A former officer of the Indian Cavalry, Harry Weber, was as good as any of them at his best, but his riding career in this country was not a long one. The Royal Navy had a triumph at Sandown in 1935 when Young Cuthbert won the Grand Military, owned and ridden by Lieutenant Richard Courage, R.N.

Among the leading National Hunt trainers in the inter-war years were naturally some who were fully established before 1914. Tom Coulthwaite, for instance, had trained two Grand National winners before the war and in 1931 he trained his third winner of that event, Grakle. Bob Gore, too, had won two pre-war Grand Nationals, but unlike Coulthwaite, who never sat on a horse in his life, he had ridden a lot in his time and had in fact won races in almost every European country. His horses invariably looked robust and well and nearly always had their tails plaited, a fashion that has now almost entirely disappeared. His stable was at Findon and so was that of Alec Law, who trained a lot of winners in the late nineteen twenties and early 'thirties, including that gallant little mare Alike.

No trainer commanded greater respect and affection than Fred Withington. The son of a parson, he was a leading amateur rider in his youth and first began to train in 1899. In 1908 he saddled Rubio and Mattie McGregor, first and second in the National, and he also trained the first Cheltenham Gold Cup winner, Red Splash. He retired from training in 1930 and it is proof of the esteem in which he was held that he was elected not only to the National Hunt Committee, but to the Jockey Club as well. He served as a Steward with the former body, being the first public trainer to do so. He had acted as trainer up to his retirement for Mr Vivian Hugh Smith, later Lord Bicester, and he was succeeded in this capacity by George Beeby, who also trained some good horses for the American owner Mr J. B. Snow.

Aubrey Hastings continued to conduct his stable at Wroughton with consistent success, but like his son Peter Hastings-Bass, he died all too young. His successor at Wroughton was Ivor Anthony, who had ridden a lot for the stable and had gone there as assistant after a bad fall at Ludlow had prevented him riding any more. Anthony fully maintained the high standard for which Wroughton was famous, his particular virtues being his unwearying patience and his attention to detail. He particularly enjoyed dealing with a difficult horse and was apt to spend more time over a 'problem child' than over the established champions of the stable. His successes included the Grand National with Kellsboro' Jack and Royal Mail, the Gold Cup with Morse Code and Poet Prince, and the Champion Hurdle with Chenango. Owen and Jack Anthony both had their share of successes, Owen winning the Grand National with Music Hall, and the Gold Cup with Golden Miller and Roman Hackle, while Jack won two Gold Cups with Easter Hero and the Champion Hurdle with Brown Tony.

A remarkable character was Percy Woodland. The son of a Hendon horse-dealer, he rode the winner of a chase at Lingfield when he was just thirteen and so small that he had to stand on a chair to take the saddle off. His riding record was a truly extraordinary one, as besides winning the Grand National twice and the Grand Steeplechase de Paris twice, he also had two victories in the French Derby. He had a big stable at Cholderton in Wiltshire, where many of his patrons were army officers or owner riders. His horses were easily distinguished in the paddock, as they were usually clipped trace high, had long, untidy tails and carried not one ounce of superfluous flesh. They were extremely well schooled, though, and fit to run for their lives.

Among the notable horses Woodland trained were Gregalach (after his 1929 Grand National victory); Drin, a high-class staying chaser that was killed in the Grand National; and Captain R. E. Sassoon's brilliant mare West Indies. Woodland was the brother-in-law of the Epsom trainer 'Vic' Tabor. The best horse Tabor trained under National Hunt rules was Sir Francis Towle's Airgead Sios. This big chestnut was the most dashing and spectacular jumper of his time, his victories including the Champion Chase, the Becher Chase (twice), the Grand Annual Chase and the Victory Chase.

Another 'character' was the American-born Morgan de Witt Blair. An individualist with no lack of pluck and self-confidence, he first came into the news in 1921 when he backed himself to complete the course in the Grand National on Bonnie Charlie. He won his bet after Bonnie Charlie had fallen four times. He made a similar wager when he rode Jack Horner in 1925 and again he won his money. He first started training at Rugby and then moved on to Ewhurst in Surrey, where he enjoyed a good deal of success although it was common gossip on the racecourse that his methods were unorthodox to say the very least. He won the Champion Hurdle in 1936 with Victor Norman and he won a lot of races with a most versatile horse, The Brown

Talisman, that, like Victor Norman, belonged to Mr Michael Stephens.

A very different type to Morgan Blair was Tom Leader, son of the Tom Leader who trained George Frederick to win the Derby in 1874. A devout Churchman, a licensed preacher, and an active and distinguished Freemason, he was one of the best-liked and most respected men in Newmarket. He won the 1927 Grand National with Sprig, ridden by his son Ted, and he won that race again two years later with Gregalach. In 1920 he achieved the unique feat of saddling fourteen winners in succession.

Stewart Wight, bewhiskered and bowler hatted, trained many good winners up North, and so did Bobby Renton. Frank Hartigan, Walter Nightingall, Stanley Wootton and Peter Thrale all ran successful 'mixed' stables, and at this period 'Towser' Gosden had not yet deserted jumping for the flat. Herbert Smyth was not only very able professionally, but a considerable wit and many of his sayings, unfortunately unrepeatable here, have deservedly won a permanent place in the lore and legend of racing. Harry Brown's brother, Frank, sent out a steady stream of winners from Bourton-on-the-Hill. Though he lacked Harry's occasional touch of ruthlessness, he tended to regard racing as a perpetual battle of wits in which the ultimate result, even when successful, probably gave him less pleasure than the various stratagems employed. George Poole was a master at placing moderate horses to the best advantage; he trained some good horses, too, winning the Grand National with Shaun Spadah, while Kingsford, a tremendously hard puller that was unfortunately killed in the Gold Cup, was a brilliant three-mile chaser. Bill Payne senior did pretty well year after year, and so did Tommy Rayson whose son Monty, a rider of the highest promise, unfortunately died very young.

It only remains to add that in the mid-nineteen thirties it was still possible to find a trainer of first rate ability whose basic training fee was four guineas a week, while many of the 'small' trainers charged considerably less than that.

Among notable members of the National Hunt Committee during this era were Lord Coventry, who was a founder-member and continued to serve till his death in 1930; Lord Gowrie, v.c., an administrator of quite exceptional ability; and Brigadier Ferdinand Stanley, brother of the late Lord Derby. Brigadier Stanley had done notable work in cleaning up jumping before 1914 and after the war he turned his attention to point-to-points. He was the inventor of the Bona Fide Hunt or Military Meeting.

When he retired from training, Mr Fred Withington, with his intimate knowledge of the sport, proved a valuable asset to the N.H.C. Everyone who knew him trusted him implicitly, and furthermore he was the kindest of men with ready sympathy for the troubles of others. It was to him that trainers and jockeys invariably turned when in need of help or advice.

II

THE GRAND NATIONAL 1919–29

Not surprisingly National Hunt racing took some little time to get into its stride again after the war and the process was hardly assisted by the fact that Ireland, the traditional nursery of jumpers, was fighting for her independence and in the bitter throes of a savage civil war. The quality of the field in the 1919 Grand National was probably well below the average standard and Mrs Hugh Peel's nine-year-old Poethlyn, who had won the substitute National at Gatwick the year before, was a hot favourite at 11–4, despite the fact that he had the burden of 12 st 7 lbs on his back. However, he fully justified the confidence of his supporters, and beautifully ridden by Ernest Piggott, who had also won on him at Gatwick, he was a ready winner from the Irish horse Ballyboggan, ridden by Willie Head, whose son Alec trained the 1956 Derby victor Lavandin. Trained by Harry Escott, Poethlyn was a bold, somewhat impetuous, jumper but an adept at putting in a short one when he happened to meet a fence wrong. The following year, again carrying 12 st 7 lbs, he was favourite at 3–1, but fell at the very first fence. Since Poethlyn, the only horses to have won the Grand National with twelve stone or over are Sprig (12 st 4 lbs) in 1927; Golden Miller (12 st 2 lbs) in 1934; and Reynoldstown (12 st 2 lbs) in 1936.

As is the case with so many Grand National winners, there was a curious story behind Poethlyn. He was bred by his owner's husband, Major Hugh Peel, who had purchased the dam, Fine Champagne, at an auction for twenty-five guineas. Mated with a somewhat obscure sire called Rydal Head, Fine Champagne produced a weakly foal that Major Peel had no compunction in selling for seven guineas. Some time later Major Peel was asked to go and have a look at a big, rather overgrown two-year-old at Shrewsbury. His wife went instead and found the two-year-old in question was the sickly foal that had been sold for so trifling a sum. He was bought back for fifty guineas and the first salmon Major Peel caught that year, and was duly given the name of Poethlyn, which is Welsh for brandy.

Conditions for the 1920 Grand National were appalling. Cold, driving rain swept the course relentlessly without a pause. There were pools of water on the track and the paddock was like a snipe bog. The thousands of spectators who had packed the unprotected top of the stand since before the first race was run to ensure securing a good view of the National suffered almost intolerable hardship and there were not a few cases, some fatal, of pneumonia and severe chills afterwards. The winner was Troytown, bred and owned by Major Thomas Gerrard of Co. Meath, a former 17th Lancer, and trained in Ireland. He was a massive horse of quite remarkable power, particularly in front of the saddle; by comparison he seemed to fall away about his loins, but as his rider Jack Anthony remarked: 'An athlete wants all shoulder and chest development. He doesn't want to be big below.'

Troytown had not been broken with any marked degree of skill and in consequence he always had a bad mouth, which, combined with his phenomenal strength, made him a terribly difficult horse to hold. Even Jack Anthony, strong and fit as he was, wondered at times during the National if his own strength and stamina were going to last out. Troytown soon pulled his way to the front and coming to the water jump he was lengths ahead of his opponents. He cleared the obstacle well enough, but slipped on landing, slithered for several yards and it was touch and go whether he recovered his legs.

This incident at least enabled Anthony to regain control and take a pull with the result that Turkey Buzzard and Ardonagh both drew level. At the first open ditch on the second circuit Troytown made a hideous mistake and lost several lengths. 'He's gone,' shouted Mr Percy Whitaker, Ardonagh's rider, in premature triumph to Bill Payne senior on Turkey Buzzard, but two fences later Troytown, going as strong as ever, jumped past them both and in fact Ardonagh and Turkey Buzzard came down soon afterwards.

From that point Anthony never saw another horse till the last open ditch four fences from home. At this formidable obstacle Troytown elected to take off almost outside the wings and landed slap on top of the fence. It looked all up with him, but his gigantic strength pulled him through and he managed to struggle safely to the landing side, leaving a hole in the fence big enough to drive a cab through. In the meantime The Bore, ridden by Mr Harry

Brown, and The Turk II passed him, but he had caught them again by the very next fence where he took off a length behind The Bore and landed a length in front of him. From that point it was plain sailing and he galloped on with no sign of diminishing vigour to give Jack Anthony, still an amateur at this stage of his career, his third Grand National success. Despite his exertions Troytown galloped almost down to the first fence before his rider could pull him up. 'He'd have won with fourteen stone on his back,' said Anthony afterwards.

In the summer Troytown was sent over to France to compete in some races there. He finished third in the Grand Steeplechase de Paris at Auteuil, an event he had won the previous year, and a few days later ran in the Prix des Drags over the same course. He did not actually fall, but jumping the post, rails and brook he broke a leg just above the knee and there was no option but to put him down. He was seven years of age and probably one of the greatest horses, certainly the most powerful one, ever to win the Grand National.

Conditions were again tough in 1921 and the going was very heavy. Of the thirty-five runners Mr T. M. McAlpine's ten-year-old Shaun Spadah, the winner, was the only one to complete the course without a fall. The favourite at 9–1 was The Bore, owned and ridden by Harry Brown, and coming to the final fence The Bore and Shaun Spadah, the latter partnered by that superb rider Dick Rees, had the race between them. Shaun Spadah landed safely but down came The Bore, breaking Harry Brown's collar-bone in the process. Inspired perhaps by thoughts of his each way bet on The Bore, Brown was quickly in the saddle again and to resounding cheers finished a gallant second with his right arm swinging loosely at his side. Third place went to All White who, like The Bore, had been remounted.

Shaun Spadah, who carried 11 st 7 lbs, was not a fast horse but he was a brilliant jumper and stayed for ever. He was trained at Lewes by George Poole, who had ridden his first winner over fences at the age of thirteen and as a young man made a reputation for himself as a maker of hunters. A shrewd, reserved and somewhat taciturn bachelor, rarely seen without a cigarette dropping from his lip, he was a specialist in the art of placing indifferent horses to the best advantage. He nearly achieved a remarkable double this year as he also trained Senhora who was second in the Lincoln. If the double had materialized, Poole and his patrons, in particular Mr Tommy Edge, the proprietor of various racing publications, would have landed a fortune.

Although the going was good in 1922 there was again a lot of grief and only the first three horses completed the course without mishap. Shaun Spadah fell at the first fence and so did Harry Brown's mount, the favourite Southampton, the property of Lord Woolavington, who won the Derby that year with Captain Cuttle. The only owner to have won the Grand National and the Derby the same season is King Edward VII who, as Prince of Wales, brought off the double with Ambush II and Diamond Jubilee in 1900.

The 1922 winner was Mr Hugh Kershaw's nine-year-old Music Hall (11 st 7 lbs), who scored from a couple of sure-footed plodders in Drifter and Taffytus. In July the previous year Owen Anthony, a brother of Jack Anthony, had taken out a licence to train and Music Hall was one of the first horses sent to him. Music Hall had in fact broken down badly and looked a poor proposition for the future, but Anthony treated him with the utmost care and it was a fine tribute to his professional skill that Music Hall was not only the winner, but a confidently backed winner, of the Grand National the following spring. In 1923 Music Hall was third in the Grand Steeplechase de Paris; the following year he carried 12 st 7 lbs in the National but found the weight too much for him and was pulled up. In his Grand National triumph he was ridden by L. B. Rees, a strong horseman who was, however, hardly in the same high class as either his brother F. B., or his son Bill, who has enjoyed a long and successful association with Peter Cazalet's stable.

Sergeant Murphy was not one of the greatest of Grand National winners, but he was certainly one of the most gallant and popular. Moreover he stands on record as the oldest winner of the race this century, being in his fourteenth year when he was victorious on that foggy Friday at Aintree in 1923. This was a great year for veterans as the twelve-year-old Shaun Spadah put up a magnificent performance to finish second under 12 st 7 lbs, while the eleven-year-old Conjuror II ridden by the owner's son, Mr C. Dewhurst, was third. It is proof of the formidable nature of the Aintree fences at this period that in the four years 1920-21-22-23 119 horses competed in the National and only just over a dozen completed the course without mishap.

A big powerful chestnut with boundless stamina and not much speed, Sergeant Murphy had originally carried the colours of the well-known bookmaker Mr M. H. Benson, who traded under the name of Douglas Stuart—'Duggie Never Owes' as the famous advertisement claimed. In the substitute Grand National at

Gatwick in 1918 Sergeant Murphy was unplaced. He failed at Aintree in 1920 and the following year he was fourth. He missed the race in 1921, but in 1922 he was again fourth despite a refusal at the Canal Turn and losing his bridle. His final appearance was in 1924 when he finished fifth. Many of his admirers thought he had earned his retirement when he won the National; his owner thought otherwise and the old horse was fatally injured in some minor event at Bogside at the age of sixteen.

In 1922 Sergeant Murphy had been bought by a rich young American, Mr Stephen Sanford, who planned to hunt him and ride him himself in the University steeplechases at Cottenham, being at that time an undergraduate at Cambridge. On hearing this notion Mr Benson is said to have given a wry smile and he was not unduly surprised when Mr Sanford found 'The Sergeant', who was not everyone's ride by a long way, too much of a good thing in the hunting field. The old horse was therefore sent over to George Blackwell's stable at Newmarket and put into training again. Blackwell, who had once been a pupil of the great Mat Dawson, had won the Triple Crown in 1903 with Rock Sand. Other trainers to have won both the Derby and the Grand National are J. Jewitt, R. C. Dawson, W. Stephenson and M. V. O'Brien.

Sergeant Murphy was ridden to victory at Aintree by Captain 'Tuppy' Bennet, a veterinary surgeon who was a top-class amateur rider. The following year he died at the age of thirty after a horrible fall on Ardeen at Wolverhampton.

Conjuror II had met with considerable interference when third in 1923, and in 1924, with Harry Brown in the saddle, he was a hot favourite at 5–2. He fell at Becher's, though, first time round. It was Harry Brown's last ride in the race and it was the final appearance, too, of Shaun Spadah, who, at the age thirteen, was seventh with 12 st 5 lbs. Winnall was twenty lengths in front second time round and going strong when he was baulked by a loose horse at the Canal Turn, while Old Tay Bridge, ridden by Hubert Hartigan, was looking very dangerous when he fell three fences from home.

The race was won by the 25–1 outsider, Master Robert, owned in partnership by Lord Airlie, who had won a race or two on him, and Colonel Sidney Green. Bred in Co Donegal, Master Robert was a great big horse standing seventeen hands and of somewhat doubtful soundness. To put it mildly he had taken a long time to come to hand and at the age of five he was pulling a plough for his breeder. He was trained at Wroughton by Aubrey

Golden Miller (Gerry Wilson up), winner of the Grand National and of five Cheltenham Gold Cups. *Copyright W. W. Rouch & Co. Ltd.*

Easter Hero (Dick Rees up). Twice winner of the Gold Cup, second in the Grand National. *Copyright W. W. Rouch & Co. Ltd.*

George Duller, on Trespasser, three times winner of the Imperial Cup. *Copyright W. W. Rouch & Co. Ltd.*

Two outstanding personalities in N.H. racing between the wars: Jack and Ivor Anthony. *Copyright W. W. Rouch & Co. Ltd.*

LEFT TO RIGHT: L. B. Rees, George Poole, Miss M. Poole, F. B. Rees. L.B. won the National on Music Hall, F.B. on Shaun Spadah, who was trained by Poole. *Copyright W. W. Rouch & Co. Ltd.*

Hastings, who had ridden and trained the 1906 winner Ascetic's Silver and had also trained the 1915 winner Ally Sloper. The ride on Master Robert, who is remembered today for the hotel named after him on the Great West Road, had been offered to Mr Peter Roberts. However, Roberts preferred to partner Palm Oil, who fell. Master Robert was therefore ridden by Bob Trudgill, who may have been unfashionable, but certainly lacked nothing in pluck and vigour. Overcome by his exertions and the excitement, Trudgill collapsed in the weighing room afterwards and had to receive medical attention.

Second to Master Robert was Fly Mask and third with 12st 2 lbs came Silvo. A brilliant horse that did not quite stay the full Grand National course, Silvo, ridden by Dick Rees, won the Grand Steeplechase de Paris in 1925. At one time he was owned in partnership by Mr W. H. Midwood and Sir Edward Edgar, and when the partnership was dissolved, Mr Midwood bought him outright for the then gigantic sum of 10,500 guineas.

To destroy a German Zeppelin and to ride the winner of a Grand National is the unique double that was completed in 1925 by Major Jack Wilson. During the war he had been awarded the D.F.C. for destroying a Zeppelin that had bombed Hull, and when hostilities were over he ran a small jumping stable in Yorkshire, riding a number of winners himself. When Ted Leader turned down the ride on Double Chance it was offered to Wilson, and despite his comparative lack of Aintree experience, no one could have ridden a better or cooler race.

Double Chance was bred by Mr Anthony de Rothschild and won a couple of races on the flat as a three-year-old. He then broke down rather badly amd Mr de Rothschild offered him as a hack to Frederick Archer, who had been a trooper in his squadron of the Royal Buckinghamshire Yeomanry in Palestine during the war and was just setting up as a trainer in Yorkshire. Archer, a nephew of the great jockey, patched Double Chance up and hunted him for several seasons with the Middleton. When the horse was thoroughly sound again Archer, who had just transferred his stable from Malton to Newmarket, decided to put him into training. Double Chance soon showed that he possessed marked ability and before the Grand National he won five races, admittedly of no great significance, in succession. Three weeks before the Liverpool Spring Meeting, Archer sold a half share in him to Mr D. Goold, a Liverpool business man.

Coming to the last fence Double Chance was only lying third, but he produced a great turn of speed in the run-in to overhaul

Old Tay Bridge, ridden by Jack Anthony, and Fly Mask ridden by E. C. Doyle—Major E. C. Doyle, D.S.O., who had just turned professional. Sprig was fourth and Silvo, carrying 12 st 7 lbs, fifth. A lot of money was won over Double Chance, who was extremely well backed at 100–9. A year or two later Archer was killed in a car crash.

It may well be that between the wars the Grand National reached the zenith of its popularity and prestige. With the Gold Cup still more or less in its infancy, the National stood out on its own as by far the most important and valuable race of the jumping season, inspiring not only the widest public interest but a weighty volume of ante-post betting. The fences were extremely severe and even to complete the course was reckoned an heroic achievement. The stands and enclosures were packed with spectators; it was difficult to find hotel accommodation for miles around, and, in addition, there was much private entertaining in Lancashire and Cheshire. Seats on special trains from London on Grand National day had to be booked weeks ahead.

Nowadays the National is run on a Saturday and once the big race is over, the crowds, meagre indeed compared to those in the old days, begin to disperse. Up till the war, though, the National was run on a Friday and there was another fine day's sport, with the Champion Chase as the main attraction, on the Saturday. For some, too, there were the raucous delights of the traditional Grand National party at the Adelphi Hotel on Friday night. Conduct at this festivity, where the wine flowed perhaps a trifle too freely, was liable to become distinctly uninhibited, and sometimes the standard of behaviour would have been more appropriate to a Bullingdon Club Dinner or, since old resentments and quarrels were liable to flare up as the evening progressed, to a clash between 'rockers' and 'mods'. On the whole, though, it was very good fun and it was rare for anyone to get seriously hurt.

It was in the nineteen twenties that the glamour of the National began to attract American owners in some strength. Possibly they were inspired by the victory of the American-owned Sergeant Murphy. Their advent certainly livened up the market for staying chasers, which was all to the good, but it undoubtedly encouraged certain owners to enter mediocre and unsuitable horses for the National in the hope of finding some American who wanted to see his colours carried on the big day, no matter how remote the prospect of success.

In 1926 the winner, Jack Horner, was owned by an American, Mr A. C. Schwartz, who bought him three weeks before the race for the appreciable sum of £4,000 and a £2,000 contingency if he won. As a young horse Jack Horner had been in the Blankney Hunt stables and had carried the Master, Colonel Vernon Willey, in the first half of a famous hunt when hounds made a fourteen-mile point and covered some twenty-six miles in all. Colonel Willey said he changed from Jack Horner after roughly fifteen miles. The horse had jumped superbly except for a fall at a very wide brook.

Later Jack Horner was drafted and sold for 160 guineas at Leicester. At one point he became very temperamental and diffi-cult and declined to jump at all, but was eventually reformed by Mr Morgan Blair, who then owned him in partnership with Mr Kenneth Mackay. With Blair riding Jack Horner ran seventh to Double Chance in the 1925 Grand National. Mr Mackay then became his sole owner for 1,250 guineas and in due course passed him on at a nice profit to Mr Schwartz.

Silvo came down at the first fence in 1926 and the gallant Old Tay Bridge, ridden by Jack Anthony and a great favourite with the public, looked all over a winner when he jumped the last fence in front, but he was twelve years of age and carrying 12 st 2 lbs and Jack Horner, an out-and-out stayer receiving 25 lbs, caught him fifty yards from the post. Bright's Boy was third and Sprig was fourth for the second year running. Only five horses finished.

Jack Horner was trained at Newmarket by Harvey Leader—better known as 'Jack' Leader—who as a very young man had trained the 1920 St Leger winner, Caligula. He is still a leading flat-race trainer today. Jack Horner's rider was W. Watkinson, a short, tough Tasmanian-born jockey who thus found fame and fortune at the somewhat advanced age of forty. The following month he had a terrible fall at Bogside and died two days later.

Newmarket at this period played a far more important part in National Hunt racing than it does today and in 1927 the Grand National was won for the fourth time in five years by a horse trained at the headquarters of sport under Jockey Club rules. The winner, and a very worthy one, was Sprig, a ten-year-old trained by Tom Leader, one of the best-liked and most respected men in Newmarket, and ridden by his son Ted, who on retirement became a successful trainer on the flat. Sprig, who carried 12 st 2 lbs and had finished fourth the two previous years, was a big, powerful chestnut of the stamp that journalists of the period used to describe as 'the approved Aintree type'. He carried the colours of a seventy-four-year-old widow, Mrs M. Partridge, and there was a touch of sadness in his background as he had been bred by Mrs Partridge's son Richard, who had been killed in the war. Mrs Partridge put Sprig into training solely because she thought it was what Richard would have wished.

Coming to the last fence Mr Stephen Sandford's Bright's Boy, ridden by that great Aintree jockey, Jack Anthony, was just ahead of Sprig and the 100–1 outsider Bovril III and it looked like being another American victory. Bright's Boy, who had been third the previous year, battled on gamely under 12 st 7 lbs but the weight was a bit too much for him and he was finally mastered by Sprig. Just as Sprig appeared to have the race well won, along came Bovril III with a tremendous late run and in the end Sprig was all out to win by a length

Bovril III, trained by J. C. Cockton in Huntingdonshire, was a chestnut hunter with one eye, owned and ridden by Mr G. W. Pennington, who had just joined the 11th Hussars and was comparatively inexperienced in the art of race-riding. Because of Bovril's disability, Pennington took him round on the outside to make sure he saw his fences and though these tactics were perfectly justified, Bovril must have travelled a lot further than Sprig and Bright's Boy. Nor, of course, could Pennington help his horse at the finish to the same extent as Ted Leader and Jack Anthony did theirs.

Nevertheless it was an extremely stout-hearted performance that came very near to pulling off one of the greatest surprises in the history of the race. Mr Pennington—now Sir William Pennington-Ramsden—is a brother-in-law of General Sir Randle Feilden, the head of the recently formed Turf Board. Other amateurs to complete the course this year were Mr J. B. Balding on Drinmond, Major T. Cavanagh on Master of Arts, and Captain R. E. Sassoon on Ballystockart.

Sprig started favourite at 8–1 and there was a lot of money at 9–1 for Grakle, who was only a five-year-old. For the first time the B.B.C. broadcast a running commentary on the race.

The 1928 Grand National was one of the most remarkable in the history of the race. Of the forty-two horses that faced the starter, the only one to complete the course was the unconsidered outsider Tipperary Tim, whose starting price was 100–1.

The going was very heavy and the visibility poor. Unseen from the stands because of the mist, the main cause of the grief was the best horse in the race, Easter Hero, who had recently been sold for £7,000 and a contingency by Mr Frank Barbour to the international financier, Mr. A. Lowenstein. Sailing along towards

Captain R. E. Sassoon, a very gallant amateur who was fatally injured at Lingfield. *Copyright W. W. Rouch & Co. Ltd.*

Billy Speck, a tough, brilliant rider who died as a result of a fall at Cheltenham. *Copyright W. W. Rouch & Co. Ltd.*

Gregalach, winner of the 1929 Grand National, with Bob Everett up.
Copyright W. W. Rouch & Co. Ltd.

Major Jack Wilson, rider
of the 1925 Grand
National winner, Double
Chance. *Copyright
W. W. Rouch & Co. Ltd.*

Sprig, who won the
Grand National in 1927
and was twice fourth in
that event. With Ted
Leader up. *Copyright
W. W. Rouch & Co. Ltd.*

Troytown, with Jack
Anthony up. Won
Grand Steeplechase de
Paris, as a six-year-old,
and the Grand National
the following year.
*Copyright
W. W. Rouch & Co. Ltd.*

the Canal Turn fence, which was then an open ditch. Easter Hero took off far too soon and landed on top of the jump. There he stuck, baulking the horses immediately behind him, who in turn baulked those behind them. In this manner more than twenty horses were put out of the race.

On the second circuit the six-year-old French mare Maguelonne, ridden by Bedeloup, was going very well indeed when she fell at the fence after Valentine's and coming on to the racecourse the probable winner appeared to be Great Span, trained by Bill Payne senior and ridden by his son, 'Young Bill', who was then only seventeen years of age. At the second last fence, though, Great Span's saddle slipped right round and deposited poor Bill on the floor.

At the final fence the only horses standing were the American candidate Billy Barton, trained by Aubrey Hastings and ridden by Tommy Cullinan, and Tipperary Tim. Both were desperately tired, but Tipperary Tim, who had never put a foot wrong throughout, got over safely, whereas to the intense disappointment of the hundreds of Americans watching, Billy Barton came down, being remounted to finish second. No horse was placed third and among those that failed to finish were Sprig, Bright's Boy and Grakle. The result brought great joy and much profit to bookmakers everywhere except in Tipperary where Tims are fairly thick on the ground and a good many of them had their shilling on the winner.

Owned by Mr H. S. Kenyon and trained in Shropshire by J. Dodd, Tipperary Tim was a very moderate plodder whose previous and subsequent form never rose above the mediocre. By a sire called Cipango who changed hands for £13, he not only had a tube, but a parrot mouth as well. He was ridden with great determination in the National by Mr William Dutton, son of a Cheshire farmer. Dutton, a gentle, modest man of great charm and intelligence, had not long left Cambridge, where he had gained his B.A. and LL.B. degrees, and was articled to his uncle, a Chester solicitor. During the nineteen twenties he had made a name for himself as a rider and in 1926 had won the N.H. Chase at Cheltenham on Cloringo, a half-brother of the famous sprinter, Irish Elegance. In 1932 he forsook the law and set up a small stable at Hednesford, moving to Malton after war service in the Middle East. He trained three very good sprinters in Pappa Fourway, Vigo and Right Boy as well as the Cheltenham Gold Cup winner Limber Hill. He died suddenly aged fifty-seven in 1958.

9

In view of the debacle at the Canal Turn, the ditch was filled in and the fence became a plain one.

If Easter Hero had been the villain in 1928 he was undoubtedly the hero in the following year, and his performance in finishing second in a field of sixty-six when he carried 12 st 7 lbs and furthermore spread a plate some way from the finish, was beyond question one of the finest in the history of the race. Trained by Jack Anthony and ridden by Jack Moloney, he carried the colours this time of the young American owner Mr J. H. Whitney, his previous owner, Mr Lowenstein, having disappeared from an aircraft during a flight to Brussels. Mr Whitney also bought Maguelonne, who had run so well in 1928 and had later been purchased by Mr Lowenstein, at the same time, paying £11,000 for the two. It was understood that Maguelonne was slightly the more expensive of the pair.

It had been hoped that by raising the cost of starting to £100 that the size of the field would be reduced, but in fact a record number took the field, many of them possessing no valid qualifications for such an exacting test. The crowd was gigantic and it is estimated that 300,000 people were present as the runners paraded in bright sunshine. The atmosphere of tension and excitement was even more pronounced than usual, no doubt because of anxiety lest wholesale disaster should occur at the first few fences. In fact all sixty-six got safely over the first, and Ardeen was the only faller at the second. Nevertheless, the field soon began to thin out and forty-seven of them were out of the race at the half-way mark.

At that point Easter Hero, a hot favourite at 9–2, was going so easily that he obviously had a great chance of success. Coming on to the racecourse the issue clearly lay between him and Gregalach, but very soon afterwards the favourite seemed to waver and become unbalanced. It was at this point that he spread a plate that was twisted into the shape of a letter S. He fought on bravely enough under this disadvantage but Gregalach, receiving 17 lbs, gradually wore him down and mastered him in the run-in to win by half a dozen lengths. Richmond II, a six-year-old that unfortunately became difficult to train, was third and nine horses completed the course without mishap, including Mellerays Belle, second in 1930, and Grakle, winner in 1931. Easter Hero's performance was all the more remarkable as he was by no means a typical massive Aintree weight-carrier, being a rather highly strung horse of outstanding quality that would not have looked out of place in the paddock at Royal Ascot. Both he and Gregalach

were by that great sire of jumpers, My Prince, but Gregalach
represented far more closely the then conventional Grand
National type.

Gregalach was owned by Mrs Gemmell, who had bought him
for 5,000 guineas as a five-year-old. He was, in fact, as his subsequent Grand National record showed, a really good horse and
very different from the usual Aintree outsider even though his
starting price was 100–1. On this occasion he was the least fancied
of Tom Leader's Grand National fleet, the best backed of which
was Ted Leader's mount, Mount Etna, who fell. Another of Tom
Leader's outsiders, Sandy Hook, ran a great race until falling
after Valentine's second time round.

Because of heavy overnight rain, there was some doubt about
Gregalach running but in the end it was decided to let him take
his chance. He was ridden by Bob Everett, who was then very
little known to the racing public and had been engaged only
five days before the race. Australian-born and tall for a jockey,
Everett served briefly as a midshipman in the Royal Navy and
rode with modest success as an amateur in South Africa and
England. His first winner in England was in February 1928 and
he turned professional in December that year. His services could
hardly be described as being in constant demand and his success
in the Grand National was his first ride over fences for several
weeks. Always keen on flying, he served in the Fleet Air Arm with
distinction in the war, being awarded the D.S.O. He was killed
in action in 1941.

Perhaps this chapter could fittingly conclude with a brief
history of Lord Wavertree's All White, one of those typical hardy
old-time Aintree chasers that used to take part in the National
year after year. According to Lord Wavertree, whose statements
and opinions on racing, particularly where his own horses were
concerned, always had to be accepted with a modicum of reserve,
All White was somewhat unfortunate never to win the Grand
National. In 1919, so Lord Wavertree used to relate, All White
was bang up with the leaders on the second circuit when his rider
pulled him up and was violently sick. Despite this unusual contretemps, All White finished fifth. In 1920 he slipped up on the flat
and in 1921 he was leading second time round when he was put
off at an open ditch by a heap of newspapers blown there by the
wind and unseated his rider, who remounted to finish third. In
1922 he was carried out at the Canal Turn by Sergeant Murphy,
and unlike Sergeant Murphy, who finished fourth after losing
his bridle and having it replaced, he was not asked to persevere

in the struggle. In 1923 he was lame and could not run and in 1924 he was carried out at the Canal Turn again. In 1925, though according to his owner he was far from fit and was further-more taken round on the wide outside by his rider, he got as far as the last fence but one. He was absent in 1926, but re-appeared in 1927; by then the old campaigner was very dicky on his legs and had to be pulled up. That was his final Aintree appearance. Unfortunately the jockeys' version of this luckless saga is not in existence.

III

THE GRAND NATIONAL 1930–1940

Shaun Goilin, winner in 1930, is shown on the records as being by a sire of unknown pedigree. It is practically certain, though, that his sire was a three-year-old called Shaun Abou who happened to be in a paddock adjacent to one in which was a mare called Golden Day. This mare happened to find a gap in a fence and joined Shaun Abou, who no doubt was delighted with her company. The result of this unplanned union was Shaun Goilin, who was sold as a yearling for 22 guineas. After winning a small race at Naas he was sold again, this time for 550 guineas, and in due course he was bought for 1,250 guineas by Mr W. H. Mid-wood, a well-known Liverpool cotton broker and a former Master of the Cheshire Hunt. Mr Midwood had previously made several attempts to win the Grand National with that good horse Silvo.

Shaun Goilin was specially laid out for the National in 1930 and was a heavily-backed second favourite at 100–8, Grakle being favourite at 100–12. Up at Aintree Shaun Goilin caused both Mr Midwood and Frank Hartigan, who trained him, considerable anxiety as his surroundings seemed to upset him and he did not eat up at all well. However, he ran the race of his life and with the appreciable weight of 11 st 7 lbs he just got the best of a tremendous finish with Mr W. Wilson's eleven-year-old mare Mellerays Belle (10 st), who had just won the Foxhunters' Cup at Cheltenham, and Mr J. H. Whitney's Sir Lindsay (10 st 6 lbs), who the previous year had won the National Hunt Chase ridden by Lord Fingall.

The early running was made by a handsome grey, Glangesia, who jumped superbly, but he began to weaken soon after Valen-tine's second time round and Mellerays Belle, who had been fourth the year before, went into the lead. She was still just in front at the last fence, but Shaun Goilin and Sir Lindsay were pressing her hard, Sir Lindsay perhaps going a shade the best of the three. Not one of them jumped the last fence well; Dudley Williams on Sir Lindsay lost both his irons, while Cullinan on Shaun Goilin and Mason on Mellerays Belle both lost one each. With their riders thus at some disadvantage, particularly Williams, the three horses battled on to the winning post. Close to home Shaun Goilin found a little bit extra and passed Mellerays Belle to win a thrilling race by a neck, while Sir Lindsay was a length and a half away third. From the stands it looked as if Sir Lindsay, who was by The Tetrarch's sire Roi Hérode, might have been a somewhat unlucky loser.

Easter Hero was unable to run as he was lame after winning the Gold Cup. Had he taken part, Tommy Cullinan would have ridden him instead of Shaun Goilin. An Irishman whose personality and character were hardly improved by this success, Cullinan was not at the top of the tree in his profession for long and he died in unhappy circumstances soon after the start of the war. Grakle, ridden by Lester Piggott's father, Keith Piggott, made a mistake at Valentine's second time round and a worse one at the next fence. Piggott lost an iron and appeared to become dislodged while groping for it. This was not Gregalach's lucky year. He threw a splint, was moved, following some disagreement, from Tom Leader's stable to that of Percy Woodland, and was given 'the bird' by the crowd at Hurst Park after finishing last there in the Trial Handicap Chase when ridden by Major Gossage. He was greatly fancied at Aintree, where he was partnered by Bob Everett, who had won on him the year before, and he fell at an open ditch where he was slightly baulked.

Shaun Goilin's trainer Frank Hartigan was the son of a veterinary officer in the 3rd Dragoon Guards and a nephew of Garrett Moore, who won the 1879 Grand National on The Liberator. A good rider in his younger days, first as an amateur and later as a professional, he was shrewd, tough and highly competent, just like his brother Hubert. For years he ran a highly successful 'mixed' stable, winning the One Thousand Guineas with Vaucluse and Roseway, while he made Lord Rosebery's Wrack into one of the finest hurdlers of all time. He also trained Old Tay Bridge who was twice second in the Grand National, and on a third occasion, with Hubert Hartigan in the saddle, looked very much like winning when he fell close home.

In 1927 the well-known Irish owner Mr T. K. Laidlaw decided, on account of his wife's health, to take a long trip abroad and accordingly he sold his two highly promising five-year-old chasers, Gregalach and Grakle, at Newmarket on Two Thousand Guineas day. Both horses were at that time trained by Tom Coulthwaite, who had had them under his care since they came to him from Ireland when they were three. Mr Cecil Taylor, a patron of Coulthwaite, was very keen to acquire one of them and he bid up to 4,500 guineas for Gregalach, who, however, was eventually knocked down to Mrs A. Gemmell for 5,000 guineas. For 4,000 guineas, though, Mr Taylor was able to buy Grakle. As has been related, Gregalach won the Grand National in 1929; his former stable companion followed suit at his fifth attempt two years later.

Conditions were perfect in 1931; the weather was fit for Royal Ascot, the going fast and true. The race, too, was worthy of the occasion. Grakle (11 st 7 lbs) came to the last fence about a length in front of Gregalach (12 st) with Ballasport, Georginatown and Kilbuck about six lengths behind them. Ballasport, Georginatown and Kilbuck all came down at that final obstacle, leaving Annandale to take third place.

It was generally assumed by those watching the race that Grakle with his speed and his pull in the weights would draw clear in the long run-in, but Gregalach, superbly ridden by Jack Moloney, one of the finest Aintree riders never to win the National, simply refused to give in. Battling on to a roar of encouragement from the stands, the big chestnut gradually closed the gap and a hundred yards from home he secured a narrow lead. By then, though, he had given all he had; his stride began to shorten and Grakle, tired as he was, re-passed him to win a memorable race by a length and a half. The victory of a high-class chaser belonging to a local owner was, of course, extremely popular. Twelve of the forty-three runners completed the course and thirty had been standing at the halfway mark. The time, 9 minutes 32 4/5 seconds, beat the record of 9 minutes 34 2/5 seconds set up in 1906 by Ascetic's Silver. The unlucky horses were the favourite Easter Hero, Drintyre and Ballasport. When Solanum fell at Becher's second time round when disputing the lead, he brought down Easter Hero with him. Easter Hero collided with Ballasport and one of the leathers was wrenched from Ballasport's saddle. In addition, that very good chaser Drintyre, owned and ridden by Captain Cecil Brownhill of the Irish Guards, was badly kicked on the knee in the mix-up. He was going extremely well at the time. Gyi lovam had been sent from Czecho-Slovakia to take part in the race, but he and his stout-hearted rider Captain Popler were tailed off right from the start and failed to finish although Captain Popler remounted more than once after falling.

It was a third Grand National victory for old Tom Coulthwaite who had deferred his retirement in the confident expectation of Grakle's success. His previous winners were Eremon in 1907 and Jenkinstown in 1910. Percy Woodland, trainer of Gregalach, saddled four other runners for the race; the most fancied of them, Drin, broke a leg and had to be destroyed. Bob Lyall, who rode a faultless race on the winner, was a sound, reliable rider whose career in the saddle was ended by a crashing fall in which he received severe injuries to his head.

In 1932, in order to cut down the number of indifferent horses entered, the race was restricted to horses that at the time of entry had been placed in a chase of three miles or over worth £200 to the winner, or in a chase of any distance at Liverpool.

Grakle, carrying 12 st 3 lbs and ridden on this occasion by Jack Fawcus who was still an amateur but later became a leading professional, made his sixth and final Grand National appearance. He started joint favourite at 100–12 with the Irish mare Heart-break Hill, but he was put out of the race by a loose horse soon after Valentine's on the first circuit and at that stage Heartbreak Hill was badly interfered with as well. Gregalach (12 st 7 lbs) was well backed at 100–9, but he came down, giving poor Fred Thackray a terrible fall. The outstanding amateur of his day and fully the equal of the best professionals, Thackray was unconscious for a fortnight and never rode in a race again.

The excitement this year lay in the great duel throughout the second circuit between the two leaders, Forbra (10 st 7 lbs) ridden by Tim Hamey, and Egremont (10 st 7 lbs), the mount of Mr Edward Paget, a London stockbroker. Both horses jumped magnificently, but Forbra, a seven-year-old carrying the colours of Mr W. Parsonage, a retired Ludlow bookmaker, gradually gained the upper hand and after jumping the last fence in front he held on to his advantage to win a fine race by three lengths. Shaun Goilin with 12 st 4 lbs was third and eight horses finished, including Annandale who fell two fences out when lying third and was remounted. Forbra, whom Mr Parsonage had bought for £1,500 the previous year from Mr H. Hunt of Uppingham, was trained at Kinnersley in Worcestershire by Tom Rimell, whose son Fred, after a brilliant riding career, trained the Grand National winners E.S.B. and Nicolaus Silver. Tim Hamey was a brave if unstylish rider, more effective over fences than hurdles.

For some time after his retirement from the saddle he conducted a small jumping stable at Cheltenham. Edward Paget was a bold, forceful rider of immense determination. In due course he became closely associated with Peter Cazalet's Fairlawne stable, for which he rode many good winners. He won the Foxhunters' Chase at Aintree in 1934 and was still race-riding after the war when he was well past forty. A sportsman of the very finest type, he served National Hunt racing devotedly, not merely as a member and Steward of the National Hunt Committee, but through his personal example. He died very suddenly at the age of fifty-eight in 1963.

It is proof of the way that Miss Dorothy Paget's Golden Miller captured the imagination of the public that as a mere six-year-old, albeit the winner of two Cheltenham Gold Cups, and with no less than 12 st 2 lbs on his back, he was favourite at 9–1 for the 1933 Grand National. Ridden by Ted Leader, he was ideally placed on the second circuit when he made a bad mistake at Becher's. He recovered cleverly, but his confidence was shaken and he fell at the Canal Turn, at which point Gregalach was pulled up with a broken blood-vessel.

Coming on to the racecourse second time round, Kellsboro' Jack (11 st 9 lbs) and the gigantic Pelorous Jack (10 st 7 lbs) appeared to have the race between them. Pelorous Jack, ridden by Billy Stott, had a very slight lead at the last, but he bungled the fence and came down. Kellsboro' Jack, a seven-year-old partnered by Dudley Williams, then seemed to have the race at his mercy, but in fact he had to be ridden right out to hold off the late challenges of Really True and Slater, ridden by Mr Frank Furlong and Mr Michael Barry respectively. Delaneige, a fine Liverpool horse, was fourth, and Alpine Hut, ridden by Mr 'Perry' Harding, fifth. Altogether nineteen horses finished, including Merriment IV and Ballybrack who had both been remounted after falling.

Kellsboro' Jack belonged to an American owner, Mrs Florence Ambrose Clark, who together with her husband—known to his friends as 'Brose'—was well-known and much liked in English racing and hunting circles. It was Mr Ambrose Clark, a leading personality in the sporting world of the United States, who had bought Kellsboro' Jack, but the horse did not thrive in America and was accordingly sent to England to be trained by Ivor Anthony at Wroughton. In the meantime Mr Ambrose Clark sold him to his wife for the token sum of £1. A son of Jackdaw, the sire of Grakle, Kellsboro' Jack lacked the speed to cope with Golden

Miller in races like the Cheltenham Gold Cup, in which he was three times third, but he was a superlative Aintree jumper and was never defeated on that course. In all probability he would have won the Grand National more than once, but his owner resolutely declined to enter him for that race again.

Ivor Anthony, brother of Jack Anthony who rode three Grand National winners, and of Owen Anthony who trained the 1922 winner Music Hall, had been a leading rider under National Hunt rules before the war. He then went to Wroughton to assist Aubrey Hastings, and when Hastings died suddenly after a game of polo in 1929, he took over the Wroughton stable. Shrewd and patient, he was an adept at having a horse at the peak of condition on the one day that really mattered. He won the Grand National again in 1937 with Royal Mail, but the most famous horse he ever trained was Brown Jack, winner of the Champion Hurdle and also of the Queen Alexandra Stakes at Ascot six years running.

Dudley Williams, who first rode as an amateur, was a beautiful horseman with the very best of hands and there was no more accomplished rider round Liverpool. Unfortunately he injured his back very badly in a fall the following year and never rode again. Subsequently he became a skilled masseur and also for some years held a trainer's licence.

Kellsboro' Jack had set up a new record by winning in 9 minutes 28 seconds, but the record only stood for twelve months. It was Golden Miller's year in 1934 and Miss Paget's great chaser put up a magnificent performance to win with 12 st 2 lbs on his back in the remarkable time of 9 minutes 20 2/5 seconds. Two really good horses, Delaneige (11 st 6 lbs) and Thomond II (12 st 4 lbs) were second and third, while the 1932 winner Forbra (11 st 7 lbs) was fourth. It was the final appearance in the race of Gregalach; in his thirteenth year and carrying 12st 7 lbs, he ran with his usual courage and finished seventh. Golden Miller started second favourite at 8–1, the favourite being Major Noel Furlong's Really True ridden by his son Frank. Really True was up with the leaders and going extremely well when he fell at the fence after Valentine's second time round.

Delaneige, a bold horse and a beautiful jumper, made nearly all the running and with four fences to go he was still in the lead, closely followed by Golden Miller, Forbra and Thomond II. At the last fence Delaneige landed first, but he was being hard pressed by Golden Miller. On the flat Golden Miller produced a turn of speed that very soon settled the issue and he drew clear of his rivals to win almost easily by five lengths, with that grand little horse Thomond II a further five lengths away third. It was a wonderful race and Golden Miller thoroughly deserved the tremendous reception he was given on his return to the unsaddling enclosure.

Golden Miller was ridden with supreme confidence by Gerry Wilson, one of the outstanding riders of the nineteen thirties. Of medium size but strongly built, he was the son of a well-known horse-dealer in the Whaddon country and had the advantage of experience in the hunting field himself. He came up the hard way, riding indifferent horses at minor meetings, but his many successes for 'Sonny' Hall's stable soon attracted attention and he began to secure a better class of mount. Always hard and fit himself, he could drive a tiring horse over the last few fences in remarkable style, and as regards sheer pluck and the will to win he had no superior in his day. Cheerful and enthusiastic, he once summed up his career by saying 'I get paid for what I like doing best'. When he retired he became a trainer, but was less successful in that sphere than might have been expected and after some years he decided to quit the racing world and become landlord of a country public house.

Bred in Ireland, Golden Miller had already changed hands a couple of times when the young Cambridgeshire trainer Basil Briscoe bought him 'in the rough' for 500 guineas. Briscoe had owned two of the earlier produce of Golden Miller's dam and had himself won races on one of them, May Crescent. As a three-year-old Golden Miller ran in a hurdle race at Southwell and then Briscoe hunted him for a bit. Hunting, though, was not a sport that appealed to Golden Miller and Briscoe was never able to make him keep up with hounds.

However Golden Miller soon began to improve and after a narrow defeat over fences at Newbury, he was bought by Mr Philip Carr, father of the famous cricketer Mr A. W. Carr, for £1,000. Mr Philip Carr died soon afterwards and Golden Miller was sold for £6,000 to Miss Dorothy Paget, who had just engaged Briscoe as her private trainer.

For some years Briscoe was extremely successful, but he then suffered two misfortunes which undoubtedly affected his career—the death of his young wife and the row after the 1935 Grand National which ended with Miss Paget removing Golden Miller from his care. Subsequently Briscoe moved his stable to Royston where he trained the Cambridgeshire winner Commander III, but he ceased to train soon after the outbreak of war and most of his racing friends had not seen him for years when he died in 1951.

Kind, generous and a bold gambler, he was perhaps too highly-strung to stand up to the inevitable ups and downs of a racing career.

Golden Miller's victory was all the more remarkable in that he was not really an Aintree horse at all. He jumped off his forehand, and that being so it is hardly surprising that he did not much fancy those big drop fences, his antipathy towards them increasing with experience. It was his class and courage that saw him through in 1934.

The following year Golden Miller was not surprisingly set to carry 12 st 7 lbs. Despite this severe burden and despite the fact that mathematically it was at that time at least 3–1 against any competitor even getting round, public faith in Miss Paget's champion was such that at the 'off' the best price available was 2–1. Alas, Golden Miller failed to complete a circuit. At the fence after Valentine's he screwed badly to the left taking off—some thought he tried to refuse—landed awkwardly and parted company with Gerry Wilson. Only those with good binoculars and keen eyesight could pick out this distant incident from the stands. It was unseen by ninety per cent of those present, who were dumbfounded to discover the favourite missing as the runners streamed on to the racecourse proper. The departure of Golden Miller inevitably robbed the race of much of its interest, but at least it brought relief to the bookmakers, who had many doubles outstanding with him and the Lincoln winner Flamenco.

At the final fence there was little in it between Reynoldstown (11 st 4 lbs), owned and trained by Major Noel Furlong, and Mr J. H. Whitney's Thomond II (11 st 13 lbs) who had been third to Golden Miller the year before. Under pressure from Billy Speck, Thomond II had put in a gallant rally coming to the last, but he was desperately tired and as he landed level with Reynolds-town he swerved to the right and collided with his rival. Being the smaller and wearier of the two, he came off second best. In the run-in Reynoldstown, ridden by the owner's son Mr Frank Furlong, drew clear, while Thomond II could find no more and in fact was beaten for second place by Blue Prince, who might well have given the winner more to do had not his saddle slipped at the last fence but one, thereby placing his rider Billy Parvin at an uncomfortable disadvantage. Bred in Ireland, Reynolds-town was by that famous sire of jumpers, My Prince, who was twenty-four years of age when he got Reynoldstown, four years older than Reynoldstown's dam. Frank Furlong, who had finished second on Really True two years previously, served for some years in the 9th Lancers. He was killed in action in the war while serving with the Fleet Air Arm.

After the race Golden Miller was examined by veterinary surgeons who could detect nothing wrong with him. Accordingly it was decided to run him in the Champion Chase the following day. The decision proved unfortunate to say the least; Golden Miller made a mess of the first fence, and though he did not actually fall, he unseated Wilson. As the horse was led back to the paddock, a storm of ugly booing arose from the stands.

In the following week a flood of rumours, some scandalous, nearly all improbable, circulated about Golden Miller and those most closely connected with him. It was perfectly true, though, that Miss Paget and Wilson were at loggerheads with Basil Briscoe. The upshot of this distasteful affair was that Golden Miller and six other jumpers belonging to Miss Paget left Briscoe's stable for that of Donald Snow. In August Golden Miller changed quarters again, this time going to Owen Anthony, with whom he remained for the rest of his racing career.

Looking back on this sad business across the years, it seems possible that Golden Miller's failures on this occasion could be attributed to two main causes. Firstly, despite his victory in 1934, he did not really like those big black Aintree fences. Secondly, the Grand National came all too soon after his desperate battle in the Gold Cup with Thomond II, a battle so severe that it may well have left a permanent mark on both contestants.

The 1936 Grand National will always be remembered equally for Reynoldstown's superb achievement in winning for the second year running, and for the cruel misfortune of Mr Anthony Mildmay on the 100–1 outsider Davy Jones, owned by his father, Lord Mildmay of Flete.

At this period Anthony Mildmay who, in the immediate post-war era, became the leading personality in National Hunt racing, was a little-known amateur with no great experience and no high degree of skill. Twelve months previously he had almost been killed by a dreadful fall in the Foxhunters' Chase, but that mishap had not diminished either his courage or his enthusiasm.

Davy Jones was a beautifully bred horse by Pharos out of a mare by Hurry On, but owing to respiratory trouble he had been tubed and Lord Mildmay had been able to buy him for £650. A big, powerful chestnut, he had won a couple of small steeplechases at Gatwick, the stiffest of all park courses, but he was really little more than a novice when he ran in the National. He was a horse that always took a really strong hold and it was Mildmay's custom to tie a knot in the reins when riding him. Just as Davy Jones was leaving the paddock at Aintree for the parade, Peter Cazalet, who really controlled the Fairlawne stable where Davy Jones was trained although Harry Whiteman actually held the licence, noticed that Mildmay had not tied his usual knot. He was about to advise him to do so when he changed his mind, thinking that Mildmay had decided not to tie a knot in order to make it easier to slip the reins when landing over the drop fences. This perfectly reasonable decision was to cost Davy Jones the race.

Right from the very first jump, where Golden Miller fell, Davy Jones pulled his way to the front and throughout the first circuit he led the field, measuring fence after fence with faultless accuracy. Passing the stands he was going very easily in the lead with the favourite, Avenger, lying second. At the first fence second time round, Avenger, a brilliant chaser, fell heavily and broke his neck.

With Avenger out of the race, Davy Jones held a clear lead and it began to occur to Mildmay that he might be going to achieve the ambition of his life and win the Grand National. However Reynoldstown, ridden by Fulke Walwyn, was making up ground and by Becher's had almost drawn level. On they went together, Davy Jones, barely a length to the good, both horses jumping magnificently for their amateur riders. It was a wonderful race to watch and in the crystal light of that perfect spring afternoon every incident could be seen from the stands.

With three fences to go Reynoldstown made his first real mistake. Walwyn recovered as only a top-class horseman can, but he lost an iron and Reynoldstown was now left with the better part of a dozen lengths to make up. Moreover Reynoldstown carried 12 st 2 lbs and was conceding Davy Jones 23 lbs. At that point Davy Jones looked as sure to win the Grand National as any horse can with two Aintree fences still ahead of him.

Tired as Reynoldstown was, he fought back with the utmost courage and by the second last fence he had succeeded in narrowing the gap appreciably. Walwyn, though, was driving him hard, whereas Mildmay had not moved on Davy Jones. At this second last fence Davy Jones pecked a little on landing and to give his horse every chance to recover, Mildmay let slip his reins to the buckle. It was then in one awful moment that disaster descended. The prong of the buckle slipped through the hasp and in a trice the reins were flapping loosely round Davy Jones's neck. Mildmay was powerless to control him and Davy Jones ran out at the final fence, leaving the gallant Reynoldstown to win comfortably from Ego, ridden by Mr Harry Llewellyn. In a few seconds the vision that must have seemed to Mildmay almost too good to be true had been cruelly erased. Lord Mildmay was in hospital at the time. For the rest of his life he loved to watch the film of the race, but its conclusion was always too much for him; after the second last fence it was his invariable custom to emit a dreadful groan and to leave the room.

Reynoldstown was the fifth horse to win the Liverpool Grand National twice, the others being Abd-el-Kader (1850 and 1851); The Lamb (1868 and 1871); The Colonel (1869 and 1870); and Manifesto (1897 and 1899). Poethlyn won the substitute Grand National at Gatwick in 1918 and the Liverpool Grand National the following year. Frank Furlong, who rode Reynoldstown to victory in 1935, had decided to give up riding owing to increasing weight so the mount this time was given to Fulke Walwyn, who had been in the same company as Furlong at Sandhurst and had been a brother officer of his in the 9th Lancers. Walwyn later turned professional, but his riding career was curtailed by serious injuries. After the war he became a leading trainer and won the Grand National with Team Spirit in 1964.

During Grand National week it was announced that the minimum weight in the following year's race would be reduced to 10 st, from which it had been raised to 10 st 7 lbs in 1931 with the object of discouraging the entry of indifferent horses. This reversion was not popular and Mr George Lambton, a great rider in his day, wrote to the press as follows: 'The Grand National is the Blue Riband of steeplechasing; it is not meant to be won by moderate horses. Before the race this year I often heard it said that this was the most interesting National for many years. Why was it so interesting? Because good horses like Golden Miller, Reynoldstown and Avenger had their fair chance and were not crushed by weight. Even then we have seen that Reynoldstown would not have been able to give 23 lbs to a tubed horse which has been beaten in selling races, so why go back to the 10 st limit? Two stone is enough for any horse to give away over that course, and if any owner thinks that he has no chance of beating one like Reynoldstown at two stone, then he should not aspire to win a Grand National. I have much sympathy for owners of bad horses (I have many of them myself), but we should not expect to win great races with them. The Grand National is no place for bad horses. If the authorities encourage owners to enter them, the race will lose its high tone and quality and revert to the farcical scramble it became some years ago.'

A great many people were in entire agreement with the views that Mr Lambton had so clearly expressed.

'There is such a thing as taking the pitcher to the well too often,' observed Major Noel Furlong and accordingly he did not enter Reynoldstown for the 1937 Grand National, while it was found impossible to train Lord Mildmay's Davy Jones for the race. Despite the fact that he was shouldering 12 st 7 lbs and had failed rather badly both in 1935 and 1936, the public made Golden Miller favourite at 8–1, but by now he definitely disliked Aintree and he refused before completing a circuit.

The winner, Royal Mail, was a very good horse on his day but he was not endowed with the most robust of constitutions and he was not an easy horse to prepare for such an exacting test. An eight-year-old black gelding and the last of My Prince's three Grand National winners, he was trained by Ivor Anthony and belonged to Mr Hugh Lloyd Thomas, who had been assistant secretary to the Duke of Windsor (when Prince of Wales) and at the time of the race held a post of importance at the British Embassy in Paris. A tall, good-looking man of great charm and distinction, he was not only a fine rider to hounds, but an accomplished race-rider, too. He won races on Royal Mail in 1934 and 1935 and his most important success was to win the Grand Sefton Chase at Aintree on his own mare Destiny Bay.

Despite his stiff weight, Royal Mail went to the front after the fourth fence on the second circuit and there he stayed to the end, winning comfortably from two mares, Mr J. V. Rank's Cooleen, ridden by Jack Fawcus, and Mr E. W. Bailey's Pucka Belle, ridden by her owner. Both Cooleen and Pucka Belle were badly hampered by Drim who careered loose round the course after falling and Fawcus was firmly of the opinion that Cooleen would have won but for the interference that she suffered.

Royal Mail was capably ridden by Evan Williams, who had formerly been an amateur and had carried out secretarial duties for the Wroughton stable. He turned professional and became one of the most successful riders of his time. After the war he trained at Kingsclere and won the Festival of Britain King George VI and Queen Elizabeth Stakes with Supreme Court. He retired from training when still comparatively young to become a master of fox-hounds in Ireland. The Knockaney Stud Co., Limerick, where the Derby winners Galtee More and Ard Patrick were bred, belongs to his wife.

Royal Mail was top weight with 12 st 7 lbs in 1938. It had been assumed that Evan Williams would ride him again, but early in

February Mr Lloyd Thomas announced that he was going to take the ride himself. The decision seemed a hazardous one as, although Mr Lloyd Thomas was a fine horseman, he was in his fiftieth year and had done no race-riding for two seasons. Later that month he rode a rather moderate horse of his called Periwinkle in a steeplechase at Derby. Periwinkle fell heavily and Mr Lloyd Thomas, whom his many friends had tried their hardest to dissuade from this venture, was killed. Royal Mail was sold at Hurst Park on 12th March and bought for 6,500 guineas by Mrs Camille Evans. It was then arranged that Williams should ride him again.

The weight, however, proved too much for Royal Mail, who never looked like winning, and in one of the most thrilling finishes in the history of the race the little American horse Battleship, owned by Mrs Marion Scott, beat the big, handsome Royal Danieli by a very short head. Workman, who, like Royal Danieli, was trained in Ireland, finished third.

At Becher's second time round Battleship, ridden by young Bruce Hobbs, and Royal Danieli, ridden by Dan Moore, who had just turned professional, were in front with Workman about half a dozen lengths behind them. Three fences from home Battleship made a nasty mistake and was headed by Workman so at that stage it looked long odds on an Irish victory. At the next fence, though, Workman blundered, while Battleship rallied to such purpose that at the final jump he was only two lengths behind the leader.

In that long run-in it was a terrific duel between Royal Danieli on the rails and Battleship in the centre of the course. Compared to his massive opponent Battleship, who stood exactly 15.2, looked a mere pony, but he had the heart of a lion and with Bruce Hobbs riding for all he was worth, he got up to win in the very last stride. Before the judge made known his verdict there were seconds of complete silence, and when Battleship's number went into the frame it was greeted by cheers from the bookmakers and groans from the huge Irish contingent present. Battleship, who started at 40–1, formed the first leg of the Tote Double, of which the sole winner was the late Lord Digby, whose success earned him over £5,000 for his 10/- stake.

The winner, an entire horse by the famous Man O'War, was trained at Lambourn by Reg Hobbs, a great rider to hounds in his day and no mean performer over fences as well. His son Bruce, who rode a wonderful race on the winner, was seventeen years old at the time and is the youngest rider ever to have won

Bill Stott, six times champion
jockey.
Copyright W. W. Rouch & Co. Ltd.

Peter Payne-Gallwey going out
to win the Grand Military
Gold Cup on Backsight.
Copyright W. W. Rouch & Co. Ltd.

ABOVE: The greatest amateur of the inter-war period: Harry Brown on The Bore. LEFT: Percy Woodland, who rode two Grand National winners, two winners of the Grand Steeplechase de Paris and two winners of the French Derby. Later a successful trainer. BELOW: Reynoldstown, twice winner of the Grand National, with Frank Furlong up, landing over a fence at Gatwick just behind Lady Sen with G. Wilson up. *Photographs copyright W. W. Rouch & Co. Ltd.*

this great race. Later that year he had a serious fall at Cheltenham, fracturing one of his spinal vertebrae. He served with distinction in the war, being awarded the Military Cross, and after a lengthy period as assistant to Captain Boyd-Rochfort, he is now a successful trainer on his own account.

Battleship, who returned to America after the race, is one of the few Grand National winners to have worn blinkers. He was about the same size as Casse Tête, who won in 1872, and Regal, who won in 1876, but he was both larger and more robustly built than Father O'Flynn, whom Captain Roddy Owen rode to victory in 1892.

In 1939 Royal Danieli fell at Becher's first time round and the race went to his Irish rival, Workman, who had been third the previous year. Second was the Scottish horse, MacMoffat, owned by Captain L. Scott-Briggs who had bought him for sixty guineas, and ridden by 'Ben' Alder, while third was the favourite Kilstar, with George Archibald up. Kilstar belonged to Miss Dorothy Paget, who had bought him from Major Mark Roddick of the 10th Hussars after Kilstar had won the Grand Military Gold Cup. In all probability Kilstar would have won but for a dreadful mistake at Becher's second time round that cost him twenty lengths. Another unlucky competitor was Black Hawk, who collided with Workman at the last open ditch, came off second best, and fell. The 1937 winner Royal Mail was among those that completed the course.

Bred by Mr P. J. O'Leary in Co Cork, Workman, who was soundly backed at 100–8, belonged to the well-known Irish industrialist Sir Alexander Maguire, who had business interests both in Dublin and Belfast. John Ruttle, Workman's trainer, was in his day one of Ireland's best cross-country riders, while Tim Hyde who rode the winner was not only a very fine rider under National Hunt rules, but equally successful in the highly competitive show-jumping world.

Despite the outbreak of war and the curtailment of racing, it was still found possible, since hostilities had not really hotted up by then, to run the Grand National in 1940. It was to be the last Grand National until Lovely Cottage won in 1946.

There were fifty-nine entries and the conditions contained a proviso that riders must have won five steeplechases under recognized Rules of Steeplechasing in any country. Royal Danieli was favourite and other well-backed horses included Kilstar, Mac-Moffat and Milano. Royal Danieli as usual forced the pace, but he began to tire from Becher's second time round, where the

10

gallant MacMoffat was going particularly well and Lord Stalbridge's Bogskar was gradually beginning to make up ground.
Even so, at Valentine's Bogskar was still a dozen lengths behind
MacMoffat, who was in the lead accompanied by a loose horse
that was clearly liable to cause trouble.

Coming on to the racecourse MacMoffat and the loose horse still
led the field with Bogskar and Gold Arrow in dogged pursuit.
Royal Danieli, beat to the world, fell heavily two out. It was some
time before he could struggle to his feet and this grand looking
horse never ran again afterwards. Alder on MacMoffat had felt
himself compelled to race the loose horse to try and get clear of
him and the effort this entailed in all probability robbed the
Scottish horse of the victory he richly deserved. He had nothing
left when Bogskar drew level at the last fence, and despite a slight
mistake there Bogskar drew clear to win quite comfortably. Gold
Arrow was third, six lengths behind MacMoffat. Altogether
seventeen horses completed the course, including Lazy Boots,
ridden by bearded Sir Geoffrey Congreve who was serving in the
Royal Navy.

An active member of the National Hunt Committee who served
two terms of stewardship for that body, Lord Stalbridge not only
owned Bogskar, who started at 25–1, but trained him himself at
Eastbury. No doubt in the moment of victory his thoughts went
back to his only son Hugh Grosvenor, who, as a young officer in
the 7th Hussars, won the Cheltenham Gold Cup on Thrown In
but was killed in an air crash soon afterwards. Lord Stalbridge
bought Bogskar, whose dam was sold for nine guineas at the age of
sixteen, from Mr Sydney McGregor as a three-year-old. Mr Mc-
Gregor, in partnership with Major G. S. L. Whitelaw, bred the
Derby winner April the Fifth, who was foaled on the fifth of
April which happened to be Mr McGregor's birthday. It was certainly his lucky day since this Grand National was run on April
the fifth and Bogskar, by his victory, earned Mr McGregor a
handsome contingency.

But for being injured shortly before the race, Eric Foley would
have ridden Bogskar, who thus provided a chance ride for twenty-
year-old Mervyn Jones, a nephew of Ivor Anthony with whom
he had been living since leaving school at the age of seventeen.
It was Jones's first ride at Aintree. He was serving as a Pilot
Sergeant in the Royal Air Force at the time and he was killed in
action two years later.

IV

An event of much significance in National Hunt history was the founding of the Cheltenham Gold Cup. In the early nineteen twenties important weight-for-age chases were rare. Bar the National Hunt Chase at Cheltenham and the Champion Chase at Liverpool all the most important races were handicaps. Some people thought that this preponderance of handicaps was not in the best interests of the sport and the Gold Cup was founded in an attempt to restore the balance, at least to a limited extent. There is no record to show who precisely can claim credit for devising the race, but it is generally believed that Mr F. H. Cathcart, at that time Chairman of the Cheltenham executive, was largely responsible. At all events the race has proved a resounding success, its prestige and importance growing steadily throughout the years. Quite rightly it is now regarded as the true championship race for staying chasers. Occasionally the Grand National is referred to as the 'Blue Riband' of steeplechasing, but that must surely be an incorrect appellation for a handicap.

Originally run over three miles and three furlongs, the Gold Cup, for five-year-olds and upwards, 11 st 4 lbs for five-year-olds, 12 st for the remainder, first took place in 1924 and was worth the comparatively modest sum of £685 to the winner, being considerably less valuable than the National Hunt Chase which was still regarded as the *pièce de résistance* of the meeting. The initial contest for this new prize went off well. The weather at Cheltenham for once was mild and springlike; there was a strong field and among the spectators was the Prince of Wales, a friend of Harry Brown who was riding Conjuror II. On the Tuesday evening that much respected trainer Fred Withington, one of the few men elected to the Jockey Club without ever having owned a horse that ran on the flat, had remarked to a friend at dinner that he was in two minds about starting Red Splash, owned by Major E. H. Wyndham, in the Gold Cup as the horse was only a five-year-old and in addition was a late foal so that in actual years he was only four. Furthermore he reckoned that Red Splash had little hope of beating Dick Rees's mount Alcazar at the weights and in any case he had not engaged a jockey and was not sure of finding a suitable one. The next morning, however, Withington learnt that Alcazar was not going to run after all and he at once engaged Rees for Red Splash. He himself had a particular interest in Red Splash as he had previously trained both that horse's sire and dam.

Forewarned, trained by Aubrey Hastings and ridden by Jack Anthony, was favourite at 3–1 and Red Splash, although his preparation had been a hurried one owing to a slight accident, was significantly backed at 5–1. Right from the start Red Splash made the running and he stayed in front for two and a half miles when it looked from the stands as if he was beginning to tire. However Rees shook him up and he at once ran on again; in fact he led coming to the last fence, where both Conjuror II and Gerald L were pressing him hard. They landed on the flat almost in line and in a desperate finish Red Splash held on to win by a head from Conjuror II with Gerald L a neck away third. It was a magnificent performance by a young horse that seemed to have a glittering career ahead of him, but unfortunately he proved difficult to train and never ran in the race again. Major (now Colonel) Wyndham, who was then serving in the Life Guards, had been a fine rider in his younger days and twice won the Grand Military Gold Cup on Another Delight. Today he is the senior member of the National Hunt Committee.

It was not a particularly distinguished Gold Cup field in 1925 when Ballinode, an Irish mare trained by Frank Morgan at the Curragh, won comfortably from three opponents. A quick but rather chancy jumper, Ballinode, admirably ridden by Ted Leader, won easily from the odds-on favourite Alcazar, at that time reckoned just about the best three-miler in England. Conjuror II, now in his fourteenth year, had to be pulled up after a disastrous mistake at the water second time round.

It was another Irish victory in 1926 when the winner was the 10–1 chance Koko, owned by Mr Frank Barbour of Trimblestown, Co Meath. A wonderful judge of a young horse likely to make a chaser, Mr Barbour had his own private steeplechase course which included reproductions of various famous fences. He was a shrewd dealer, too, who was rarely averse to parting with a horse if he thought the price was the right one.

A fine big bay by Santoi, Koko was a hard-pulling front-runner that took years off the lives of his backers by taking hair-raising liberties with his fences. At Cheltenham, though, he was at his best, and forcing the pace, he won easily from Old Tay Bridge, who more than once came close to winning the Grand National, and the favourite, Ruddyglow, who was ridden by his owner Mr W. Filmer-Sankey. At the end of his racing career poor Koko had

ABOVE: Landing over the water in the 1921 Grand National. The winner, Shaun Spadah, with Dick Rees up, is in the centre, The Bore with Harry Brown up is on the left. BELOW: Sprig with T. Leader up winning the 1927 Grand National from the one-eyed Bovril III with Mr. G. W. Pennington up. *Photographs copyright of W. W. Rouch & Co. Ltd.*

Red Splash, winner of the first race for the Cheltenham Gold Cup. *Copyright W. W. Rouch & Co. Ltd.*

sunk to running in soldiers' races at Aldershot and Windmill Hill.

Lord Stalbridge, a great supporter of National Hunt racing, won in 1927 with Thrown In, admirably ridden by his son Mr Hugh Grosvenor, a young officer in the 7th Hussars. It is a remarkable fact that Mr Grosvenor, a formidable boxer, had only ridden in eight steeplechases previously, one of them being the Grand National in which he finished fifth. Possibly luck was on Thrown In's side as the five-year-old Grakle, who was pressing him hard coming to the final fence, swerved badly at that obstacle yet was only beaten by two lengths. The once brilliant Silvo, who was a shade past his best, was third. Thrown In had been useless on the flat. For two seasons he was hunted by Mr Morgan Blair whose unconventional methods were sometimes remarkably successful with difficult horses. Mr Grosvenor never rode at Cheltenham again; after the Grand National, in which Thrown In was brought down at the first fence, he went out to Australia to take up a military appointment and not long afterwards was killed in an air crash.

The going was very heavy in 1928. Koko, reckoned a better horse, and in particular a safer jumper, than when he had won two years previously, was an odds-on favourite. Coming to the last fence Patron Saint, a five-year-old trained by H. Harrison and ridden by Dick Rees, was in front but he was under pressure whereas Koko, hard on his heels, was apparently still on the bit and looked certain to win. On the flat, though, Koko stopped to nothing in a couple of strides and it was later found he had broken a small blood-vessel. Vive finished strongly, but Patron Saint stayed on well to win by four lengths. Unfortunately Patron Saint proved difficult to train afterwards and never ran in the race again.

From 1929 to 1937 only two horses won the Gold Cup, Easter Hero and Golden Miller. Both were chasers of the highest class and both possessed in a remarkable degree that rare capacity for capturing the imagination of the sporting public. Through their exploits they not only raised the prestige of the Gold Cup, earning for that race general recognition as the championship of the staying chasers, but in addition they did much to elevate the whole status of National Hunt racing and increase what had previously been its somewhat limited appeal.

A brief background to Easter Hero's career has been given in the section dealing with the Grand National and it will suffice to say that he had passed into Mr J. H. Whitney's ownership and was nine years of age when he ran in the Gold Cup in 1929. His preparation that season had been planned specifically with the object of winning the Grand National and the Gold Cup was his first outing over fences. He had, however, run in some minor events over hurdles and won them all.

It had been a very hard winter and because of frost and snow it was found necessary to postpone the Cheltenham meeting for a week. The field of ten, the biggest for the race so far, included some good horses such as Grakle, Bright's Boy and Koko, and chiefly because of the heavy support for Grakle, Easter Hero started at the remarkably liberal odds of 7-4 against.

Ridden by Dick Rees, Easter Hero put up one of his most brilliant performances, completely outjumping and outgalloping his opponents. At halfway he was thirty lengths clear and he eventually won at his leisure by twenty lengths from Grakle. Koko, who might conceivably have made a fight of it if he had been permitted to stride out from the start as he really liked, was unfortunately restrained and made mistake after mistake in consequence. A fortnight later Easter Hero, with 12 st 7 lbs on his back, was second in a field of sixty-six in the Grand National, being beaten by that fine chaser Gregalach, to whom he was conceding 16 lbs.

In 1930 Easter Hero, this time ridden by Cullinan, again won the Gold Cup by twenty lengths, but the race was not without exciting, even disquieting, moments for his backers. Starting off with a zest and impetuosity that his rider seemed unable to check, he hit the first fences hard though without losing much ground and he made another mistake at the second. Fortunately this second blunder sobered him down and from that point he never put a foot wrong. His chief opponent was Gib, a big, rangy horse that had originally belonged to that good amateur rider Lord Fingall, who sold him to Mr B. D. Davis, a patron of Percy Woodland's stable. Gib had won the Cranford Chase at Newbury with 12 st 7 lbs and the Troytown Chase at Lingfield, a far more important event then than it is now, with 12 st 9 lbs, and these efforts may have taken a good deal out of a seven-year-old that was having his first season in top-class chasing. Ridden by Dick Rees, he put up a great fight, and despite a number of mistakes was up with Easter Hero when he fell at the last fence but one. He was under pressure at the time, though, whereas Cullinan had not moved on the favourite. He was never as good again afterwards and eventually he was reduced to competing in sellers. Cullinan, apart from riding the Gold Cup winner, also rode the Champion Hurdle winner Brown Tony, while three weeks later he rode Shaun Goilin to victory in the National.

Easter Hero, by then in his twelfth year, might well have won his third Gold Cup in 1931, but he was unquestionably shedding a little of his brilliance and at Lingfield, starting at 6–1 on, he was beaten by Major Colin Davy's Desert Chief, his first defeat on a park course in England. However bad weather caused the Cheltenham meeting to be abandoned. In the Grand National Easter Hero was knocked over at Becher's, and in the Champion Chase the following day he could only dead heat with the outsider Coup de Chapeau, who was meeting him at level weights. Mr Whitney kindly and wisely decided to retire him forthwith. 'The best horse that never won a National,' said Dick Rees; 'The best horse I ever knew,' was the eloquent verdict of his trainer Jack Anthony, who had ridden the mighty Troytown to victory at Aintree.

From 1932 to 1938 the Gold Cup was dominated by Miss Dorothy Paget's Golden Miller and though something of his background has been described in the pages dealing with his Grand National victory, he was such an outstanding horse that it is perhaps worth relating here the curious story of his breeding as told by John Welcome in his book *The Cheltenham Gold Cup*.

In 1914 a Dublin businessman with the somewhat un-Irish name of Mr Julius Solomon came to the conclusion that there were more improbable ways of making money than by having an interest in bloodstock. He therefore decided to buy a brood mare and with that object in view summoned his car and was driven to the farm of Mr James Nugent, who had a number of mares for sale. Mr Solomon did not pretend to know anything about horses so he sat in the car while his chauffeur went off to select a mare. The chauffeur, whose identity has not been recorded, was apparently no bad judge and he chose a mare called Miller's Pride, for whom Mr Solomon paid £100.

Mr Solomon sent the mare to board with Mr Laurence Geraghty of Drumree, Co Meath, who had her covered by quite a well-known sire but unfortunately she proved barren. As the war intensified and the demand for bloodstock almost vanished, Mr Solomon completely lost interest in his mare. However Mr Geraghty treated her as if she was his own and bred several foals from her, mostly by sires from the Flat House Stud. When that stud closed down, Mr Geraghty had her covered by Goldcourt, a five-guinea sire owned by Mr P. Byrne of Copperally, Maynooth, Co Meath. In 1927 a colt foal by Goldcourt was duly produced and Mr Geraghty at once saw that the foal was a good one. As a yearling it was sent to be sold at Ballsbridge and was sold to Mr P. Quinn for 1,000 guineas, a good price in those days for that stamp of horse.

Some years later, when Golden Miller had established his reputation in England, Mr Solomon decided that the opportunity was at hand to earn a little prestige for himself, so he took steps to have himself officially named as Golden Miller's breeder. This he eventually succeeded in doing, but all the credit of course really goes to Mr Geraghty, who had kept the mare, arranged the mating and paid the service fee.

Golden Miller was five years old and trained by Basil Briscoe when he ran in the Gold Cup in 1932. He had only run in four steeplechases, winning three of them (he was in fact disqualified in one on technical grounds) and being narrowly beaten in the other. This was a promising record, but it was felt that he was still too inexperienced to take on seasoned chasers in a top-class race. Ridden by Ted Leader, he was easy to back at 13–2, Grakle being favourite at 11–10 on, while there was no lack of support for the brilliant, hard-pulling Kingsford.

This year the Cheltenham fences were unduly severe. A few days before the meeting began the Inspector of Courses visited Cheltenham and as the result of his distinctly critical observations, six inches were lopped off the top of each obstacle with the result that the tops were much stiffer than was usually the case. Fifty-six horses fell during the three days in the steeplechases and a rather enigmatic character called Count Louis Bernheim was killed when Summer Song came down.

At the fence after the water in the Gold Cup, Aruntius made a bad mistake; Kingsford, just behind him, was unsighted and took a crashing fall, receiving fatal injuries. Grakle, ridden by Jack Fawcus who at that time was still an amateur, cleared the fence but swerved sharply on landing to avoid the prostrate Kingsford and unseated his rider. After this debacle Golden Miller only had to stand up to win and this he did, passing the post a comfortable four lengths in front of Inverse with Aruntius third. Golden Miller had in fact made two mistakes in the first two miles but he was always very clever at recovering and never really looked like coming down. In fact he never fell at a park course throughout his entire career.

It took some little time for the racing public to accept Golden Miller as the great horse that he was, possibly because he lacked the almost insolent panache of Easter Hero. In a race he was inclined to be idle, while his jumping was quick and economical rather than brilliantly spectacular. He was accustomed to jump off his forehand and was therefore not the ideal horse for Aintree. His class and his cleverness, combined with courage and stamina, earned him one Grand National, but in fact he was essentially a park course type. Cheltenham was a track that suited him to perfection, his long stride and apparently boundless stamina earning a rich dividend in that stiff uphill climb to the winning post.

Golden Miller had improved considerably by 1933 and had impressed everyone with his magnificent victory in the Troytown Chase at Lingfield with 12 st 10 lbs. In the Gold Cup he was a hot favourite at 7–4 on and although opposed by such good horses as Kellsboro' Jack, admittedly more formidable at Aintree than at Cheltenham, Thomond II and Delaneige, he won with the utmost ease by ten lengths in the hands of Billy Stott. Thomond II had led on sufferance at the last open ditch but immediately afterwards the favourite took command and from two out, the race was at his mercy bar a fall.

Short, tough and as brave as a lion, Billy Stott had ridden Golden Miller in all his races that season but in the Grand National he was taken off on the rather flimsy excuse that he was not the ideal jockey for Aintree and Ted Leader rode Golden Miller in his place. Golden Miller fell at Becher's second time round. Stott rode the gigantic Pelorous Jack who was slightly ahead of the winner Kellsboro' Jack when he toppled over at the last. The racing public took the view that Stott had been unjustly and unkindly treated and it would have been tremendously popular had he won on Pelorous Jack.

Gerry Wilson was chosen as Golden Miller's partner in 1934 when Golden Miller's main target was the National. The new partnership won a race at Lingfield in November, beating Thomond II, but a month later Thomond showed that he had become a force to be reckoned with in beating Golden Miller at Kempton at a difference of only 7 lbs. Golden Miller was defeated again in January, this time by Southern Hero at Hurst Park, but there was no disgrace about that as Southern Hero, who belonged to Mr J. V. Rank, was a good horse and was receiving 28 lbs. Southern Hero's favourite race was the Scottish Grand National which he had won on three occasions, the last time at the age of fourteen with 12 st 3 lbs on his back.

In the Gold Cup, despite the absence of Thomond II, Golden Miller started at the surprisingly generous price of 6–5 against, largely on account of sustained support for the handsome El Hadjar, a French seven-year-old from Percy Woodland's stable that had won the Coventry Chase at Kempton most impressively. It is impossible to say precisely how good El Hadjar was as he fell three fences from home just as he was moving up to challenge. He fell, too, in his next race, the Champion Chase at Aintree, and on that occasion he received fatal injuries.

Kellsboro' Jack made his effort at the same time as El Hadjar and actually headed Golden Miller for a few strides but he had been mastered by the time the last fence but one had been reached. At the last the brilliant young five-year-old Avenger, destined to be killed in the 1936 Grand National, did his best to make a fight of it, but Golden Miller shook him off without difficulty and won by half a dozen lengths with his ears pricked. Seventeen days later The Miller put up the finest performance of his career by winning the Grand National in record time with 12 st 2 lbs.

Golden Miller's main objective in 1935 was again the Grand National. This year he seemed better than ever and at Sandown he won the three-mile five-furlong Grand International Chase with 12 st 7 lbs, conceding 14 lbs and 18 lbs respectively to Delaneige and Really True, who had both finished second in the National, Delaneige with 11 st 6 lbs. The Gold Cup was regarded as hardly more than a winding-up race for Miss Paget's horse, particularly as it had been announced that Royal Ransom would carry Mr Whitney's colours in that event, the far more formidable Thomond being detailed for the two-mile Coventry Cup. At the eleventh hour, however, Mr Whitney changed his mind and decided to run Thomond in the Gold Cup. It was only on the evening before the race that this unwelcome news reached Basil Briscoe's ears; naturally disturbed at the prospect of Golden Miller being subjected to a hard race with Aintree so close, he tried to induce Mr Whitney to change his mind, but to no avail.

Besides the two main protagonists, there were three other runners in the Cup, all good horses, Kellsboro' Jack, Southern Hero and Avenger, but they attracted little support in the market, the bulk of the money being for Golden Miller, who started at 2–1, and Thomond who was 5–2 against. The crowd was enormous; the supply of racecards was rapidly exhausted and cars were still pouring into the parks long after the first race had been run. The sun shone and the going was fast, a bit too fast, some thought, for 'The Miller'.

Southern Hero forced the pace and it was a fierce gallop right from the start. All five horses jumped faultlessly and with just under a mile to go they were all in the race with a chance. After the last open ditch, though, the pace began to tell; Southern Hero dropped back beaten and though Kellsboro' Jack showed no sign of weakening, he was unable to accelerate and it was clear that the issue lay between Golden Miller and Thomond.

With three fences still to be jumped Wilson was having to push the always rather indolent Golden Miller, whereas from the stands it looked as if Speck had the much smaller Thomond still comfortably on the bit. Over the last fence but one, amid growing excitement, they landed level, but on that stiff uphill climb Golden Miller's tremendous stride began to tell and before long he led by half a length. Speck, though, refused to admit defeat. Drawing his whip he rode Thomond into the last with all the strength and courage for which he was famous, and with Thomond responding in the bravest manner possible the two horses took off neck and neck. They landed together and as they fought it out on the flat, the Cotswold Hills re-echoed to cheering such as is rarely heard on an English racecourse. Gradually the bigger horse, giving everything he had, obtained the mastery over his lionhearted opponent and at the finish of one of the greatest races in steeplechasing history Golden Miller was three parts of a length to the good.

It was the hardest race of Golden Miller's career and his light never shone quite so brightly again. Soon afterwards came the Aintree debacle with its ugly rumours and stormy repercussions, incidents that have been related in the section dealing with the Grand National.

The following year Golden Miller was trained by Owen Anthony. In December he won a National Hunt flat race—fortunately those inordinately dreary events exist no longer—and later that month, carrying 12 st 10 lbs and ridden by Gerry Wilson, he won a two-mile chase at Newbury with all his old brilliance. In February he ran again at Newbury with Wilson up, this time over three miles, but he never appeared to be enjoying himself and he ran out five fences from home. The immediate sequel to this was an announcement that Evan Williams would ride him in the Gold Cup in place of Wilson. Williams was an excellent horseman— he won the 1937 Grand National on Royal Mail—but he was hardly of the same calibre as Wilson. He certainly possessed, though, one curious record; he rode two winners at Cardiff on Easter Monday in 1933, the first one as an amateur, the second as a professional. Incidentally in the course of his racing career Golden Miller had seventeen different riders, fifteen professionals and two amateurs, Mr Hector Gordon and Mr Robin Mount.

In the Gold Cup Golden Miller's task, with Thomond an absentee, was clearly easier than it had been the year before but his reputation did not stand quite as high as it did, and largely on account of his lapse at Newbury, his starting price was only fractionally under evens. However on his favourite course he proceeded to win in quite his old style, having a dozen lengths to spare over Royal Mail, partnered by Fulke Walwyn.

Because of bad weather there was no Gold Cup in 1937, but Golden Miller was back at Cheltenham in 1938 for what was to be his final appearance on that track. Now in his twelfth year, he had inevitably shed some of his old-time brilliance, but he was nevertheless still formidable and started favourite at 7–4. Macaulay, bought from Lord Rosebery by Mr H. A. Steel and trained by Peter Thrale, was heavily backed at 3–1 and there was good money, too, for that spectacular jumper Airgead Sios and also for Lt-Colonel D. C. Part's Morse Code, trained by Ivor Anthony and ridden by Danny Morgan, one of the best riders that never won a National. Coming to the last fence Golden Miller, ridden this time by 'Frenchie' Nicholson, was just in front but he was clearly under pressure whereas Morgan on Morse Code was sitting very confidently close behind him. On the flat the speed of the younger horse soon proved decisive and courageously as Golden Miller battled on, he had to admit defeat by a couple of lengths. Despite the occasional lapses and disappointments of his later years, he still retained to the full the affection of the racing public and as he stood in the unsaddling enclosure, beaten for the first time at Cheltenham, the old champion was cheered again and again and even the toughest professional backer found it hard not to show some emotion.

Golden Miller remains to this day the only horse ever to have won both the Grand National and the Gold Cup though Mont Tremblant came close to bringing off the double. Altogether he won twenty-nine races and over £15,000 in stakes. Comparisons between champions of different eras tend to be inconclusive, even pointless, because of the difference in conditions. Possibly Dr W. G. Grace would have found difficulty in coping with top-class leg-spin bowling, but on the other hand would Sir Donald Bradman have been seen to advantage against really fast bowling on the appallingly rough wickets that were the general rule at Lord's in the eighteen seventies? In comparing Golden Miller with Arkle it must be remembered that the structure of National Hunt racing has completely changed. In the nineteen thirties a chaser, to win big money, had to take his chance in the National.

Young Prince (grey horse), with G. Hardy up, and Castletown, with W. Stott up, taking the water jump in the Southern Double Handicap Chase at Lingfield, 1930

A bad fall at Becher's Brook during the 1930 Grand National

Battleship, one of the smallest Grand National winners, ridden by the seventeen-year-old B. Hobbs.
Copyright W. W. Rouch & Co. Ltd.

If there had been then the many rich prizes on park courses that stand to be won today, Golden Miller might never have gone to Aintree at all. He very probably would not have gone back there after once proving he could win the toughest, most exacting race in the Calendar. It is arguable that Arkle is the greater horse of the two, but he has never been asked to perform at Aintree, the supreme test for a chaser still even though the fences are nothing like as formidable as they were. No single victory of Arkle's equals in sheer merit Golden Miller's win in the 1934 Grand National in record time.

Perhaps at this stage something should be said of Golden Miller's owner Miss Dorothy Paget, a unique and remarkable personality in the racing world for almost thirty years. The second daughter of Lord Queenborough, who won the Two Thousand Guineas with St Louis, she was a genuine eccentric, her eccentricity being largely due to the fact that she was morbidly shy and outside her own small and devoted female entourage she took every possible step to avoid human contact. She was already a legend during her own lifetime and everyone on the racecourse had stories to tell of her extraordinary existence, almost that of a recluse, at her house at Chalfont St Giles; of her voracious appetite; of the unconventional hours that she kept; and of her interminable conferences with her trainer of the moment, often in a racecourse restaurant long after everyone else had gone home. She was certainly not without a sense of the ridiculous, she was often extremely generous, and the few people who knew her really well were unquestionably very fond of her indeed.

Her appearance was distinctive and no one could ever have accused her of being a slave to fashion. Stout and ungainly, she invariably wore a blue felt hat and a long blue coat that eventually terminated within easy reach of her ankles. Her face, large, round and pallid, was framed in hair that was dark and austerely straight. She had a disconcertingly retentive memory, a sound knowledge of bloodstock breeding, and she habitually betted in very large sums indeed. She was not easy to get on with and her career on the turf was punctuated by sudden and occasionally painful breaches with those who served her. She had to be treated with firmness tempered by tact and patience and Charlie Rogers held his post as her stud manager and her trainer in Ireland for twenty-three years.

This is not the place to comment on her activities in racing under Jockey Club Rules, but there is no doubt that the money she so lavishly poured into National Hunt racing afforded that sport a highly stimulating shot in the arm, just as her betting of which some people affected to disapprove, certainly livened up the market. In the course of time she became a familiar and easily recognizable part of the English racing scene and like most eccentrics in this country that do no harm to others, she was eventually regarded with something approaching affection. She was certainly very much missed when she died in 1960 at the age of fifty-four.

It had been planned to run Golden Miller again at Cheltenham in 1939, but he ran poorly in a preparatory outing at Newbury and as he failed to satisfy Owen Anthony in his work at home subsequently, he was taken out of the Cup and in fact he never ran again. It was a poor field this year and Morse Code was thought certain to win again, but in a slow-run, somewhat featureless contest he was soundly defeated by Mrs Arthur Smith-Bingham's Brendan's Cottage, trained by George Beeby and ridden by George Owen, who subsequently trained the Grand National winner Russian Hero.

In 1940 the National Hunt meeting was restricted to two days and part of the course had been ploughed up. Miss Paget won her sixth Gold Cup, this time with Roman Hackle, a big, powerful rather plain horse ridden by Evan Williams. Miss Paget had already won the two other main events at the meeting, the Champion Hurdle with Solford and the National Hunt Handicap with Kilstar. Roman Hackle was expected to win again in 1941 but was unplaced behind Poet Prince, owned by Mr David Sherbrooke, a practising veterinary surgeon. Trained by Ivor Anthony and ridden by Roger Burford, whose father was for many years a faithful servant of the Wroughton stable, Poet Prince was touched in the wind and had cost his owner only forty guineas. But for a bad fall the previous day, Mr Sherbrooke would have ridden Poet Prince himself. In 1942 there were only eighteen days steeplechasing and the Gold Cup was run on a damp, foggy Saturday before a very small crowd. At the last open ditch the race seemed to be between Broken Promise and Solarium but they both came down at that point and Red Rower, who was lying third, very nearly fell over them. This paved the way for Lord Sefton's Medoc II, who, ridden by 'Frenchie' Nicholson, won smoothly by eight lengths from Red Rower.

On 10th September, 1942, the following notice appeared in the *Racing Calendar*—'The Stewards of the National Hunt Committee have received notification from His Majesty's Government that they are unable to sanction National Hunt Racing during the season 1942–43.' Steeplechasing did not start up again until January 6th, 1945. The Gold Cup was run at a one-day meeting on 17th March. Spirits were rising now that the war was almost over and despite the difficulties over transport a huge crowd assembled to see the first important steeplechase for nearly three years. Sixteen runners turned out, a record for the race, and a closely contested struggle between moderate horses was won by Red Rower who overhauled Schubert and Paladin at the final fence. Red Rower was bred, owned and trained by Lord Stal bridge and ridden by the lightweight D. L. Jones who had to carry three stone dead weight in order to do twelve stone. Jones subsequently gave up riding over fences and hurdles and took to the flat where he met with a fair measure of success.

Once it became apparent that the Gold Cup was a success, it was only natural that a race of similar type should be established for hurdlers. The Champion Hurdle was first run in 1926 and was won by Blaris, owned by Mrs Hollins, a great supporter of jumping, and appropriately ridden by George Duller, greatest of all hurdle-race riders. It took, however, some little time before the Champion Hurdle showed even a hint of approaching the Gold Cup in respect of prestige and of public interest. The fact is that the hurdlers in the late nineteen-twenties and in the nineteen thirties were not particularly good. Not one of them could compare with the mighty Trespasser, who had won the Imperial Gold Cup at Sandown three years running, and no hurdler of that time was of comparable stature to those giants of steeplechasing, Easter Hero and Golden Miller. However, one great name appears among the early winners of the race, that of Brown Jack, who won as a four-year-old in 1928. When it was discovered what a good horse Brown Jack was on the flat, he was never permitted to run over hurdles again, but for which he might have set up in the Champion Hurdle a sequence of victories as long as the one he established in the Queen Alexandra Stakes at Ascot. Insurance, who won in 1931 and 1932 for Miss Paget, was a pretty good hurdler and so was Free Fare who won in 1937, but by and large there were no hurdlers in this era that could measure up to postwar Champion Hurdle winners such as National Spirit, Hatton's Grace and Sir Ken.

Up till the war the big race at Cheltenham, at least as regards prize money, was the National Hunt Steeplechase, a four-mile race for maidens at entry ridden by amateurs. At one stage the race was for maidens at starting, but the disadvantage of having one of the most valuable races of the entire season restricted to horses of that description was all too obvious. Some of the preliminary outings for National Hunt Chase candidates were apt to end in an undignified struggle between horse and rider, with the horse's jaw at the point of fracture in the battle to maintain its maiden certificate. The National Hunt course was a unique and attractive one, not a single fence being jumped twice and the runners streaming off into the country up by the racecourse station and away behind the stands before coming on to the racecourse proper for the final circuit. That course has, alas, been done away with and inevitably the race has lost much of its special and attractive character. No doubt, though, it was an unjustifiable expense maintaining a particular course that was only used in its entirety for two races during the season, the other one being the Foxhunters' Cup.

Some good horses won the National Hunt Chase in the nineteen thirties, one of the best being Mr J. H. Whitney's Sir Lindsay who in 1930 started at 5–4 in a big field and scored with ease, admirably ridden by Lord Fingall. Sir Lindsay was third in the National the following year and was reckoned unlucky not to have won. The winner in 1931, Merriment IV, owned and ridden by Lord Haddington, was a good horse, too, and gave his owner a winning ride in a chase at Aintree. Ego won in 1933 and three years later Mr Harry Llewellyn, later a famous name in the show-jumping world, rode him into second place in the Grand National. Crown Prince, who at one time carried a hunt servant out with the Whaddon, won for Lord Rosebery in 1934. He was ridden by Lord Rosebery's step-son Mr Ronald Strutt (now Lord Belper) and with Mr Strutt again riding him he was fourth in the Grand National the following year. Pucka Belle, winner in 1936, was an exceptionally good mare that carried her owner, Mr E. W. Bailey, into third place in the Grand National in 1937.

On the whole the hunters that ran at Cheltenham between the wars seem markedly inferior to more recent performers such as Halloween, The Callant, Colledge Master, Freddie and Baulking Green. Perhaps the pick of the pre-war hunters seen out at Cheltenham although he never won one of the big races there, was Don Bradman, a big handsome chestnut that won many prizes in the show-ring and in 1936 dead-heated with Delaneige in the Grand Sefton at Aintree. In 1935 Don Bradman, partnered by a highly competent rider in Mr Alec Marsh, was confidently expected to win the United Hunts Cup at the National Hunt meeting. He was cruising along comfortably in front when to the horror of his supporters, Mr Marsh took the wrong course. Don Bradman had to be pulled up and turned round, and when he joined in the race again he must have lost a furlong. Even so he finished a creditable second. Another famous hunter of this period was Major H. P. Rushton's O'Dell, a gallant grey that won over forty point-to-points and hunter-chases. In those days the Fox-hunters' Chase at Aintree was run over the full Grand National course and O'Dell won in 1936 at the age of fifteen. He won again in 1937 and in 1938 he was second. On each occasion he was ridden by Major O. L. Prior-Palmer of the 9th Lancers.

PART IV

Since 1945

BY JOHN LAWRENCE

I

IN January 1945, as the last German offensive of the second world war ground to a halt in the Ardennes, National Hunt racing, abandoned entirely for two and a half years, became, once more, a part of the English scene.

It was, inevitably, a hesitant beginning. Only four courses, Cheltenham, Windsor, Wetherby and Catterick, were operational in the spring of 1945—and the weather did its best to spoil what sport there was. In the winter 1945-6, 144 days' racing were held on twenty-six different courses but, quite apart from the large number which did not survive the war at all, several of the major tracks, including Sandown, Kempton, Hurst Park and Newbury were still unusable.

Nevertheless a start was made and it immediately became apparent that, whatever else might be in short supply (petrol, foodstuffs and clothing were, of course, still rationed) enthusiasm for jumping was at least as great as ever. After five long years of war the public was hungry for entertainment. Those to whom the sights and sounds of N.H. racing were already familiar came flooding back, and many new racegoers found, in a day's jumping, the perfect antidote to grim and painful memories.

So despite everything—primitive racecourse accommodation and very considerable difficulty in getting from A to B—the stands at most of those early meetings were crowded. And, more remarkably, there were from the first more than enough men and horses to provide both entertaining and competitive sport. In fact, in the first full post-war season 1,830 horses took part and the average field had nine or ten runners—very little lower than today and an extraordinary figure in a country only just emerging from a struggle for its life.

Of the horses bred just before and during the early years of the war a large proportion had been turned out for want of more profitable occupation and these now provided a nucleus of mature, if inexperienced performers.

Another factor in the rapid renaissance of National Hunt racing was that the farming community came out of the war considerably more prosperous than it had been in the 'thirties—and its security was further reinforced by the Agricultural Act of 1947. Those farmers who had already owned jumpers could now afford to do so on a much bigger scale, and many who had not took to the game with enthusiasm. They have been its backbone ever since, and although professional trainers are nowadays understandably apt to look askance at the permit holder who trains his own and his family's horses 'on the Farm'—in the economic sense as well as the physical—there can be no doubt that, without such small private stables, jumping would be a much narrower, less sporting affair than it is.

And, with the horses in those early years, came the men, often still in uniform but with fingers itching to feel the reins once more. No less than 240 amateurs rode in 1945-6 (Anthony Mildmay headed the list) and among the leading professional jockeys were names that have been in the winter headlines ever since—names like Fred Rimell, Frenchie Nicholson, Bryan Marshall, Bob Turnell and many more.

But despite all outward signs of a thriving sport the future of National Hunt racing was by no means certain. Prize-money was still pathetically small—about £178,000 in 1945-6, of which more than £30,000 was accounted for jointly by Cheltenham's first post-war National Hunt meeting and the Grand National meeting at Liverpool. The whole season still hinged almost entirely on three climactic weeks in March. For the rest of the winter jumping was still very definitely small beer. Excluding the two big meetings, 830 races run elsewhere that season averaged about £125 to the winner. Prince Regent, coming from Ireland in the evening of a great career to run away with the 1946 Cheltenham Gold Cup, earned only £1,130 for Mr J. V. Rank. And the £8,805 won by Lovely Cottage in the 1946 Grand National was enough, with one other small prize, to give Mr J. Morant winnings almost double those of his nearest rival in the owners' list.

Then, as now, unlike the flat, jumping lacked the solid foundation of a breeding industry with a more or less guaranteed international demand for its products. It had to depend instead on the readiness of some people to pay large sums of money (with precious little hope of profit) for the privilege of owning a jumper—and the keenness of others to pay to watch those jumpers perform. These two—or even one without the other—would no doubt have been enough to keep National Hunt racing alive, at least roughly on its pre-war scale. But how could that scale be much expanded?

As usual the root of the problem was money. The National Hunt Committee itself was still operating on a shoestring. Racecourses, though some made large profits in the post-war years, had shareholders to satisfy and faced huge capital expenditure if their stands and other accommodation were to be improved. From neither of these two sources could any substantial increase in prize money be expected.

So where else was it to come from?

Anyone who, in the late nineteen forties, had predicted that, in 1965 an eight-year-old chaser might bring his total earnings to more than £60,000—without going near Aintree—would have been considered optimistic to the point of lunacy.

A National Hunt course at Ascot, a Tote turnover for National Hunt racing alone of eleven million pounds in a single season, a handicap hurdle worth £7,000, an offer of £25,000 refused for a six-year-old chaser, a National Hunt jockey honoured by the Queen, a central Turf Board jointly responsible for policy both on the flat and under National Hunt rules—all these would, in those days, have seemed mere dreamlike specks on a make-believe horizon.

Yet all have come to pass. The last twenty years of the century just completed have been by far the most eventful in the whole history of National Hunt racing and of the committee which controls it. They have seen a transformation—not yet complete, not yet secure in its results, but none the less miraculous—and it is the story of those twenty years that I now have the honour to tell.

The period begins with the end of the second world war and war itself had wrought one vital, lasting change. In 1939, seventy-nine courses (not including bona fide Hunt meetings which, in any case, soon disappeared entirely) were licensed by the National Hunt Committee. In 1947 only forty-six of these remained. Some, like Newbury, had yet to be reclaimed from wartime servitude but the vast majority of the casualties were permanent. And, with a few exceptions (Gatwick was perhaps the most serious loss) they were smallish country meetings differing only from point to points in that a charge could be made for admission—and from bona fide Hunt meetings in that professionals were allowed to ride.

The very considerable fun and entertainment such courses provided has been described in an earlier chapter. For those who took part and for the local crowds who came to watch they served a very real purpose—education and practice without much publicity for the former, rough and ready entertainment for the latter. By both their departure was doubtless much regretted and if the trend towards centralization ever killed off the many country meetings which still exist the whole character of National Hunt racing would be altered very greatly for the worse.

But some measure of streamlining was, without much doubt, desirable. The standard of organization, local stewards and discipline had, pre-war, been variable to say the least. There were then two categories of meeting: those in Appendix A of the

National Hunt rules, at which a basic minimum of prize money and official control was demanded and those outside at which the requirements were very much less stringent.

After the war, and accelerated by it, the proportion of meetings in Appendix A was steadily increased until, quite soon, the distinction became meaningless and was abolished. So, sad though it may have been to see these meetings die, the National Hunt Committee's job was made a good deal easier by their departure. They had been a happy hunting ground for that element in racing to which neither the ten commandments nor the National Hunt Rules were exactly sacrosanct and, although some of these gentlemen were colourful, amusing characters, their activities had not been calculated to improve the public image of the sport. Needless to say they are not even now extinct but many things have helped to make their lives more difficult and the first of these was the degree of centralization introduced by the second world war.

But this change alone could not have brought about the transformation I am attempting to describe. Men, women and horses all played a part in it as well, and even they would have been powerless without three crucial events: the advent of television, the rise of the sponsored race, and the formation of the Betting Levy Board.

The overall effect of television upon racing is a thorny subject. Undoubtedly it can, particularly when the weather is bad, keep potential racegoers at home by the fire, and the racecourses quite rightly demand fair compensation for this loss of revenue. But there is another much brighter side to the coin.

On 24th January, 1948 two steeplechases and a hurdle race were covered at Sandown by B.B.C. Television in the first broadcast of its kind in the world. It quickly became apparent to those responsible that National Hunt racing provided an exciting spectacle ideally suited to the medium, and the number of meetings televised increased steadily from that time on. The immediate result of this skilled and highly effective coverage (commercial television soon appeared to compete with the B.B.C.) was to bring the sights and sounds of jumping, its thrill, its dangers and its charm, to an entirely new, far wider public.

Countless people in whose lives horses and riding had hitherto played little or no part became fascinated by a sport which, in a mechanical age, depends not on machines but on creatures of flesh and blood. The names of the horses and men who, throughout the winter, risk limb and sometimes life for such trifling material rewards became for the first time household words. Before the war the Grand National and the occasional outstanding figure such as Golden Miller had been more or less the only points of contact between National Hunt racing and the sporting public as a whole. Now that contact was enormously extended and, not surprisingly, many whose interest had at first been aroused by television wanted to go and see for themselves.

There is no way to measure the profit or loss in terms of race-course attendance caused by television. Probably, taking into account the fees paid by the two T.V. companies, they balance out.

But in every other way, to television and to its commentators, men like Peter O'Sullevan, Clive Graham, John Rickman and Tony Cooke, National Hunt racing owes a tremendous debt. There has, as we shall see, been at least one harmful side effect—the decline in the fortunes of Aintree in general and attendance at the Grand National in particular—but compared to the overall increase of public interest in jumping this is of minor importance.

And the debt becomes ever heavier if, as is almost certainly the case, commercial sponsorship of N.H. races would never have materialized on anything like its present scale without the wider audience, and therefore wider scope for advertisement, that television gives.

It was in 1957 that Colonel W. H. Whitbread, a lifelong supporter of jumping who had himself ridden in two Grand Nationals (and got round both times when to do so was still a real achievement), conceived the idea of a top-class steeplechase at Sandown sponsored entirely by the famous brewery of which he is Chairman.

The date chosen for the first Whitbread Gold Cup, 27th April, was in itself a sign of the times. After the running of the Grand National at the end of March, National Hunt racing had hitherto been very much thrust into the background as the flat got under way. But that day in 1957, of the huge crowd which watched Mr M. H. Draper's Much Obliged beat a six-year-old called Mandarin, at least a large proportion was drawn to Sandown not primarily by the five flat-races on the card but by the steeplechase.

Some of the magnificent contests which the Whitbread Gold Cup has since produced will be described elsewhere. Its place as an integral part of the National Hunt season is now assured. What matters here is that Colonel Whitbread's example was immediately followed by other firms and the stream of which his brainchild was the source has now become a flood, surging all winter long and swelling National Hunt prize-money to a level which, without commercial sponsorship, it would never have achieved.

Next season, for instance, the Hennessy Gold Cup did for the autumn what the Whitbread had done for the spring. First run in November 1957, and won appropriately enough by Mandarin in Mme Kilian Hennessy's colours, its sponsors deserve a share of credit only slightly less than Whitbread's. These two races proved to the business world that sponsorship was well worth while and, I'm thankful to say, nothing has happened since to alter that conviction.

Quite apart from the example they set and the badly needed transfusion of prize-money they injected, the Whitbread and Hennessy Gold Cups together completed a transformation already begun in the National Hunt Calendar by races like the Queen Elizabeth Chase, first run at Hurst Park in 1949, and the King George VI Chase run, weather permitting, at Kempton on Boxing Day since 1951. Before the war, and for several years after it, the Grand National was by so far the richest prize of the jumping season that any steeplechaser with pretentions, however remote, to winning at Aintree was trained more or less exclusively with that one target in mind. He might, it is true, have a dress-rehearsal in the Grand Sefton or one of the other races at the Aintree November meeting but the rest of the season—even, in many cases, the Cheltenham Gold Cup itself—was apt to be little more than a means to one all-important end.

This situation had begun to alter in the late 'forties and early 'fifties but it was the appearance of the first big sponsored races that finally changed the whole emphasis. The Grand National (itself a sponsored race from 1961-4) remained the summit of many owners' ambition (it became worth over £13,000 to the winner in 1958 and this was raised to £20,000 in 1961) but by 1957 it had become quite possible to frame a programme for a top-class staying 'chaser which kept him profitably and busily employed from October to April without going anywhere near Aintree.

The consequent decline in the class and prestige of the Grand National will be examined later. In every other way the change was entirely for the good. It meant that public interest, which always centres around the best, could now be kept alive virtually throughout the whole National Hunt season, and certainly throughout those months when jumping holds the stage un-challenged by the flat. Instead of creeping round in minor races, often threequarters fit, avoiding each other wherever possible and waiting hopefully for the Grand National weights to be published, the best staying 'chasers have, since 1957, had four main targets to aim at: the Hennessy in November, the King George VI Chase

in December, the Cheltenham Gold Cup in March and the Whitbread in April. No one horse, at the time of writing, has ever won
all four in the same season, but it can't be long odds against Arkle
doing so before you read these words.

So, no sooner had television begun to make familiar public
figures of the steeplechasing stars and the men who rode them than
commercial sponsorship began to broaden the stage on which
those stars performed. Nor have the three-mile 'chasers been the
only objects of the sponsors' bounty. For hurdlers—hitherto
miserably treated in terms of prize-money—two mile 'chasers,
novices and four-year-olds, a whole new crop of sponsored races
has sprung up. Scarcely a Saturday now passes all winter long
without a main event which owes its existence to commerce.
Colonel Whitbread certainly started something that April day at
Sandown—and, come to think of it, Much Obliged was no bad
name for the first beneficiary of his generous enterprise. The
National Hunt world is deeply grateful and, since by far the most
prolific sponsors have been purveyors of various alcoholic bever-
ages, it is able to show its gratitude whenever there are successes
to be celebrated, sorrows to be drowned or simply the rigours of
winter to be warded off.

Prize-money is not the be-all and end-all of National Hunt
racing. Even nowadays, if owners demanded a reasonable expectation of profit there would be precious few jumpers in training;
National Hunt jockeys are still grossly under-rewarded by comparison with their plutocratic flat-race colleagues and National
Hunt trainers work on a margin of profit which, without successful
betting, is still unhealthily narrow. Though the sport still *is* a
sport and many who follow it would do so for even smaller rewards, prize-money is its life-blood and, inevitably, one of the
yardsticks by which its progress must be measured.

It follows that a major milestone in the story of that progress
was the passage through Parliament in 1963 of the Betting, Gaming
and Lotteries Act. For the first time in the history of British racing
the resources of off-course betting with bookmakers were tapped
for the good of the sport under both rules. It is no part of my
brief to discuss whether the bookmaker's contribution is, at present, adequate or whether it is being used to the best advantage.
What matters is that the total prize-money competed for under
National Hunt rules in the season 1947-8 was £390,650. In 1964-5
it was £1,055,152 and of that total owners put up 39% in entry
fees and forfeits, commercial sponsors gave nearly 12% and the
Betting Levy Board over 20%. Part of this, being revenue from

the greatly increased Tote turnover, was, of course, nothing new, but the Levy Board's assistance was nevertheless substantial. From it £10,000 is now added to the Grand National prize, £5,000 to the Cheltenham Gold Cup and £5,000 to the Champion Hurdle.

Even with all the aids described above it cannot honestly be claimed that National Hunt racing is yet on anything like a sound financial footing. The racecourses themselves put up only 28·79% of the total prize-money in 1964-5—considerably less than the owners—and the average prize per race, £510, does not compare all that favourably with £250 in 1947-8 when the rise in costs and fall in the value of money are taken into account.

This is a history, not a crystal ball prophecy, but it takes neither great imagination nor a brilliant head for figures to see how quickly even a slight business depression might cause the situation to deteriorate. Commercial sponsorship would be cut, there would be less spare cash both for betting and for ownership, and the sport might find its present outward prosperity little more substantial than the South Sea Bubble.

But nothing like that has happened yet. Although owners are still paying through the nose for their (and our) amusement, there is no sign of a fall in the numbers of those prepared to do so and higher prices are now being paid for young potential jumpers than ever before. Whatever the other weaknesses of its position, the popularity of jumping as a spectacle and the dream of having a good horse to carry one's colours over fences or hurdles is more firmly entrenched than ever in English hearts. And in that fact the National Hunt Committee, looking back on the first hundred years of its existence, can take both pleasure and pride.

II

Any sport or business in which large sums of tax-free money are at stake must be controlled by rules, and when a sport involves people from as many different walks of life—and takes place in as many different far-flung places as British National Hunt racing—the enforcement of those rules is, to say the least of it, no easy matter.

It is often a cause for wonder abroad—and from time to time for complaint at home—that the control of a great sport like racing should, in Great Britain, rest entirely in the hands of unpaid amateurs—the members of two self-elected bodies, the Jockey Club, and its younger brother the National Hunt Committee. But however odd the supremacy of these autocratic (and, so far as the word has any meaning nowadays, aristocratic) bodies may seem in a modern democracy the fact remains that no one has ever yet been able to think of a much better alternative.

Racing needs strong central control and offences against its code of rules are seldom susceptible of strict legal proof. A jury of twelve good men and true, asked to decide 'beyond reasonable doubt' that, for example, a horse had not been allowed to do his best in a certain race would, nine times out of ten, find the accused not guilty for want of sufficient evidence. Such 'crimes' are best judged by men with the widest possible experience of racing and, while not all stewards of the National Hunt Committee have been as fully qualified in this respect as, for instance, Lord Mildmay was, they do all have the best interests of the sport at heart. What is more they give their time and services free of charge. Just conceivably the job could be done as well or even better by paid professionals, but the best brains and experience would have to be bought and the price would be very high indeed.

So, although the National Hunt stewards are often bitterly criticised both by word of mouth and in the Press, such criticism, even on the rare occasions when it is both informed and justified, should not be allowed to obscure the very real feeling of gratitude and respect that exists in the racing world for those who bear so cheerfully the burden of its government.

For the fact is that the system *works*, and the brief survey I am about to attempt of the major changes in rules and policy since the war shows a continuous trend towards tighter discipline, better management and more consistent, more centralized control. Often the changes have come too slowly for many of us but those responsible can fairly argue that the right change a year too late is better than the wrong one a year too soon.

When the war ended in 1945 there were still six stewards of the National Hunt Committee, each serving for three years, and the whole Committee met only three times each season. For obvious reasons it is twice as difficult to get clear-cut policy decisions from six men as from three, particularly when their services are only given part-time, and from 1950 the number of stewards was progressively reduced. Soon, falling into line with the Jockey Club, there were three National Hunt stewards, each rising in rotation to be senior steward in his third year of office—and the number of Annual General meetings was at the same time increased from three to five.

The obvious weakness in this system was lack of continuity. Three years, part-time, is all too short a period in which to grasp a job as many-sided and complex as that of senior steward and it wasn't till 1964 that, with the setting up of a nine man Turf Board official steps were taken to combat this problem. The Board consists of a Chairman serving for five years, two planning vice-chairmen, one from the Jockey Club and another from National Hunt Committee, each serving for two years, and the three executive stewards of each body serving for three years as before. The chairman and one other member of the Levy Board sit in on all its meetings with a watching brief.

In the meanwhile a measure of continuity had been provided by Messrs Weatherby, secretaries to both the Jockey Club and the National Hunt Committee. Ever since he returned (wounded) from the war Mr Peter Weatherby and his assistants Messrs Watts and Marshall have given invaluable help and counsel to succeeding National Hunt stewards. Like the Civil Service, the family firm of Messrs Weatherby is constantly sniped at by those whose lives it so greatly affects; but here too, if the critics are honest, they have to admit that the benefit to the sport of a central, continuous, enormously experienced secretariat outweighs the minor irritations its methods sometimes cause.

Nor have all senior stewards come fresh and without previous knowledge to their task. Several, like Lord Abergavenny and both Lord Willoughby de Broke (three times a steward) and Lord Cadogan (twice a steward and now the National Hunt vice-chairman of the Turf Board), have been more or less constantly engaged in the service of National Hunt racing since the war and its debt to them is correspondingly great.

The first sign of a tightening up in the somewhat amateurish pre-war system of control came in 1948 when permits were issued to all those previously unregistered owner-trainers who wished to train only their own or their family's horses. Until 1965 a man could still train hunter-chasers only without permission and the qualifications for holding a permit were not particularly strict. Judging, in fact, by some of the dangerously ill-schooled half-fit animals one sees running at minor meetings they are not, to this day, half strict enough.

A parallel change was introduced in 1961 when all amateur riders were brought under permit. Originally allowed to ride anywhere (and some said anyhow!) amateurs had for some time been required to apply for a permit after riding ten winners. From 1961 there have been 'A' permits for those who have not done so and 'B' permits for those who have.

Quite rightly, since the war, the stewards have taken pains to see that no amateur, because of his unpaid status, is allowed to compete unfairly with the professionals. The ever-increasing modern need to earn a living sees to it that very few nowadays become skilled enough to reach that level, but those few who do, must either prove 'independent means' or turn professional.

The result is that although the standard of amateur riding will never again achieve the heights it did in the days of Mr Harry Brown its practitioners are, in the true sense of the word, 'amateurs'—something that can be said for precious few other sports. There have, it is true, been one or two who can afford to keep their amateur status only by wielding the pen more freely than the whip, but perhaps the less said about them the better.

The abolition of the Appendix A classification of racecourses has already been mentioned. With it came an extension of official control at all meetings. More stewards' secretaries—professionals who advise and assist the unpaid local stewards—were appointed and now, except occasionally on Bank Holidays, there is always at least one at every National Hunt meeting. The requirements for medical and veterinary officers were also stepped up soon after the war and, with the invaluable voluntary assistance of the St John Ambulance Brigade (recognized in 1965 by a sponsored charity meeting at Ascot), the treatment of injured jockeys has been raised to a standard few who rode pre-war would recognize.

As regards the physical comfort of the winter racegoer, little could be done for racecourse reconstruction until the Levy Board began to assist in it, but in other ways his lot had long ago been considerably improved. The broadcasting of runners, riders and other information became general in 1946, broadcast running commentaries of races were introduced in 1953 and the photo-finish began to operate under National Hunt rules in 1957—not quite soon enough for those who will always maintain that, in the first Whitbread Gold Cup, Mandarin beat Much Obliged instead of the other way round!

Many members and stewards of the National Hunt Committee rode themselves as amateurs and the interests of the jockeys, on whose courage and skill so much that is good about jumping depends, have always been near their heart.

Fees were raised in 1947 to seven guineas for a losing ride and ten for a winner (in races worth over £85) and in 1961 this was modified, at the jockeys' request, to a flat basic fee of ten guineas win or lose. In that year also the rates of compensation paid to injured jockeys from the National Hunt Accident Fund were improved and in 1964 the Levy Board introduced its own comprehensive insurance and pension scheme for all jockeys and stable employees under both rules. Inspired by the tragic accidents to Paddy Farrell and Tim Brookshaw, a further fund was set up in 1963 with the blessing of the National Hunt Committee to protect against hardship those jockeys so seriously hurt that they were forced to give up riding. The risk of injury, unavoidable though it will always be, was also materially lessened when, in 1962, a new and far more effective form of crash-helmet was devised. It is kept on by a chin-strap which, though unflattering to the wearer's profile, ensures the protection of his skull in even the most head-long fall.

To the satisfaction of all who rode in them, one and a half mile hurdle races—a perverted form of amusement which did no good to man or beast—were abolished in 1953 and the National Hunt Juvenile Chase for Four-year-olds went the same way, equally unlamented, in 1958.

From 1953 to 1955 experiments were carried out on several courses with a new 'French' type of hurdle, made not of wood but of birch, not unlike a small steeplechase fence. Though by no means a complete failure, these were eventually discarded—largely because of the fear, expressed by the opposition group of trainers, that jumping them might give future steeplechasers too flippant an attitude to the larger obstacles.

A valuable change was, however, introduced in 1959 when the top bars of all hurdles were padded with rubber. This lessened the risk of injury to horses' legs, caused fewer hurdles to be broken and muffled the machine-gun rattle, so alarming to a young horse (or rider) which had hitherto signalled the passage of a big close-bunched field.

Various other minor alterations have been made in the rules for construction of fences including one to the water-jump which, if I may be excused for letting a personal prejudice creep in, has signally failed to prevent the special, avoidable, type of accident that obstacle involves!

In most other changes of rules and policy the National Hunt Committee has kept in step with the Jockey Club, though in at least one case, the sensible rule which allows a horse disqualified on objection to be placed second or third instead of last, they took the lead.

Doping has, alas, been a constant problem under both Rules and though the use of drugs to improve a horse's ability is prob-ably, owing to regular official tests, a thing of the past no effective deterrent has yet been found to the horrid crime of 'nobbling' or doping to stop. A horse ridden by Lord Mildmay called St Neots

Lord Mildmay

The first fence at the 1950 Grand National

was sprayed with acid in the paddock at Worcester back in 1946, and since that time no one can say how many jumpers have gone out to race half-blind and drugged, with all the dangers to themselves and their riders that this involves.

Until the Duke of Norfolk's Committee in 1961 any trainer of a horse found to have been doped—with whatever motive—automatically lost his licence, and of the men who suffered under this rule some were probably, by modern standards, blameless. In 1962, consequent upon the Norfolk report, the rule as to a trainer's responsibility was altered, routine sampling for dope was introduced and measures for improving the security of racecourse stables set in train. Regrettably the problem is not yet solved but the authorities are at least more alive than ever before to its seriousness.

In pursuit of a different kind of security the use of the film patrol camera was extended to National Hunt racing in 1962. It is of enormous value in helping stewards to decide objections and also acts as a deterrent to that small minority of jockeys and trainers who, hoping to hoodwink either the handicapper or the bookmaker or both, neglect to observe rule 132 'that every horse shall run on its merits'.

Though by no means extinct, the non-trier is far less common now than ever before and, in my opinion, less so in jumping, than under Jockey Club rules. With the exception of the doping menace, in fact, the ordinary punter gets a better, fairer run for his money than at any previous time.

The overnight declarations scheme, designed to help those who bet off the course, was brought into force for jumping in 1961. No unmixed boon to owners and trainers struggling to place a moderate horse successfully, it has at least removed the 'surprise runner' and, to that extent must have helped swell the betting turnover from which the Levy comes.

This catalogue of progress, brief and incomplete, is nevertheless enough to show that the ruling body of National Hunt racing has been far from idle since the war. I cannot hope to mention by name all those who have worked so hard and long at what is, too often, a thankless task. But without them the game could not have come so successfully through the difficult post-war years. Its present health and popularity is the best testimonial to their efforts and the only reward they ever sought.

III

As Roger Mortimer has written, National Hunt racing used to be known in some uncharitable circles as a sport for 'the needy and greedy'. If, which I doubt, that slander was ever deserved, it certainly isn't today when even the most biased advocates of rival pastimes are apt to regard jumping and those who take part in it, if not with actual admiration then at least with some respect.

But an army is only as good as its soldiers and a game as good as the men who play it. Since the war the National Hunt scene has been adorned by many admirable characters men, women and horses alike; among them are three to whom the sport owes so much that in any story of its progress they deserve a chapter to themselves.

They are, in order of appearance on the scene, Lord Mildmay, Fred Winter and Queen Elizabeth the Queen Mother.

Anthony Mildmay's early exploits as an amateur rider—and in particular his luckless experience on Davy Jones—have already been described. After serving throughout the war in the Commandos, the Welsh Guards and, latterly, in the Guards Armoured Division, he and his lifelong friend Peter Cazalet came back to England with one objective in their minds. They had jointly decided to build up at Fairlawne, Cazalet's house in Kent, a stable of jumpers run on the best conceivable lines, to win as many races as possible and, above all, to win the Grand National with Mildmay in the saddle. That last ambition was never to be realized, but in his efforts to achieve it Anthony Mildmay carved for himself a place in the hearts of the racing world which has not, since his death, been filled.

Leading amateur in each of the five seasons from 1945-50 Lord Mildmay (he succeeded to the title on his father's death in 1947) rode 133 winners during that period and had ridden sixty-nine before the war. Six foot two and inevitably handicapped by his height, he was never an elegant rider and never, in a finish, the equal of the best professionals. But the finish isn't everything and, by sheer hard work and dedication Lord Mildmay acquired almost all the other weapons in a first-rate jumping jockey's armoury. He was, from first to last, despite many serious and painful falls, completely fearless. Though, in his own words, 'a born worrier', his worries vanished as the gate went up. Thereafter, cool and supremely determined, he went the shortest way whenever possible and, in the latter part of his career was not easily dislodged.

But it was not these qualities alone—they have after all been possessed by many riders past and present—that endeared him both to the racing public and to the men with whom he rode. To the ordinary racegoer a horse ridden by Lord Mildmay meant one which, whatever happened, was doing its level best to win. They loved him for this and even more for the fact that he, a rich man, was 'having a go'—risking his neck, not for money, not even for glory, but just for the thing he wanted most from life, the joy of riding good horses at speed over fences and hurdles.

It was this mixture of respect, admiration and affection which inspired the cry 'Come on, M'Lord' whenever the famous light blue and white colours were seen with a ghost of a winning chance. Whether they had backed him or not the public loved to see him win. To them he personified all that was best and most honourable in National Hunt racing and, as their regard for him grew over the years, so did the reputation of the sport to which he gave his life.

Lord Mildmay became a member of the National Hunt Committee in 1942 and served as a steward twice, from 1944-7 and from 1949 until his death. He was also elected a member of the Jockey Club in 1947. No conflict ever existed between these positions and his life as an amateur jockey. Those who rode against him, professional and amateur alike, knew him for a hard, determined competitor who gave no quarter and expected none. Incapable of meanness on a horse or off one, he often served as a steward at meetings where he was also riding but would never dream of using in his official capacity knowledge gained in the cut and thrust of a race.

To my infinite regret I never met Lord Mildmay but have talked to those who did in many different walks of life. And no man I ever knew or heard of had more devoted friends or inspired more universal undiluted affection. From them one gets a picture of a natural, unaffected man—the sort who is equally at ease in Windsor Castle or the weighing-room—talking to a viscount or a valet, a steward or a stable-lad.

'A gentleman,' Herbert Tree once said, 'is a man whose courtesy is not regulated by his interests.' By that definition, or by any other, Anthony Mildmay was a gentleman, for his courtesy was unlimited. He treated all those with whom he had to deal on their merits as men, and expecting no favours by virtue of his unique position, asked only to be treated likewise. Though supremely serious about his riding he was in every other way a gay, utterly unselfconscious man whose charm and kindness warmed the hearts of all who knew him.

It was in the 1948 Grand National riding his own great favourite Cromwell that Lord Mildmay came, for the second time, within striking distance of his lifelong dream.

Always a slow beginner, Cromwell was kicked at the start and it wasn't till well into the second circuit that he began to get going in earnest. Then, making ground fast down the long straight that ends at Becher's, he closed steadily on the leaders and, still full of running, was poised by the Canal Turn in a perfect position.

At the start of that season, falling heavily at Folkestone Lord Mildmay had broken his neck and, in at least one race since then, the after-effects of this injury had produced an agonizing cramp which rendered him quite unable to lift his head. And now, when it mattered most, with a mile to go and Cromwell needing all the help he could get, this same disability reasserted itself. From then on Lord Mildmay was able to do little more than sit and hope. Over the last two fences, his head bowed on his chest, he rode virtually blind—and still finished third only six lengths and one length behind Sheila's Cottage and First of the Dandies. In his own opinion—though he never complained—and in that of Peter Cazalet, Cromwell was every bit as unlucky a loser as Davy Jones.

Early the next season Lord Mildmay did at last win a steeple-chase round Aintree—the Grand Sefton on Lecale Prince—and the welcome he received that day bore eloquent witness to the crowd's delight.

Then in the last months of his life he rode, on Cromwell again, perhaps the finest of all his many memorable races. Forty years old at the time, he was already past the age when most National Hunt jockeys, professional or amateur, decide to call it a day. The war had taken nearly six of what should have been the best years of his riding life and yet, at this stage, by common consent, he was a better all-round horseman and jockey than ever before. And anyone who has ridden regularly under National Hunt rules, for however short a time, will appreciate the sheer tough-ness—of mind as well as body—involved in that achievement.

On 21st January, 1950, Cromwell's chief rival in the valuable Prince's Chase at Sandown was Freebooter, one of the best staying 'chasers then in training and certainly best of the post-war Grand National winners.

Going to the Pond, three fences from home at Sandown there is an open space where the flat and hurdle courses branch away uphill. A bold man on a horse sufficiently full of running can get through on the inside here and this was what Jimmy Power on Freebooter tried to do.

But Lord Mildmay, second at the time to Fighting Line (who fell a moment later), saw the danger coming and acted promptly. With every justification he cut Power off before the Pond and Freebooter had to be checked and brought round the outside to challenge. Even so, rallying gamely, he landed first on the flat—but Lord Mildmay had one more card to play. Up the final hill he drove Cromwell for all he was worth and, amid tremendous cheering, got home by a desperately hard-fought neck. It was a victory of which the greatest jockey ever born could reasonably have been proud.

Four months later, on the morning of Friday, 12th May, staying at Mothecombe, his beautiful home in Devonshire, he went down to the beach to bathe, calling at the stables en route to say he would not ride that day. He was never seen alive again and it seems almost certain that the same injury that robbed him of the 1948 Grand National also caused his death.

I cannot do better than end this brief account of the best loved character in National Hunt history by quoting from *The Times* leading article published the day after his memorial service. It finished with these words:

'There never was a harder rider, a better loser or a more popular winner; and although he always valued the race more than the victory and the victory more than the prize, he would not perhaps have disdained the reward he has won—which is a kind of immortality among the English.'

Two years later at Sandown—two years almost to the day after Cromwell's victory in the Prince's Chase—the same horse, now eleven years old and ridden by Bryan Marshall, went out with eleven others to run for the first Mildmay Memorial Chase. And storming up the hill, fighting for all the world as if he knew how much depended on him, Cromwell struggled home in front to win for Lord Mildmay's sister Helen the trophy given by his riding friends. It was a moment in which happiness and sadness were inextricably mingled—a scene entirely worthy of the man it commemorated and one which none who witnessed it will easily forget.

By the force of his personal example Lord Mildmay had lifted National Hunt racing to a position in the English sporting scene it had never occupied before. Had he lived he would only now be fifty-seven years old and his value as a member and steward of the National Hunt Committee would be incalculable. During his lifetime riding understandably occupied a much larger part of his energies than administration, but time would inevitably have altered that. It could never have altered his utter dedication to the best interests of the sport.

Apart from the impact of his career and personality Lord Mildmay left another priceless legacy behind him—one which, in the years since his death, has helped carry the prestige and popularity of jumping to heights unthinkable before the war. For the supremely happy connection between Queen Elizabeth the Queen Mother and National Hunt racing was in no small measure due originally to him.

It was while staying at Windsor Castle for a Royal Ascot meeting that, communicating his own enthusiasm to his hostess, he encouraged the Queen as she then was and her daughter, Princess Elizabeth, to consider owning a jumper.

Lord Mildmay assisted and advised upon this new extension of the Royal interest in racing, and Monaveen, the first horse Peter Cazalet bought for Queen Elizabeth (who gave a half share to her daughter), was an immediate and considerable success.

Then an eight-year-old gelding (by Landscape Hill, sire also of Cromwell), Monaveen won his first race in Princess Elizabeth's colours at Fontwell in October 1949 and then, after finishing second to Freebooter in the Grand Sefton, was an appropriate and enormously popular winner of the first Queen Elizabeth Chase at Hurst Park.

In this valuable race, one of the many imaginative contributions made to jumping by Sir John Crocker Bulteel, Monaveen was ridden by Tony Grantham, then Peter Cazalet's stable jockey. Freebooter was again in the field but Hurst Park did not suit him anything like so well as Aintree and, making much of the running, Monaveen turned the tables in no uncertain fashion.

After this and another victory on the same course in February, hopes were high that year of a Royal Grand National. Monaveen, running freely as usual, led to the fourteenth fence (one before the Chair), but he blundered so badly there that Tony Grantham hung for an awful moment 'betwixt the stirrup and the ground'. In fact, as the poem goes on, 'mercy he asked and mercy he found', for with a nice mixture of patriotism and sportsmanship Arthur Thompson riding Wot No Sun, reached out and hauled him back into the plate. But this experience had doubtless knocked a lot of steam out of Monaveen and, a tired horse from Becher's second time round, he could only plug on to finish fifth in the end, far behind his old rival Freebooter.

Monaveen's career was to end in tragedy for, trying to win a second Queen Elizabeth Chase the following season, he fell at the

water jump, broke a leg and had to be destroyed. He had, however, already given his owners a tantalizing first taste of the
pleasures of National Hunt racing and for that as well as his
courage and speed he deserves to be gratefully remembered.

Only two months before he died Lord Mildmay won a division
of the Broadway Novices Chase at Cheltenham on a brilliant
French-bred five-year-old called Manicou. The winner of five
other races that season, Manicou was passed on after his owner's
death to Queen Elizabeth the Queen Mother, whose now famous
colours he was the first horse ever to carry.

It was on Boxing Day 1950 that Manicou won the last and greatest
of his victories when, in the King George VI Chase at Kempton
Park, he beat the subsequent Gold Cup winner, Silver Fame.

Because Tony Grantham, injured in Monaveen's fatal fall, was
still out of action Manicou was ridden at Kempton by Bryan
Marshall. For a five-year-old it was a remarkable achievement to
beat so good and experienced a jumper as Silver Fame and John
Hislop, describing the race, gave it as his opinion, that 'Manicou
is the best steeplechase horse in training and Marshall the best
steeplechase jockey riding'.

For the latter, incidentally, riding in the Royal colours used to
pose a special problem. Like those of many National Hunt jockeys
Marshall's own teeth had long ago become casualties to the
hazards of the game and under normal circumstances he used to
remove their false replacements before going out to ride. But no
man wants to face his Queen with a toothless grin and Marshall
hit upon the solution of keeping a special 'Royal' set which after
mounting he would hand to the stable lad leading him out. Then
if excitement or exasperation did not cause the lad to drop them
in the mud he could rearm himself in time to enter the unsaddling
enclosure with a suitable Pepsodent smile!

Having inherited from her father the very considerable Royal
flat-race stable the young Queen soon chose to devote herself
primarily (and with great success) to that branch of the sport,
leaving National Hunt racing to her mother. The second jumper
the Queen Mother owned entirely herself was M'as-tu Vu, a
tough consistent French-bred; and the third was the horse whose
tragic and mysterious fate was to earn for his owner the heartfelt
sympathy and admiration of millions all over the world. His name
of course was Devon Loch.

Bought in Ireland from Colonel Stephen Hill-Dillon, for whom
he had won a two-mile 'bumpers' flat race, Devon Loch, by
Devonian out of a mare by Loch Lomond, was a fine strong

'chasing type with a bold and honest head. Arriving at Fairlawne
as a five-year-old, he ran well though without success in three
hurdle races and then, first time over fences at Hurst Park, was
second only four lengths behind Mont Tremblant. Since Mont
Tremblant won the Gold Cup easily two months later this was,
to say the least, the performance of a horse with a future.

But that future was soon to be rudely interrupted. In his first
and only race next season Devon Loch damaged a tendon in
one of his forelegs and had to be fired. More important he had to
be rested—and Peter Cazalet, recognizing in him the raw material
of greatness was quite prepared to wait.

His patience and skill were rewarded for when after nearly two
years' convalescence Devon Loch reappeared in 1954-5, it was to
win two of the season's top novice chases. And in one of these he
gave Linwell, winner of the 1957 Cheltenham Gold Cup, 12 lbs
and a twelve lengths beating. So, in the autumn of 1955, Peter
Cazalet once again mapped out a programme with Aintree and
the National as its aim and object. After winning twice before
Christmas Devon Loch was held up in his work by a hard winter,
but, though not fully fit, finished third in the National Hunt
Handicap Chase at Cheltenham. He was staying on like a lion,
the National was only two weeks off and, at Fairlawne, whence
Davy Jones and Cromwell had gone in vain to Aintree, it seemed
the luck might, at last, be on the turn.

The 1956 Grand National was not televised and, in perfect
weather a crowd of almost pre-war size assembled at Aintree on
24th March. It included the Queen, Queen Elizabeth the Queen
Mother, Princess Margaret, the Princess Royal and a group of
distinguished Russian statesmen, notably Mr Malenkov, whose
impressions may, for all I know, have inspired the abortive Soviet
challenge five years later.

Although Quare Times who had won the year before was withdrawn at the eleventh hour, two previous winners, Early Mist and
Royal Tan, were in the field. So were M'as-tu Vu and Sundew
who was to win a year later, but in all Devon Loch had only
twenty-eight rivals—fewer than usual for a National.

Dick Francis, who had been Peter Cazalet's stable jockey since
1953, knew from experience that despite the risks involved in a
slow beginning he must give Devon Loch time to settle down.
But in fact, so magnificently did his mount jump from start to
finish that, gaining ground time after time in the air he was
always going easily on the bit.

By the Canal Turn second time round Devon Loch had moved

up close behind the leader Armorial III and for the first time in
his life Francis found himself in the rare and unforgettable position of having actually to steady a horse with a mile to go in a
Grand National. Beside him E.S.B., Eagle Lodge, and Gentle
Moya were all being hard ridden, the rest were out of it one way
or another, and, jumping the last fence as perfectly as all the
previous twenty-nine Devon Loch landed in front, full of running,
with the world almost literally at his feet.

What happened next is history. Halfway up the long run-in
Dave Dick on E.S.B. had dropped his hands, content with second
place. Devon Loch's relentless stride had never faltered and towards him from the crowded stands there rolled a thunderous
roar of welcome like nothing ever heard before or since on an
English racecourse.

Is it possible I wonder that the very rapture which greeted the
royal 'chaser's apparently certain triumph was also the cause of
his defeat? Poor Dick Francis, searching in vain for another explanation is inclined to think so.

In earlier races, when winning on M'as-tu Vu, he had been
amazed by the volume of cheers a Royal victory produces. Now
it was the same thing multiplied a thousandfold and Francis
believes that Devon Loch, pricking his ears as he passed the water
jump, was so startled by the tidal wave of sound engulfing him
that he hesitated, lost his footing and fell.

None of the many other possible explanations—a mistaken
attempt to jump the water, a heart attack or a sudden onset of
muscular cramp—seems to fit the facts much better. Devon Loch,
though tired, was not exhausted. He recovered almost immediately,
never suffered from a defective heart and was far too good a
jumper to fall at a 'phantom' fence.

No one will ever know the answer. All we do know is what the
records say—that as Devon Loch and his heartbroken rider
walked sadly back Dave Dick and E.S.B. went on to win from
Gentle Moya and Royal Tan.

We know too the calm and wonderful sportsmanship with
which Queen Elizabeth the Queen Mother bore her bitter disappointment. For Francis and for Peter Cazalet—who for the third
time had seen the prize he wanted most in all the world snatched
from him by blind chance—she had only words of sympathy. For
the winning owner Mrs Leonard Carner congratulations, and for
the world at large, a smiling face. 'What a woman,' we said—
and, in victory and defeat alike have been saying it ever since
with all our hearts.

For although no one could have blamed Queen Elizabeth if this agonizing experience had sickened her for ever of National Hunt racing it had, in fact, precisely the opposite effect. Almost immediately she gave Peter Cazalet orders to buy more jumpers and since that ghastly day at Aintree her enthusiasm has never wavered.

It has also, I'm delighted to say, been rewarded. Magnificently served by her trainers, chiefly Peter Cazalet but also Jack O'Donoghue, and by her jockeys who down the years have included Tony Grantham, Bryan Marshall, Dick Francis, Arthur Freeman, Bill Rees, David Mould and several others, Queen Elizabeth has also had many good brave horses to carry her colours.

Double Star II, a gallant all-rounder full, at his best, of fire and courage, won her no less than seventeen races. The Rip, Laffy, Gay Record and Super Fox have each done more than their share and Makaldar, quite conceivably best of them all, is still going strong with at the time of writing eleven victories to his credit.

On 20th October, 1964 Gay Record at Folkestone became the Queen Mother's 100th winner under National Hunt rules while both in 1961-2 and 1964-5 she won more races than any other owner. But these are mere statistics. They tell nothing of the pleasure and encouragement Her Majesty's presence has given to men and women in every branch of National Hunt racing. In 1954 she and the Queen became patrons of the National Hunt Committee but if patronage suggests a patronizing attitude there never was a more misleading word.

For the Queen Mother does not merely follow jumping, she lives it. Whenever official duties permit she comes in person to see her horses run and, however foul the weather, is there in the paddock to wish them luck and afterwards to congratulate or console. Many a shivering jockey down the course with his heart in his boots at the start of a three-mile chase has suddenly been made to feel that it is all worth while by the sight of that radiant, smiling face.

For jockeys, owners, trainers and stable-lads alike her charm and knowledge of the game make it hard to remember they are talking to a Queen. To the public who watch and cheer and back her horses she stands, as Lord Mildmay did, for all that's best in jumping. If one day a Royal horse succeeds where Devon Loch so gloriously failed he had better be fitted with ear-plugs, for the cheers that greet him will waken the dead.

On 27th December, 1947 Lord Mildmay won the Corinthian Handicap Chase at Kempton Park on Cromwell and, as he changed to go out for that race, it is doubtful whether he took much notice of a stocky uniformed figure walking somewhat apprehensively into the weighing-room. Thirty minutes later he must have noticed—and doubtless appreciated—the timing with which a young jockey, claiming the full 7 lbs allowance, brought an old horse called Carton up from behind to win the Kenton Handicap Chase. But neither he nor anyone else, unless endowed with second sight, can have realized the significance of this moment in the history of National Hunt racing. For the jockey's name was Frederick Thomas Winter. Then an officer on leave, shortly to be demobbed from the Parachute Regiment, he had ridden for the first time under National Hunt rules the day before. Carton (who nine years earlier had given an apprentice called Dave Dick his first success on the flat) was Fred's first ride in a steeplechase and his first jumping winner.

On 11th April, 1964 Fred Winter, c.b.e., walked into another weighing-room at Cheltenham. This time, when the valet pulled off his muddy boots it was for ever—and this time, although Lord Mildmay was not there to see, everyone else took a very great deal of notice.

For in the seventeen years between Fred Winter had ridden more than ten thousand miles over fences and hurdles. He had won 929 races in England, France, America and Ireland, had suffered over 300 falls, broken most of the major bones in his body —and become by far the best known figure in British National Hunt racing.

And during all that time, in victory or defeat, on the good days or the bad, on a horse or on the ground, he had never once reflected anything but credit on the sport. Four times champion jockey, honoured by the Queen, respected by all, he went out as a champion should—at the top—and left National Hunt racing as much the poorer by his going as it had been the richer for his presence.

No success worth having was ever lightly gained and Fred Winter's career had at first been clouded by doubt, disaster, fear and pain. In his fifth ride, he dislocated his shoulder and at least one observer swears (Fred doesn't deny it) that the injury was caused not by the fall itself but by diving under the rails to avoid a rival's hooves! Then, after only eleven rides, falling at Wye on an animal with the uninspiring name of Tugboat Minnie he broke three vertebrae in his back.

In the painful months of convalescence that followed Fred came within an ace of giving up. Courage, they say, is like a bank account. You can draw only so many cheques before your body calls a halt and Fred Winter's account was, in a sense, overdrawn before it was opened. The measure of the man is that, once he decided to go on, no cheque drawn on it was ever dishonoured.

He had ridden briefly on the flat before the war and, increasing weight having put a stop to that, Fred was in his early days more a jockey than a horseman—and acquired a reputation, only partly deserved, for insecurity over fences. Anyone who ever watched a film of Sundew winning the 1957 Grand National knows how completely that tendency, if indeed it ever really existed, was eradicated over the years.

And in any case, secure or not, discerning observers soon began to notice the combination of great physical strength and a highly developed will to win that became the hallmark of Fred Winter's riding. Among the first to do so was Captain Ryan Price. In November 1949, then training a small string at Lavant in Sussex, he asked Fred to ride for him and the association formed that day flourished without interruption (or a single serious disagreement) for fifteen brilliantly successful years.

This was the first break and increasing opportunity brought with it an ever-increasing flood of winners. In 1950-1 Fred Winter finished fourth in the jockeys' list. In 1951-2 he was second, only nineteen behind the champion Tim Molony and, next season (his sixth) he headed the list with 121 winners, a record unbeaten to this day.

He had forty-one falls that winter—and was never sick or sorry for more than a few hours. Going down to Newton Abbot on the first day of the new season the future must have looked set fair— but the wayward Fates who govern jumping jockeys' lives were laughing up their sleeves. At the very first fence of the first race Fred fell—and broke his leg so badly that, for a whole year, there could be no question of his riding.

Even for a champion, to get going again after such a lay-off, is never easy. The Jeremiahs are only too ready to say 'he's gone, he'll never be the same' and at that crucial stage one owner did, for a while, refuse to let Fred ride his horses. But he was soon in a minority of one. Beaten by a whisker for the title by Tim Molony that season, Fred was champion again for each of the next three and in 1957 won his first Grand National on Sundew—leading almost throughout, surviving several horrible mistakes and driving his gallant exhausted companion up the long run-in with the tireless energy no man in my memory has ever been able to excel.

To those who never saw him in action Fred Winter's peculiar

greatness is not easy to describe. He had all the normal qualities a jockey needs—courage, good hands, a cool head, judgment of pace and tactical skill—but it was above all strength in the finish which singled him out from his contemporaries.

There is in my mind for instance, a picture of Fred on a little hurdler called Pouding one January afternoon at Sandown. Going to the last the favourite Dandy Scot is in the lead and Pouding, two lengths behind him, is only gradually closing the gap—hard ridden already for half a mile and apparently near the end of his tether. Somehow, with what seems the last ounce of his strength he lands on the flat in front but halfway up the run-in Dandy Scot comes again. For ninety-nine men out of a hundred the race would be over—but Fred Winter is the hundredth. Head bowed and shoulders hunched, legs almost motionless—but grinding inwards like the jaws of a steel trap—he seems to sink for a moment into his horse. There's no great flourish—only a relentless rhythmic punch and drive. The whip though waved is hardly used, but suddenly with yards to go Pouding is tossed forwards like a leaf before an autumn gale. His head's in front, the prize is won—and another race goes in the record books, a victory where for any normal man defeat would have been no disgrace.

'Come on Fred', the words so often shouted till our throat were sore, bring back a hundred memories of moments such as this. And, to those lucky enough to have been there, they bring back above all that steaming overheated day in June of 1962 when, on Madame Kilian Hennessy's Mandarin, Fred Winter won the Grand Steeplechase de Paris. They bring back the unbelieving horror with which, in the stands, we realized halfway through the twisting four-mile marathon that Fred had neither brakes nor steering. The rubber bit in Mandarin's mouth had broken long before—at the fourth of the thirty strange and varied obstacles that make Auteuil so totally unlike an English steeplechase.

From then on with the snaffle useless under Mandarin's neck, Fred had only balance, the strength of his legs and the little horse's own good sense to keep them in the race. To their eternal credit the French jockeys never took advantage of his plight— some even helped—and only once, just before the final turn, did Mandarin look like losing his way. There, with no rails to guide him—only a marker passed with equal ease on either side in front—he headed right instead of left and Fred had to wrench him back, throwing his whole weight sideways like a racing cyclist on a hairpin bend.

We know now that the awful strain of that manœuvre was too great for the tendons of Mandarin's forelegs—and what followed is as much a tale of his unquenchable courage as of his rider's skill.

Round the bend, forced to sit still for fear of running wide, Fred could not make a yard of ground. The leaders turned for home six lengths in front, the Bullfinch loomed ahead, and as Mandarin crashed through it like a tank we English in the stands began to scream our heads off. 'Come on Fred'—and on he came to land over the last fence, miraculously in front. Every yard of the long run-in must have been agony. A Frenchman, Lumino, was gaining stride by stride and as with a last titanic heave Fred lifted Mandarin across the line we did not even know if they had won.

But all *was* well and, as I wrote that day, no man or woman at Auteuil could doubt that they had seen a feat of courage, skill and horsemanship never excelled on this or any other racecourse.

Forty minutes later Fred Winter was back in the same crowded hectic unsaddling enclosure on Beaver II, having just won the Grande Course de Haies for four-year-olds, and it was only after-wards that we learnt in full the odds he had overcome. For, wasting hard to do 9 st 10 lbs on Beaver, he had gone to the Turkish Baths in London the day before and, attacked there by a volcanic stomach upheaval, spent most of the night either in the lavatory or sweating, sleepless on his bed. Half a bottle of champagne (the wasting jockey's friend) did something to repair the damage next morning but Fred arrived in Paris—in an atmosphere not far removed from the Turkish baths he had just left—feeling like a bit of chewed up string.

Sitting in the Bois de Boulogne that night—a hero not just to his English friends but to all Paris too—he may well have reflected that the frightened man who broke his back on Tugboat Minnie had come a long, long way. The milestones on that road are far too numerous to be recorded here. They include two Grand Nationals (Sundew and Kilmore), two Cheltenham Gold Cups (Saffron Tartan and Mandarin), two Champion Hurdles (Clair Soleil and Fare Time), three King George VI Chases (Halloween twice and Saffron Tartan), the Grand Steeplechase de Paris, the Galway Plate and the New York Turf Writers' Cup, a hurdle race at Belmont Park in which the winner broke the course record by several seconds!

But Fred Winter's story is much more than that of just a great and supremely successful jockey. Far more important is the indelible imprint left by his character and code of behaviour on the sport in general and on his brother riders in particular. Even when no longer champion he was universally acknowledged among those who rode against him as the leader of his profession—and his modesty and kindness killed stone dead the sort of jealousy that lesser men so often feel towards the great.

I remember one day, as an unknown amateur, riding a winner at Chepstow. Fred can hardly have known my name—but he knew I'd broken a collar-bone not long before and, as we pulled up, he said with a broad grin: 'Well done John—a great come-back.' In fact, of course, I had precious little to come back to—but those words made my day and many others, I know, have been given the same cause to feel a heart-warming glow of pride and gratitude.

One final memory is of a day at Newbury in Fred's last season. He rode four winners, two of which few other men would have got home, and as he came back into the changing-room a cheer went up in which delight, respect, yes, even love, were mingled.

Most people would agree, I think, that the general standard of National Hunt jockeyship is higher nowadays than at any previous time. For this and for the wonderful spirit of friendly rivalry, hard but fair, that exists in the English weighing-room, Fred Winter deserves the lion's share of credit. He set the mark at which all others aim. No one has yet achieved it, perhaps no one ever will; but from the attempt to do so nothing but good has come.

Already established as a successful trainer, with a Grand National winner in his very first season, Fred will, I sincerely hope, adorn the game for many years to come. But when he hung up his boots, for many something irreplaceable was lost. The words are hackneyed but their meaning true: 'we shall not see his like again'.

IV

Looking back, in 1966, down the twenty-one years that separate the Grand National victories of Lovely Cottage and Anglo it is not hard to produce some account of the world's greatest steeple-chase during that post-war period. There are enough tales of triumph and disaster to fill a book, let alone a couple of chapters. To look back is one thing, to look forward quite another. We have already seen two 'last' Grand Nationals and there may be more to come. So should this chapter take the form of an obituary? Can it really be that in this strange eventful history the final page will soon be turned?

I don't propose to take that gloomy view but the fact has to be faced that Aintree's future does hang in the balance. And Aintree

by common consent *is* the Grand National. It could never be the
same on any other course and the stewards of the National Hunt
Committee have expressly stated that no pale transplanted shadow
of the real thing will ever be allowed.

The long-drawn legal battle between Messrs Topham, who own
Aintree, and Lord Sefton, who sold it to them in 1949, has now
been decided in the House of Lords. But it seems unlikely that even
their Lordships' decision, however irrevocable in law, will in fact
be final. Probably the ultimate answer lies not in a law court, not
even in Parliament or No. 10 Downing Street, but in the hearts
of men and women all over the world. If we, the sporting public,
are prepared to stand aside while Aintree and the National die,
well, they *will* die, and the ghosts of Lottery, Jem Mason and
Captain Becher will surely haunt our dreams.

But is that really likely to happen? A more optimistic view is
that under all the arguments, recriminations and petty personal
motives there exists an enormous fund of enthusiasm for the Grand
National which, if properly channelled, would sweep away the
doubters and launch Aintree on a new, more prosperous era. How
best this can be done remains an unsolved problem. But if it isn't
done, if factories and bungalows are really to mushroom where so
many famous feats have been accomplished, then something priceless and irreplaceable will be lost, a part of England's sporting
heritage which she can ill afford to lose.

The present plight in which Aintree finds itself is due to many
things, not all of them avoidable. A certain rigidity and lack of
imagination on the part of the management in general and of
Mrs Mirabel Topham in particular may or may not have been a
contributory cause. All English racecourses have gone through a
difficult period since the war and Aintree's problems have been
worse than most. Mrs Topham has not been able to overcome
them, but until someone else succeeds where she failed it is both
pointless and unjust to blame her.

To an outsider, nevertheless, it must seem strange that over
a period in which National Hunt racing as a whole has gone
steadily from strength to strength, its most famous attraction has
gone equally steadily downhill. But the explanation is not far to
seek.

We've already seen how television and the sponsored race came
hand in hand and how both, on balance, were of value to the
sport. At Aintree by contrast, one was at best a mixed blessing,
while the other was the germ of what may yet prove a mortal
sickness. For, by providing less hazardous and almost equally

The Master of Aintree—Freebooter with J. Power up winning the
1950 Grand National
'Aubrey's up! the money's down!' Cottage Rake with A. Brabazon up
winning his third Gold Cup in 1950

The 1951 Champion Hurdle with Hatton's Grace (T. Molony) jumping the last flight and National Spirit (D. Dillon) about to fall

Cheltenham 1951. Lord Bicester's Silver Fame (M. Molony) beating Freebooter (J. Power) on his favourite course

attractive alternatives, the big sponsored races have gradually undermined the Grand National's absolute pre-war supremacy. They kept the best staying 'chasers busily employed on Park courses and, once given the choice, more and more owners shrank from asking a good horse to carry big weights in the chancy free-for-all of a National.

And in the second decade of the post-war period, spurred on by the need to compete with sponsored handicaps, the great condition races, the Gold Cup and the King George VI Chase, grew steadily in value and prestige. Both, and particularly the Gold Cup, were true steeplechasing championships in a way no handicap can ever be. Of twenty post-war Gold Cup winners only five have even run in the Grand National and of those only two, Prince Regent and Mont Tremblant, managed to gain a place.

But although progressively deprived of great names and the glamour that goes with them, the National has remained the most valuable prize in the National Hunt Calendar. It has also remained—and still remains—the summit of almost every jockey's and trainer's ambition. There has never been any shortage of runners or of men whose dream it is to ride the winner. If that were enough the great race would still be flourishing. But a racecourse, like a theatre, depends not only on the quality and quantity of its actors, but also, more heavily, on the size of the audience that pays to watch them. And once the post-war boom began to wane, so did the Aintree crowds, both at the minor meetings and on National day itself.

For this sad phenomenon many factors were in part responsible but television must take its share of the blame. The Grand National course has never been ideal for spectators. Even when visibility is good, far too much of the action takes place out of sight of all but the most powerful binoculars. Once the B.B.C. developed their coverage to its present high standard many who had hitherto struggled (and paid) for a view, if they were lucky, of four or five fences found that, by staying at home, they could watch the National in hitherto undreamt of detail. And, not surprisingly, a large proportion preferred this to the expense, trouble and, all too often, discomfort of visiting the course itself.

Needless to say television also brought revenue to Aintree (volumes could be written about Mrs Topham's battles to get what she considered her due) but the damage, in this case, almost certainly outweighed the advantage. Aintree had always relied on a huge attendance at the Grand National meeting in March. Now, with even that golden goose laying fewer and fewer eggs, its subsidiary meetings, both flat, mixed and National Hunt have become increasingly unsuccessful. For want of prize-money the flat-racing, once a top-class feature of the Jockey Club year, has degenerated into boring mediocrity.

In 1953 the Mildmay course, designed as a stepping stone between conventional steeplechases and the Grand National itself was used for the first time and, in the same year a motor-racing track was built. Neither, alas, was able to halt the downward trend in Aintree's fortunes.

The Mildmay fences, smaller replicas of those on the National course (though without the drops that are their most important feature), seemed a sensible idea at the time. For various reasons however, they have never been popular with jockeys or trainers. Built on a small rectangular circuit inside the big course they are a severe test for an inexperienced jumper and, as less hazardous alternatives multiplied elsewhere the risk of damage to a promising young horse's confidence seemed, to many trainers, particularly in the South, more considerable than the incentives.

And so the sad story went on until, in 1964, Mrs Topham announced to a horrified racing world that she could no longer keep Aintree going as a racecourse. Her intention was, and, as I write, still is, to sell the property as building land to Capital and Counties Ltd. But when in 1949 Lord Sefton sold Aintree to Messrs Topham he imposed a covenant that the place should not be used for purposes other than racing or agriculture. The House of Lords, reversing two previous decisions, has now held that that covenant was not binding, but no planning permission to build at Aintree has yet been given by the local authorities concerned.

So there for the moment the future must be left—in doubt and danger but not yet in despair. Whatever the shortcomings of its home and despite the decline in class among its contestants, the Grand National still stands high among the worlds' great sporting spectacles. Nothing has happened since the war to alter that.

Nor was there any sign of things to come in the huge crowd that gathered at Aintree in 1946 for the first post-war National. Then and for several years thereafter the stands were as full as they have ever been and it is perhaps permissible to wonder whether, had the profits and goodwill forthcoming in those days been more wisely used, Aintree would ever have come to its present pass.

Irish 'chasers and those who had been trained in Ireland during the war understandably tended to dominate their English rivals in 1946 and Mr J. V. Rank's Prince Regent started a red-hot favourite that year to follow in Golden Miller's footsteps and complete the Gold Cup–Grand National double.

Then eleven years old, Prince Regent might well, but for the war, have equalled not only that but some of the Miller's other feats as well. For several seasons he had towered above his Irish contemporaries and until the coming of Arkle his trainer, Tom Dreaper, considered him, with the possible exception of the brilliant but ill-fated Royal Approach, the best horse ever to grace his famous yard. Ridden by Tim Hyde who had won on Workman in 1939, Prince Regent looked for most of the 1946 Grand National like living up in full to his tremendous reputation. Storming into a clear lead when Limestone Edward blundered at Valentine's second time round, he was constantly plagued by loose horses from then on (only six of the twenty-nine runners finished), but jumped the last fence alone and started up the long run-in a good four lengths ahead of his closest rival, Lovely Cottage.

But Prince Regent was carrying 12 st 5 lbs—25 lbs more than Lovely Cottage; and now once more the sad old truth was hammered home that, in the last dragging mile of a Grand National, every pound over twelve stone counts double if not treble.

As Lovely Cottage's rider Captain Bobby Petre said afterwards, Hyde had been forced to ride at least three finishes to avoid interference before the last fence—and these repeated efforts were too much for even Prince Regent's tremendous strength. As he faltered halfway up the straight, Lovely Cottage forged dourly past to win by four lengths and in the end Jack Finlay deprived the exhausted favourite of second place.

Bred in Ireland by Mr L. Hyde and a winner there of the Conyngham Cup over banks at Punchestown, Lovely Cottage had been advertised for sale at a price of £2,000 with another thousand to be paid 'when (not if) he wins a Grand National'. Doubtless impressed by such confidence, Mr John Morant bought the eight-year-old and sent him to Tommy Rayson, to whose distinguished career as a trainer, described in an earlier chapter, his victory was a notable climax.

Captain Petre, who until Tommy Smith in 1965 was the only amateur to win a post-war National, was thirty-three years old at the time and just demobbed from the Scots Guards. He had been at Sandhurst in the vintage years (vintage from a riding if not from a military point of view) of Frank Furlong and Fulke Walwyn and won the 1938 National Hunt Chase on St George II. His subsequent career as a trainer was, alas, terminated prematurely when one of his horses was found to have been doped but Captain Petre is now back on the racecourse and I remember taking it as a hopeful omen when he wished me luck going out to ride Carrickbeg in 1963.

From the point of view of weather the 1946–7 National Hunt season was one of the worst on record. Torrential rain and flooding followed a prolonged freeze-up and altogether sixty-seven days were lost. The main races of the National Hunt meeting had to be postponed till April and, although Aintree escaped the general holocaust by the skin of its teeth, not many of the fifty-seven starters who lined up on 29th March (a Saturday for the first time, by Government request) can have been exactly trained to the hour.

The usually well-drained turf was all but waterlogged, it rained throughout the race and the fact that, of sixteen runners for the Becher Chase two days before, not one had got round without being remounted was hardly calculated to produce an air of joyful expectation in the weighing-room.

Nor can most of the spectators have much enjoyed their day. Wet and cold, they stood peering hopefully through a thick curtain of mist; precisely the sort of conditions, in fact, which, with the coming of television, made a seat at one's own fireside seem so attractive.

Despite his failure in 1946 and the 12 st 7 lbs on his back Prince Regent again started favourite—and again ran a heroic race to be fourth. But when, after the long agonizing wait which, in these circumstances, makes seconds seem like hours, the first grey shape loomed out of the murk by Anchor Bridge it was seen to be that of a small horse wearing a huge sheepskin noseband and ridden by a jockey whose colours were unfamiliar to the vast majority of watchers. His name was Caughoo and pitching hazardously over the last fence he scampered home twenty lengths ahead of his fellow Irishman, Lough Conn, who had made much of the early running. Kami, ridden by that great amateur rider and highly professional writer Mr John Hislop, stayed on to pass the tiring Prince Regent and take third place.

Owned by Mr. J. McDowell and trained by his brother, Caughoo had won two Ulster Grand Nationals and never fell throughout his career. Looking back and considering that, trained on Portmarnock sands, he was probably one of the fittest horses in the race it seems surprising that he started a 100–1 outsider.

Of E. Dempsey who rode him not much has since been heard in England, but I believe that someone was once unwise enough to make in his presence the ignoble and totally unjustified suggestion

that Caughoo had stopped somewhere out in the fog and only re-
joined the field as they came round a second time. Dempsey, they
say, treated his accuser, as he richly deserved, with a punch on the
nose that Caughoo himself could not have bettered. And who
shall blame him?

Prince Regent ran in one more Grand National in 1948 (he
was carried out by a loose horse at Becher's second time round)
and, with Easter Hero, must be counted among the best horses
never to win one. He went on running till the age of fourteen when,
ridden by Bryan Marshall at Lingfield, he was still good enough
to be preferred in the betting to Cromwell, then an eight-year-old
in his prime. Prince Regent fell that day and was at last retired.

His chief importance in the post-war Grand National story is
probably that the lesson of his two gallant failures was not lost on
owners and trainers. They had seen a great horse run himself into
the ground on two occasions under 'impossible' weights—and,
many of them, not surprisingly, refused in future years to ask of
their own favourites a comparable question.

The 1948 Grand National has already been referred to—but
Cromwell's was not the only hard luck story involved. For Eddie
Reavey will always be convinced that, but for taking the wrong
turn after the second last, he would have won easily on Mr Norman
Gee's Zahia. Walking round on the morning of the race Reavey
had seen the rails in position for the first circuit—leading, that is,
from the last fence to the Chair. Not realizing that they are moved
back after the field has passed first time round, he concluded that
the finish must run to the *right* of the water jump—over a fence that
was in fact only used in those days for one of the minor races.

And so, coming on to the racecourse that afternoon, hard on the
heels of the leader, First of the Dandies, poor Reavey jumped the
second last and, going to win his race pulled right—away from the
last. 'I was only cantering', he says, 'and First of the Dandies was
out on his feet. I must have won, no question.'

He is probably right; and ever since the course has been railed
to prevent such a mistake. But what might have been does not pay
training bills so Zahia must join Cromwell, Davy Jones and all the
many others robbed by sheer bad luck of the chance that seldom
comes twice in a lifetime.

First of the Dandies is not quite eligible for the hard luck club,
but belongs to another, of which Purple Silk and Carrickbeg are
the most recent numbers. For he, like them, was always winning
while there was a fence to be jumped and was only beaten by the
featureless 494 yards of Aintree's long run-in.

Trained by the former champion jockey, Gerry Wilson (who had won on Golden Miller in 1934 and was never to come so close again as he did this day), First of the Dandies had led from half-way jumping superbly and, after Zahia's unexpected departure, landed on the flat still several lengths in front. But there, without the spur of a fence ahead, his stride began to shorten and Sheila's Cottage who had never been far behind stayed on doggedly to wear him down a hundred yards from the line.

A nine-year-old mare by Cottage (sire also of Workman, Lovely Cottage and Cottage Rake, and the outstanding jumping stallion of the day,) Sheila's Cottage had previously shown herself a safe conveyance with abundant stamina but so little speed that she started at 50–1. She was the first of three National winners trained by Neville Crump whose jovial Falstaffian figure and tremendous enthusiasm have been such a feature of National Hunt racing since the war, mainly in the North but also in many successful Southern forays. No trainer puts more of his heart and soul (and voice) behind his horses and it is no surprise to hear that as Sheila's Cottage passed the post Crump's hat was flung high in the air, never to be recovered.

Arthur Thompson who rode Sheila's Cottage (and won again on Teal in 1952) was for many years after the war the best and most successful jockey riding principally in the North. A tall Irishman with a hawk-like profile which might, in later days, have got him the part of James Bond, he had a notable preference for being in front and, once there, was desperately hard to overtake.

Dave Dick tells the story of how, coming into Fulke Walwyn's house one night he heard a somewhat heated conversation between the trainer and his stable jockey Bryan Marshall, who had got beaten that day by making too much use of a fancied horse. That, anyway, was Walwyn's view and he expressed it forcefully as follows: 'When I want Arthur Thompson I'll something well get him!'

Many did want Thompson, and those for whom he rode were seldom disappointed. After his retirement he trained for a while but had little luck—in striking contrast to Eddie Reavey who now controls a small but extremely successful string in Berkshire and won the 1965 Nunthorpe Stakes with Polyfoto. So fate does, just occasionally, repay its debts.

Of the beaten horses in 1948 the most distinguished was Happy Home who, trained by Walwyn and owned by Miss Paget, finished fourth with 11 st 12 lbs on his back. His heroic struggle against Cottage Rake in that year's Gold Cup will be described later.

The 1949 race produced an even bigger surprise for the winner, Mr W. F. Williamson's Russian Hero, had not only turned a somersault last time out before the National but was also thought barely to stay three miles let alone four and a half. Like many others, however, he had the sense to realize that the great Aintree fences are not to be trifled with and jumped them so well that his suspect stamina was more than adequate.

Ridden by Larry McMorrow, the high watermark of whose career this was, he won easily from Lord Bicester's Roimond, a massive chestnut typical of the wonderful type of 'chaser which bore the famous black, gold and red colours with such distinction in the post-war years. Lord Bicester was, alas, never to realize his lifelong dream of winning a National and Roimond, who carried 11 st 12 lbs, came closer than any of his other horses to achieving it.

Russian Hero was trained by George Owen, a modest charming man who, beside turning out a steady stream of winners from his Cheshire yard, has given three champion riders, Dick Francis, Tim Brookshaw and Stan Mellor, their early chances and experience. He did the same for Stephen Davenport, leading amateur in 1963/4 and now a successful professional—and of modern trainers only Bob Turnell has anything like so good a record as a guide and mentor of jumping jockeys.

The 1950 Grand National was memorable for several reasons. It was the last in which Lord Mildmay was to ride, Monaveen carried Princess Elizabeth's colours in it for the first time—and the winner, Mrs L. Brotherton's Freebooter, was the best horse round Aintree of the post-war era. Then nine years old and at the height of his powers, Freebooter had already won the Champion Chase and Grand Sefton and was in fact unbeaten over the big fences. If there is such a thing as an 'Aintree type' he fitted that description perfectly—a powerful deep-chested, short-legged bay by Steel-Point bred in Co Waterford, bought first as an unbroken three-year-old for 620 gns and two years later sold to Mrs Brotherton for 3,000 gns.

With 11 st 11 lbs on his back and ridden by Jimmy Power, Freebooter started joint favourite with Roimond and at the Chair, after one circuit, came within an ace of blotting his copybook. Standing too far back from the biggest fence on the course he crashed headlong through it and, though too strong and well-balanced to fall, shot Power up between his ears. For an awful moment the tough little Irishman who had lost both his stirrups struggled like a boy on a greasy pole to get back. But then, by a combination of luck, horsemanship and sheer tenacity, all was well.

Cloncarrig, an almost equally fine powerful type of 'chaser who used to take a tremendous hold, went clear at Valentine's and, round the long bend to the second last, still sitting with a double handful, his rider Bob Turnell felt as confident as any man can be of victory.

Then close behind, he heard the thud of hoofbeats and, looking sideways, saw the one sight he least wanted to see—Mrs Brotherton's colours and Freebooter's sturdy determined head. Cloncarrig saw them too and, quickening to meet the favourite's challenge, misjudged his take-off at the second last, hit it hard and toppled over. What would certainly have been an epic finish became a triumphal procession and although Turnell is convinced to this day that Cloncarrig was going the better, Freebooter finished so full of running that no one can say for sure what the outcome would have been.

The winning trainer Bobby Renton was and still is one of the most popular and respected members of his profession. In a career spanning fifty years he has saddled the winners of every steeplechase at Aintree and his cheerful attitude to life is demonstrated by the fact that, when over seventy, he still used to have at least one ride as an amateur each season.

Freebooter never won another Grand National. One of the many sufferers in the catastrophic start next year he was brought down at the second fence and then, in 1952, fell at the Canal Turn second time round when upsides in front with Teal and going every bit as well as the eventual winner. In both those races he carried 12 st 7 lbs and, with the same huge weight, had won a second Grand Sefton in 1951. In 1953 when twelve years old he came back to his favourite course for the last time. George Slack who rode him in the Becher Chase had never won over the big fences. 'I think you will today,' said Bobby Renton and sure enough he did. Dismounting amid the tumultous welcome that greeted the old horse's return Slack told his trainer, 'I've just had a conducted tour round Aintree.' Though never quite so good on Park courses (he had a particular dislike for Cheltenham) Freebooter won twenty races in all and was pensioned off in 1954 to spend a happy retirement in the hunting field. He died two years ago and no horse since the war has beaten his record across the stiffest country in the world.

If with Freebooter's triumph the Grand National reached the peak of its post-war prestige and popularity, the disastrous events of 1951 did a lot to lower it in the eyes of the public. For some unknown reason the starter pressed his lever when half the field of thirty-six were still milling round in no sort of line and the result was a ragged undignified scramble in which several, among them Freebooter and Cloncarrig, were left the best part of a hundred yards.

Arriving over the first fence they found a scene reminiscent of the Charge of the Light Brigade. No less than twelve horses either fell or were brought down in a horrid struggling mass—and the details, needless to say, were faithfully reproduced in next morning's newspapers.

The favourite Arctic Gold, one of the few six-year-olds to run since the war, escaped the first fence fracas only to fall when in front at the Canal Turn. He did not cause quite the same wholesale carnage as Easter Hero in 1928, but at least four horses, including Cloncarrig, got no farther. Indeed only a handful, reached the Chair where Russian Hero and Dog Watch fell—a double blow for poor George Owen who trained them both. Soon after Becher's only two were left, Nickel Coin and Royal Tan. They rose at the last together but Royal Tan blundered horribly and although Mr 'Fonsie' O'Brien stayed aboard, Nickel Coin and Johnny Bullock were gone beyond recall. Derrinstown, remounted, was the only other to finish.

Owned by Mr John Royle and trained by Jack O'Donoghue who, in recent years has handled several of Queen Elizabeth the Queen Mother's horses, Nickel Coin started life as a show jumper and once finished second in that role to the great Foxhunter himself. Like Sheila's Cottage she was a nine-year-old mare when she won and, like her, had always been a safe, if not very fast, conveyance.

Through no fault of Nickel Coin's the 1951 Grand National had left a distinctly unsatisfactory taste in everyone's mouth and, although in 1952 Mr Harry Lane's Teal won a fine race in a time only one fifth of a second outside Golden Miller's record, the general impression of confusion and disaster still hung heavy over Aintree.

Very little of the running could be seen through a damp clammy mist and this was the year in which, following a dispute over copyright with the B.B.C., Mrs Topham staged her own private—and supremely unsuccessful—broadcast. The resulting comic cross-talk act told listeners precious little about the race and did even less for its reputation.

A tough little ten-year-old, Irish-bred, Teal learned to jump out hunting and was a top-class point to pointer before Mr Lane bought him. Ridden by Arthur Thompson he was up in the first two throughout in 1952 and, after Freebooter fell at the Canal Turn, engaged in a desperate battle with Legal Joy all the way to the last fence. Here Royal Tan fell—only four lengths behind the leaders and closing fast—and, staying on like a lion, Teal drew away to beat Legal Joy by five lengths. Wot No Sun, who had finished second to Freebooter in 1950 and later won the Grand Sefton, was a distant third. He, like the winner, was trained by Neville Crump who headed the trainers' list that year for the first time.

Teal himself looked like going on to even greater heights when, first time out next season, he ran a tremendous race at Doncaster against the subsequent Gold Cup winner, Knock Hard. But a failure at Cheltenham followed and not long after, while being trained for a second National, Teal fell desperately ill. A major operation revealed a twisted gut but could not repair it and two days later he had to be destroyed. Comparative merit between generations is impossible to measure but at his best Teal was probably at least the equal of all but a few post-war National winners and a great deal better than most.

V

When in 1948 a handsome but rather light-framed, nine-year-old called Cottage Rake came over from Ireland to win the Cheltenham Gold Cup, the name of his young trainer Michael Vincent O'Brien was virtually unknown in English jumping circles. Seven years later, as Pat Taaffe and Quare Times ploughed through mud and rain to win the 1955 Grand National this same small quiet-voiced Irishman had become a byword wherever men talked or thought of steeplechasing.

He had, during that short time, saddled the winners of three Grand Nationals, three Champion Hurdles, four Cheltenham Gold Cups and, over a slightly longer period, no less than eleven divisions of the Gloucestershire Hurdle at the National Hunt meeting. He had twice headed the English trainers' list and it is no exaggeration to say that he had dominated the sport more completely than any trainer, English or Irish, before or, with the possible exception of Tom Dreaper, since. Having done all he set out to do, O'Brien vanished from the National Hunt scene almost as suddenly as he had burst upon it. In 1959 he turned his attention entirely to flat racing and if his jumping colleagues breathed a sigh of relief their contemporaries under

Jockey Club rules soon learnt the reason why. But that is another story.

The son of a farmer in Co Cork, Vincent O'Brien started from scratch in 1940, training a couple of horses at Churchtown—about four miles from the same Buttevant church whence, in 1752, Messrs Blake and O'Calloghan had ridden across country to St Leger Steeple—the earliest recorded 'steeplechase'.

In his very first season O'Brien sent out one horse to win the Irish Cesarewitch and another to dead heat in the Irish Cambridgeshire. His reputation was made and in 1945 Doctor T. J. Vaughan of Mallow asked him to train a gelding by Cottage who, at that time, had run unplaced in one two-mile flat race.

Then six years old, Cottage Rake had nothing much to recommend him, but less than three years later he turned up at Cheltenham, still little more than a novice over fences, and in one of the Gold Cup's greatest finishes ran Happy Home out of it by a length and a half.

This was the first Gold Cup I ever saw and even to my untutored eye the strength and skill with which Martin Molony hurled Happy Home at the last fence was jockeyship at its finest. Conjuring from Miss Paget's horse a tremendous leap he gained a length and landed in front—but it wasn't enough. For Cottage Rake who had already won a Naas November Handicap on the flat and was later to win an Irish Cesarewitch had a turn of speed few chasers could match. And in Aubrey Brabazon he had a jockey with the style and balance to use it.

> 'Aubrey's up, the money's down,
> The frightened bookies quake.
> Come on, my lads, and give a cheer
> Begod, 'tis Cottage Rake.'

I don't know what immortal bard deserves the credit for those lines, but he must have been at Cheltenham in 1948. For now, up the famous hill, Cottage Rake and Brabazon were irresistible. Poor Happy Home had played his last card and, brushed aside a hundred yards from the line, he was beaten decisively.

Cool Customer, a bold and brilliant front-runner trained in the North by Jack Fawcus and owned by that popular member of the National Hunt Committee, Major 'Cuddy' Stirling-Stewart, had started favourite for the 1948 Gold Cup—but stood a mile off the very first fence and paid the penalty.

He made no such mistake in 1949 (when the Gold Cup, abandoned owing to frost in March had to be run in April), but Cottage

Rake was better than ever now, and though apparently going the better between the last two fences, Cool Customer, like Happy Home, could find no answer to his acceleration on the final hill.

Cottage Rake was not beaten that season. He disposed of Roimond rather comfortably in the King George VI Chase and had his hardest race a month earlier in the Emblem Chase against Lord Bicester's other more reliable servant, Silver Fame. This finish was again fought out between Brabazon and Martin Molony, and the latter again got the best of it at the last fence. Cottage Rake blundered there and Brabazon lost his whip. But gallantly though Silver Fame struggled to hold his advantage the Rake's great speed on the flat was just too much.

On the first day of the National Hunt meeting that season Vincent O'Brien had produced perhaps the most remarkable of all his extraordinary horses—Mrs M. H. Keogh's Hatton's Grace who, at nine, an age when most hurdlers are past their best, proceeded to run clean away with the Champion Hurdle. Except perhaps to the most discerning eye—or in the winner's enclosure where they all look good—Hatton's Grace would never have excited much notice in a selling hurdle let alone the Champion. A small, rather undernourished looking character he used to wander mouse-like around the parade ring before his races— but in action the mouse became a lion.

O'Brien took Hatton's Grace over from B. Nugent as an eight-year-old and proceeded to win with him, not only three Champion Hurdles at nine, ten and eleven but also two Irish Cesarewitches on the flat, in the second of which the old horse carried ten stone. With Sir Ken and National Spirit, Hatton's Grace was the out-standing hurdler of the post-war period and, without disrespect to his previous trainer it is surely permissible to wonder whether, if trained by O'Brien throughout his career, he might not have monopolized the Champion Hurdle as completely as Golden Miller did the Gold Cup before the war. More than any other horse—even Cottage Rake himself—it was he who built up for Vincent O'Brien the reputation of a man to whom miracles were child's play.

Cottage Rake's third and last Gold Cup in 1950 was also by far his easiest. When in the King George VI Chase earlier that season he failed by three-quarters of a length to give 11 lbs to Lord Bicester's Finnure (who, as a young horse, had beaten him in an Irish Cesarewitch), it seemed his powers might conceivably be on the wane. Nor did his next race at Leopardstown, in which he was brought down, do much to disprove that theory. Finnure, meanwhile, had gone from strength to strength and, unbeaten in five outings before the Gold Cup, started, in a six-horse field, at only fractionally longer odds than the champion.

It was widely held at the time that, at Kempton, Finnure had beaten Cottage Rake for speed—helped by a slow early pace—and doubtless sharing this belief, Martin Moloney kept Lord Bicester's horse behind his great rival on Gold Cup day. As things turned out a pekingese might as well have waited to pounce on a greyhound. For the race was never really a race at all. Cruising in front from half-way, Aubrey Brabazon suddenly pressed the switch on Cottage Rake and, with four fences to go, shot clear, never to be challenged thereafter. Finnure was beaten ten lengths and the third horse Garde Toi only deserves a mention because his rider, the Spanish Marquis de Portago, was the only man ever to go round Aintree both on horseback and in a racing motor-car. The second form of conveyance came to occupy his whole attention and, alas, he was killed while driving in the Mille Miglia some years later.

Cottage Rake never won again but, latterly trained in England by Gerald Balding, went on running to within three weeks of his fifteenth birthday. Though the old speed was gone his jumping never deserted him and, in that last season, when beaten by Halloween at Wincanton, Chaseform say of him 'looked well, jumped well, going on finish, good race'. Not many great champions are asked to labour on so long and even fewer have earned a more fitting epitaph. Until the coming of Arkle it was not possible to say for sure that any post-war Gold Cup winner was better than Cottage Rake.

Owned throughout his active career by Mr F. L. Vickerman, he combined to an exceptional, perhaps a unique, degree, the art of jumping fences safely (if not always brilliantly) with the ability to produce at the end of a three-mile chase, the speed of a high class flat-racer. Even those outstanding qualities would have been useless without courage but of that too Cottage Rake had more than his share. Time after time other horses used to lead him over the last fence and it was not only his speed and Aubrey Brabazon's superlative jockeyship that pulled so many races out of the fire. It was guts as well—the one characteristic without which no real steeplechaser was ever worth a light.

Retired at long last to Ireland, Cottage Rake lived happily, beloved by all who knew him, on a farm near Fermoy until his death at the age of twenty-three. A race named after him is still run at Kempton Park.

It is perhaps worth noting, for the benefit of those who listen to racecourse gossip, that before Mr Vickerman bought Cottage Rake the talk in Ireland was that the horse 'made a noise', i.e. was wrong in his wind. In fact a veterinary examination did reveal a slight noise but the vet responsible gave it as his opinion that this would never affect Cottage Rake. Mr Vickerman believed him—and had no cause to regret it.

I have digressed a long way from the Grand National—in which Cottage Rake, for the sort of reasons discussed earlier, was never asked to run. But Vincent O'Brien had long ago set his sights on the greatest prize of all. Royal Tan's two near-misses have been described. His turn was to come, but in 1953 he was temporarily out of action and the stable, now moved to new quarters near Cashel in Co Tipperary, had another formidable representative.

The story of Early Mist's youth makes ironic reading. Bred in England he was bought twice as a yearling, first at Newmarket and then in Ireland by that great judge Harry Bonner acting on behalf of Mr J. V. Rank. After searching for years for a National winner Mr Rank now had the right horse—but Early Mist, carrying his colours at Aintree in 1952, fell at the first fence. Before he could try again Mr Rank was dead.

At the dispersal sale of his horses Vincent O'Brien bought Early Mist for 5,300 guineas—and, a second irony—the under bidder was Lord Bicester who, like Mr Rank, never won a National and never gave up trying to do so.

Mr Joe Griffin, on whose behalf O'Brien bought Early Mist, was already the owner of Royal Tan and was by all accounts a colourful character as well as an extremely lucky one. Known in Ireland as 'Mincemeat Joe', he had made a considerable fortune just after the war in the manufacture of that delicacy and was to be winner of two Grand Nationals.

The purchase of Early Mist paid a rich and rapid dividend. In his last outing before Aintree the big lop-eared, still rather immature-looking eight-year-old won a three-mile chase at Naas, only to be disqualified. But by National day O'Brien had him better than ever before and, ridden by Bryan Marshall, he was in fact one of the easiest winners in the recent history of the race.

When Ordnance fell two fences before Becher's second time round Early Mist was left alone in front. There he stayed but, coming on to the racecourse with two more fences to jump began to look about him, doubtless thinking the race was over. Marshall had to sit down and ride for dear life, but once woken up Early

Mist stormed away again and, despite hitting the second last, finished sufficiently full of beans to shy at a stray piece of paper!

Throughout the final circuit Mont Tremblant, winner of the 1952 Gold Cup, had been struggling valiantly to get on terms with the leader but, under the terrible burden of 12 st 5 lbs, could never quite do so. In the end, dog-tired but infinitely game, he finished second twenty lengths behind Early Mist—a triumph of class and courage over weight only equalled since the war by Prince Regent's third in 1946. Dave Dick who rode Mont Tremblant for Miss Paget had finished third twelve months earlier on Wot No Sun—but had only three more years to wait before his luck changed with a vengeance on E.S.B.

Patient endeavour, by man or horse, does not always get the reward it deserves in racing but if ever justice was done it was in the 1954 Grand National. Royal Tan might already have won once, but for blundering at the last in 1951, and would certainly have finished second to Teal but for falling at the same fence in 1952. Fired for leg trouble after that race he had a year's well-earned rest and came back in 1954 one of the best backed horses by virtue partly of his record and partly of a highly promising run at the National Hunt meeting. The level of class was exceptionally low that year and Royal Tan with 11 st 2 lbs had, in the end, to give weight all round. Early Mist had gone wrong before Cheltenham, the Gold Cup winner Knock Hard was withdrawn and Mont Tremblant damaged a suspensory in almost his final gallop for the race.

So the stage was set for triumph of honest stamina and safe jumping as opposed to speed, and Royal Tan had with age acquired both the first two qualities in abundance.

After a race marred by four fatal accidents—among them poor Legal Joy and the massive Coneyburrow who, after dropping his hind legs in the water, broke his neck a few fences later—three horses came to the second last with a chance, Tudor Line, Churchtown (Vincent O'Brien's well fancied second runner) and Royal Tan.

Churchtown blundered there and, as Tudor Line jumped right-handed at the last, Bryan Marshall who had ridden a superbly patient race drove Royal Tan clear on the flat. There followed a finish as thrilling as any in the history of the race. For Tudor Line was not beaten. George Slack, the man to whom Freebooter had given his 'conducted tour', got every ounce out of him and up the long run in they gained on Royal Tan inch by agonizing inch.

There is a famous picture of these two brave horses locked

together at the post. Both jockeys are in perfect unison, alike with each other and with their mounts, both horses' forefeet are off the ground, both heads are straining forward. But this time Royal Tan was not to be denied. Helped every yard of the way by the best and strongest finisher in the game he dredged up from some hidden source the final vital ounce and as they crossed the line his neck showed clear in front.

This is perhaps the moment to attempt a description of Bryan Marshall, with Fred Winter and the Molony brothers the out-standing National Hunt jockey of his day. An Irishman born and bred, Marshall was apprenticed to Atty Persse and rode his first winner on the flat (at the age of thirteen) in 1929. After a short period in America and five years with Hubert Hartigan he served before the war as combined box-driver, stable-lad and occasional jockey to no less a personage than Noel Murless, then training a comparatively humble string of jumpers in Yorkshire. In one particularly bad winter they brought some horses down to Berkshire and Marshall, riding one of them at Newbury, got a taste of the hard realities of jumping when, well behind in a novice hurdle, he was summarily put into the wing by a senior leading jockey who shall be nameless!

The war followed and, commissioned in the 5th Royal Innis-killing Dragoon Guards ('the Skins'), Marshall went to Normandy shortly after D-Day, got sniped through the neck in his first action and having recovered, fought on to the end of hostilities in Europe.

When demobbed in 1948 he was thirty years old, weighed 12 st 7 lbs stripped, and, although he had ridden about twenty winners before the war, mostly for Noel Murless, was relatively unknown as a National Hunt jockey. Hardly a probable starting point, you may think, for a man who only two seasons later was to head the list with sixty-six winners out of 237 rides!

But the luck no National Hunt rider can do without soon came Marshall's way. He got a 'spare' ride at Catterick on an old plater called King's Gap whose regular jockey Jack Bissill was hurt. King's Gap won and his rider's style made a lasting impression on Fred Rimell, then champion, and on Mrs Fulke Walwyn who happened to be present. It was an incident with far-reaching results. For at the end of that season (in which Marshall rode twenty-two winners) Fulke Walwyn asked him to ride Leap Man in the Cathcart Challenge Cup at the National Hunt meeting. Chaseform records the highly significant comment 'ran on inside, took lead three out, made rest'. Next year, with his stable jockey Frenchie Nicholson on the verge of retirement, Walwyn offered

The disastrous first fence in the 1951 Grand National . . .

And its aftermath . . . from left to right: P. Fitzgerald, B. Marshall,
R. Francis, P. Taaffe, M. O'Dwyer (bending), Mr. R. McCreery,
J. Dowdeswell and M. Scudamore

The greatest hurdler of post-war years. Sir Ken with T. Molony up, winner of three Champion Hurdles, 1952–4
Copyright W. W. Rouch & Co. Ltd.

Mandarin and Fred Winter coming back after winning the Grand Steeplechase de Paris. The broken snaffle is dangling under Mandarin's neck
Photograph by
Reportage Photographique A. Well

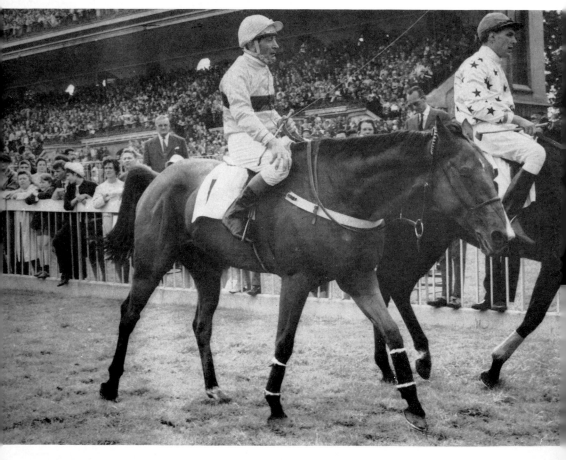

Marshall the job and their partnership, which lasted five years, gave him all the opportunities he needed.

A superlative horseman in every sense of that word Marshall's chief qualities were complete fearlessness, the ability to make horses jump (and to stay on when they didn't), fine tactical sense and tremendous strength in the finish. Famous for going the shortest way (as on Leap Man) he took the view that 'the two safest places to be are either the inside or the outside—and you don't win many races on the outer'.

First jockey in turn to Fulke Walwyn and Peter Cazalet, the two most consistently successful trainers of the era, Bryan Marshall suffered many terrible falls (he had broken his back before the war) and, throughout his career had to waste furiously to do as low as 10 st 7 lbs. Three weeks before Royal Tan's National he fractured his upper jaw in five places at Kempton and was told by a specialist that he was mad to ride. But that form of madness is not uncommon in National Hunt racing and it carried Bryan Marshall to his second and greatest triumph round Aintree. At the same meeting he had, incidentally, won two top-class hurdle races (both for O'Brien and Mr Griffin)—mainly, he says, 'to show them I was fit . . .'

Of the jockeys riding regularly since the war only Fred Winter and the Molonys can be compared with Bryan Marshall—and the comparison is not really useful. All four devoted their lives to what Will Ogilvy called 'a game made by the Gods for brave men's playing', and they played it as well and as bravely as it can be played.

I should not leave the Grand Nationals of Early Mist and Royal Tan without mentioning Irish Lizard who finished third in both. A small courageous horse belonging to Lord Sefton he was all but a patent safety over the big fences and only lack of size and speed robbed him of the highest honours.

The four fatal accidents in 1954 caused something of a public furore over the alleged 'barbarity' of the Grand National. The subject was hotly debated in the House of Lords—and agitation (which gave rise to the particularly enlightened proposal that the race should be run at Epsom) continued on and off throughout the post-war period. It accomplished little or nothing until 1961 when, as we shall see, it was among the factors that caused the Aintree fences to be modified.

The 1954–5 season was a deplorable one for weather—and the National itself was run in foul conditions after nearly three days of ceaseless rain. Vincent O'Brien had four runners—his two previous winners Early Mist and Royal Tan, Oriental Way ridden by Fred Winter, and a newcomer to Aintree, Mr W. H. Welman's Quare Times. A big Irish horse called Copp started favourite and Quare Times, originally very strongly fancied, drifted somewhat in the betting because it was thought he would not like the heavy ground.

In fact he liked it far better than any of his twenty-nine opponents and galloped home a very easy winner, twelve lengths in front of the luckless Tudor Line who, though he would not have won in any case, again jumped out to the right at the last few fences.

O'Brien's third successive Grand National marks the first appearance in this story of another formidable Irish figure: Pat Taaffe who rode Quare Times to victory. Although his name will now forever be associated with one horse, Pat Taaffe had already been riding in the top flight for years when Arkle was no more than a twinkle in Archive's eye. Since 1947 when he rode his first winner he has repeatedly headed the jockeys' list in Ireland and, quite apart from many famous English triumphs at Cheltenham and elsewhere, has won every single steeplechase over the big fences at Aintree.

Tall and long in the leg Taaffe rides exceptionally short for a jumping jockey and a picture of Quare Times at the last fence in 1955 shows his knees cocked well above the horses' withers. It is an inimitable style which, for most other men, would lead not only to repeated falls but probably to painful cramp into the bargain. Though never particularly polished or strong in a finish, Taaffe can have had few equals in the art of presenting a horse at a fence. And, in a steeplechase, when you come to think of it, far more ground and energy can be saved by good accurate jumping than was ever made up on the flat. I may be wrong but it seems to me that this fundamental truth is more often recognized nowadays by Irish trainers than by their English colleagues.

Nearly killed in a dreadful fall some years ago, Taaffe came back as cool, fearless and skilful as ever. Some men, with two horses like Arkle and Flyingbolt to ride, might be objects of jealousy—but not this one. His charm and modesty have made him tremendously popular both in the English weighing-room and with English crowds. Like Arkle himself Pat Taaffe has qualities which easily transcend any petty national rivalry. To be Irish is no longer, in the world of National Hunt racing, to be a 'foreigner'.

Quare Times's career is as good an example as any of the

combination of judgment with infinite patience which lay behind
Vincent O'Brien's extraordinary record. When Mrs Welman sent
him the horse as a three-year-old O'Brien told her that, given
sufficient time, he would make a top-class 'chaser. The owner
agreed and Quare Times, not seriously trained until he was rising
seven, won the National Hunt Chase at eight and the National
itself at nine. Six weeks later he and Early Mist started first and
second favourites for a two-mile hurdle race at Leopardstown—
an event which may well be unique in National Hunt history,
Quare Times won it easily and although he never accomplished
much on the racecourse thereafter retired at the age of twelve to
make a magnificent hunter across the fearsome banks of Southern
Ireland.

One more horse must be mentioned in this account of Vincent
O'Brien's golden years—Mrs M. H. Keogh's Knock Hard who in
1953 had given the great Irish trainer his fourth and last Cheltenham Gold Cup.

Like Cottage Rake, Knock Hard was a flat-race horse turned
steeplechaser and although he never jumped quite as safely or
fluently as his famous predecessor he may have had even greater
speed. Second in an Irish Cesarewitch (to Hatton's Grace) and
beaten by a head in the Manchester November Handicap, he won
the Irish Lincolnshire by five lengths and was also in, or very near,
the top class as a two-mile hurdler.

In 1952, moving up to challenge Mont Tremblant in the Gold
Cup Knock Hard fell at the second last—and all the usual heated
arguments raged about what might have been. Mont Tremblant,
then only six years old, ran many fine races thereafter, notably in
the 1953 Grand National, but in fact, owing to trouble with his
legs, was probably never quite so good again. He beat Knock Hard
in the King George VI Chase (though both were beaten by
Halloween) but at Cheltenham, on ground much faster than the
year before, the Irishman got his revenge.

It was a spectacular, eventful race run at a furious gallop and at
the top of the hill with Rose Park, Mont Tremblant and Galloway
Braes going great guns in the lead Tim Molony was riding the
ears off Knock Hard without any noticeable response.

But then, as so often at Cheltenham, the second and third last
fences completely transformed the picture. Rose Park, still on a
tight rein, fell two from home and suddenly, as the leaders came
under pressure, Molony got Knock Hard into top gear. In front
before the last he met it dead right and flashed over at full stretch
—as fine a leap as was ever seen at Cheltenham. Halloween came

from behind to beat Galloway Braes for third place ahead of Mont Tremblant, but Knock Hard was five lengths clear.

Because, by some strange freak of fate, he was never even placed in a Grand National Tim Molony has hardly been mentioned so far. And this is a shameful omission for, champion five times, he was never once out of the first three in the jockeys' list from 1948 to 1957.

That statement alone represents a staggering feat of sheer physical hardihood—for few had more crashing falls and none was less affected by them. In fact, unbelievable as it seems, the fractured thigh which, in 1958 ended Molony's career was the first major injury he ever suffered. In twenty-two years' riding over fences and hurdles he never once broke a collar-bone; a record of resilience which surely deserves its place in a medical history, let alone one of National Hunt racing.

Like his younger brother Martin, Tim Molony learnt to ride in the Irish hunting field—and acquired there a relaxed, almost casual-looking seat which made him, of all the great jockeys I have been privileged to watch, perhaps the hardest to dislodge. Strong as an ox he was blessed too with a pair of hands which could make the hardest puller look like a child's pony. He rode long by modern standards and was in his element on bad or inexperienced jumpers —attacking each fence as if it was an enemy, kicking harder and harder the more mistakes they made and winning dozens of races by a length or less gained somewhere far out in the country where the horseman comes into his own.

Though unlucky in the National itself (he rode in eleven and only got round four times) Molony won two Grand Seftons and many other races at Aintree. Two days before Knock Hard's Gold Cup he had won his third successive Champion Hurdle on Sir Ken—and went on next year to make it four in a row. His battles with Fred Winter for the championship enlivened the end of several post-war seasons and when he retired to hunt, farm and train in Leicestershire jumping lost one of its best loved most outstanding characters. I can see him now, swinging down to the post on a long rein—and storming back whether in victory or defeat with the same wide cheerful grin on his battered weather-beaten face.

Although, unlike his brother, Martin Molony was never champion jockey in England, he had during an all too brief career a tremendous and far-reaching effect on the reputation of the sport. Light enough to ride on the flat (he was third on Signal Box in the 1951 Epsom Derby) he had been apprenticed to Martin

Hartigan before the war and, combining flat-race polish with all his brother's robuster qualities, became the supreme stylist of the post-war years, if not, as many would say, of all time.

One of Martin Molony's finest hours—in defeat on Happy Home—has already been described. Another and, alas, almost the last seen in England, came in 1951 when, on Silver Fame, he won the Gold Cup for Lord Bicester, to whom, whenever his Irish loyalties permitted, he was then first jockey.

Silver Fame, twelve years old in 1951, really deserves a chapter to himself. If not necessarily the best of all the fine handsome horses who carried Lord Bicester's colours, he was certainly the bravest and most faithful—and there have been few more consistent 'chasers in the history of the game. In the seven seasons that followed the war Silver Fame ran forty-four times against almost all the best of his contemporaries. Trained throughout his career by George Beeby he won twenty-six races, went through the '49–50 season without defeat and would have done the same in '47–8 but for falling in the Grand National. Though desperately hard to beat on any Park course he was above all a Cheltenham specialist. Dick Francis tells how, turning for home at the top of the hill there, the old horse would suddenly, without being asked, take off as if the devil was behind him. He did this once in a four-mile 'chase and, finding to his surprise that there was another circuit, calmly dropped the bit, only to seize it again at the self-same place and battle on to win by a head. His other peculiarity was the habit of making one serious mistake in every race. This aberration seldom worried him but his jockeys used to hope it would come as early as possible to put their minds at rest!

Small wonder then, with such a record and Martin Molony on his back, that, despite his age, Silver Fame started favourite for the 1951 Gold Cup—run in April on firm ground because of frost in March.

Although his rivals included Freebooter, Manicou and the very useful northern 'chaser Lockerbie, it was a comparative outsider, Greenogue who so nearly proved the experts wrong. He, Lockerbie and Silver Fame jumped the last fence in line abreast and, as Lockerbie fell away beaten, the other two stormed up the hill shoulder to shoulder fighting as if for their lives.

There was no photo finish in those days and perhaps a dead heat would have been the fairest result. But the judge said Silver Fame —by a short head—and no one could possibly grudge the old hero this reward to crown his years of cheerful, arduous endeavour. Nor, I think, can anyone doubt, without the slightest disrespect to

Greenogue's rider Glen Kelly, a tough, determined and first-rate jockey, that Martin Molony's skill, never more evident than in a finish such as this, may just have turned the scale.

A little later that same season, riding at Thurles in Ireland, Molony fractured the base of his skull so badly that he was forced into premature retirement.

Like no other rider of his day this little Irishman had caught the imagination of the public. Off a horse he was quite unlike the conventional picture of a steeplechase jockey—teetotal, deeply religious, utterly dedicated to his profession and with little time for the more hectic forms of relaxation favoured by his colleagues. And if that makes him sound a bore nothing could be further from the truth. Many good things—both horses and men—have come out of Ireland to adorn the English National Hunt scene and on that Roll of Honour the names of the Molony brothers stand very high indeed.

VI

Quite apart from the central disaster of Devon Loch's collapse the 1956 Grand National had several other notable features. It was for one thing Royal Tan's third and last appearance in the placings and his record deserves to be set down. Second, and perhaps unlucky, in 1951, he fell at the last in 1952, came third in 1956 and in 1957 at the age of thirteen was baulked so badly at Becher's that even he could not jump it. There certainly have been horses who took a dislike to Aintree—but this epic story hardly suggests that the great fences present an unfair or unbearable test to one with the necessary strength and courage.

Then again no history of jumping would be complete without some description of E.S.B.'s rider David Victor Dick, one of the sport's most remarkable and colourful characters in this or any other age.

As an apprentice doing 7 st 4 lbs and wasting hard at the age of seventeen to do it Dave (he does not approve of those who call him Dick) won the Lincolnshire Handicap on Gloaming in 1941 which, incidentally, makes him the only man ever to ride both 'Spring Double' winners. By all accounts as good on the flat as he later became over fences, he was spotted and retained by that great trainer George Lambton, but weight and the war soon put a stop to his career under Jockey Club rules.

After a period of military service, which probably accounts for some of the haggard white-haired ex-N.C.O.s you see about, Dave, like his father before him, turned to jumping. Though successful

at once, his big chance came in 1951, when, after a major disagreement over Bryan Marshall's defeat on Lanveoc Poulmic at
Sandown, he was asked to ride all Miss Dorothy Paget's horses.
Their association lasted until Miss Paget's death and of all the
many jockeys who rode for this highly individual lady none knew
better how to humour her whims and smooth her often ruffled
feathers. For her Dave won the 1952 Gold Cup on Mont Tremblant, a brilliant and handsome chesnut who, with Fortina and
Mill House, is the only six-year-old to win the great Cheltenham
race since the war. Earlier that season, again riding for Miss Paget
(on her fine two-mile 'chaser Prince of Denmark), Dave had
suffered a horrible injury when at Cheltenham a splintered rail
ran deep into his leg. Throughout the long and painful convalescence that followed, Miss Paget, with the generosity which was
often a feature of her complex character, kept his hospital bed
surrounded with every kind of luxurious refreshment. There is not
space here to tell the story of Dave Dick's life. If it could only be
told as he tells it the book would be a best-seller overnight. What
can and should be said though, is that, but for his size and weight,
this magnificent horseman might well have played as big a part in
post-war National Hunt racing as any of those who headed the
jockeys' list—even his lifelong friend Fred Winter.

Fred and Dave attended (from time to time) the same school at
Epsom, learnt to ride on the same ponies and rode their first
winners, one jumping, the other on the flat, on the same horse,
Carton. Dave has always been a good shot and Fred Winter tells
how as a boy, imitating George Duller's crouch one day on Epsom
Downs, he received a well-aimed air gun pellet in the seat of his
carefully poised jodhpurs. The incident did not spoil their friend-
ship which endures as strong as ever to this day.

Six foot tall and a natural 12 st 7 lbs, Dave Dick has been
wasting almost all his adult life. The Turkish baths are his second
home and for many years now his minimum riding weight has
been around 11 st 4 lbs. Neither this constant battle nor the usual
jockey's crop of broken bones has had the slightest effect on his
strength in the saddle—or on his zest for the lighter side of life.
Dave's presence in the jockeys' changing-room is guaranteed to
brighten even the gloomy introspective moments before a novice
chase. At the start of a National some years ago he spotted a
banner bearing the ominous words: 'Repent or your sins will find
you out'. 'Well if that's the case,' said he, 'I won't get as far as the
first.' A noted performer in the pursuit of various types of wild-
life—the sort you hunt, the sort you shoot and the sort you take

out to dinner—he lives each day as if it was his last and the prospect of having to sweat off several pounds as a result is never
allowed to spoil his enjoyment.

In 1965, at the age of forty, when all his leading contemporaries
had long ago hung up their boots, Dave Dick was called on to ride
for Peter Cazalet, both of whose stable jockeys, Bill Rees and
David Mould, were injured. The skill and evident delight with
which he took this chance, on Dunkirk and several other good
horses, gave enormous pleasure to his many friends. It proved
what we had always said—that, if God had only constructed him
on a slightly smaller scale, Dave Dick would have made the best
of them go.

1957 was Fred Winter's turn, and Sundew's too, a well
deserved one, for this massive chestnut had run well in both the
two previous years and a ghastly headlong fall at Becher's in 1956
had totally failed to affect his courage. He was owned by Mrs
Geoffrey Kohn who had once had a half-share in E.S.B. but disposed of it before he won at Aintree. She also sent Sundew up to
the December Sales but here the luck turned for no bid of £2,500
could be found.

So Sundew went back to Frank Hudson's small yard near
Henley-in-Arden—where he was in fact the only steeplechaser.
Hudson who had held a trainer's licence for over thirty years pro-
duced him at Aintree in magnificent condition—though Fred
Winter tells me that, at the end of his final gallop up the testing
'Faringdon Road' outside Lambourn, Sundew could barely raise
a canter.

Landing clear over the last fence in the National, having led
from the fourth, he was almost equally exhausted, so much so that
Winter thought something was bound to catch them. But nothing
did. E.S.B.'s challenge had already been beaten off and two
horses whose names were to become synonymous with Aintree—
Wyndburgh and Tiberetta—followed Sundew home at a respect-
ful distance.

Sundew, alas, did not live to enjoy the retirement he had earned
for next season, dropping his hind legs in the water-jump at Hay-
dock he broke his back and had to be destroyed. He was eleven
years old when he won the National and carried 11 st 7 lbs—more
weight than all but two of the post-war winners, Freebooter (11 st
11 lbs) and Royal Tan (11 st 7 lbs).

Tiberetta, Wyndburgh and E.S.B. all ran again in 1958, and
finished 2nd, 4th and 6th respectively. But neither they nor anything else could hold a candle to the little Irishman, Mr What,

who won with insolent ease by thirty lengths carrying 6 lbs over-weight to rub salt into the handicappers' wounds.

Mr What, an eight-year-old owned by Mr D. J. Coughlan and trained by Tom Taaffe, the father of Pat and Tos, had started the season as a novice over fences. In thirty-three races after the National, passing through the hands of various trainers including Peter Cazalet, he never managed to win again, but had undoubtedly been a real good horse on the day that counted most.

He was also ridden by a real good jockey: Arthur Freeman, whose father Will Freeman hunted the Grafton for many years and whose uncle Frank was even more famous as huntsman of the Pytchley.

Freeman, first jockey to Peter Cazalet for several seasons, had all his family's skill across country—and needed it at Aintree when Mr What, still virtually running away, hit the last fence a perilous thump. Extremely strong in a finish, Freeman, like Tim Molony, knew only one way to approach a fence—kick, kick and keep on kicking. His courage got him a lot of dreadful falls but it also won many races, some of which few others would have won. I remember for instance a little French-bred called Le Petit Roi ploughing through fence after fence one day at Sandown. Nine men out of ten would have either fallen off, pulled up or at least dropped their hands—but Arthur Freeman, his body battered by half-healed injuries and constant wasting rode a 'finish' throughout the last mile and, treating the obstacles as if they were six inches high, drove home to a memorable victory.

In 1957 Willie Stephenson who since the war had trained a large and consistently successful string at Royston (including Sir Ken, of whom more later) paid 3,000 gns. on behalf of Mr J. E. Bigg for a big point to point horse called Oxo. When asked what he meant to do with Oxo, Stephenson replied simply 'win the National'—and, a man of his word, two years later he did just that.

Mr What started favourite in 1959 but the handicapper had not forgotten his treatment twelve months earlier and, with an extra 17 lbs to carry, the little horse could only plod on into third place. Behind him came the gallant Tiberetta and, ahead, the Aintree crowd were watching a feat of horsemanship seldom equalled in the history of the race.

For, landing over Becher's on Wyndburgh second time round, Tim Brookshaw felt the light metal of one of his stirrup irons snap. Slipping the other foot free he called across to his friend Michael Scudamore (on Oxo) 'Look, no feet'—and rode, from there to the finish, as near bareback as makes no difference.

Scudamore could not wait to sympathize. In front five fences out he went for his life and it was well he did so. For Brookshaw, whose seat at the last might serve as a model of how a fence should be crossed, stirrups or no stirrups, had never given up. And, down the long run-in as Oxo began to tire, Wyndburgh cut his lead with every stride. Beaten in the end by only one and a half lengths he must be counted among the unluckiest losers ever. As for his rider, well, a friend, visiting Brookshaw's farm at six o'clock next morning found him out milking the cows. His only comment on an epic ride was that it had left him 'a little bit stiff'.

The two heroes of this race, Tim Brookshaw and Michael Scudamore, have much in common. Both are farmers and the sons of farmers, learnt their trade out hunting and as amateurs at little meetings like Bangor, Ludlow, Uttoxeter and Woore. Neither would ever lay claim to flat-race style in a finish but both over the years evolved a method which, combined with determination and utter nervelessness, got horses home whenever they were good enough and, not infrequently, when they weren't.

Champion jockey in 1958–9, Tim Brookshaw was riding as well as ever if not better when on 4th December, 1963 he crashed through a wing at Liverpool and broke his back. Paralysed from the waist down, he greeted this ghastly injury with the same cheerful lack of respect as he had always shown for the last fence of a steeplechase. Told he would never walk again, he calmly set about proving the doctors wrong and in six months was hoisting himself on the back of a pony to ride around his farm. And now, though we shall never see again the memorable sight of a tired horse galvanized by the Brookshaw 'treatment', we have instead the object lesson of his absolute refusal to admit defeat. In a sport where toughness is no rare commodity they don't come any tougher.

Michael Scudamore who rode his first winner at the age of seventeen in 1949 is still going strong, the senior member, apart from Dave Dick, of the English weighing-room. After Oxo's National—and Linwell's Gold Cup in 1957—he survived a period in which, when nothing would go right, trainers deserted him and the 'experts' in the stands (who never ride a loser) wagged their hoary heads and said 'he's gone'. I only hope some of them saw him recently at Ascot getting the better, on John's Wort, of the promising eighteen-year-old Doug Barrott, who wasn't born when Michael first rode in a hunter chase.

There have always been two types of National Hunt jockey— those who graduated from the flat and those thrown up by point to points and hunting. Of the second group Tim Brookshaw and

Michael Scudamore are as good examples as you could hope to find.

The years 1960 and '61 were crucial ones in the history of the Grand National and its home. In 1960, when Miss W. H. Wallace's Merryman II ridden by Gerry Scott gave Neville Crump his third success, the race was televised for the first time—and watched by an estimated ten million in Britain and many more on the Eurovision link abroad.

Only four horses had got round in Oxo's year and when on the first two days of the 1960 meeting four were killed, the anti-cruelty agitation reached a hysterical crescendo. Lord Sefton, the senior steward at Aintree, gave the National jockeys a special warning before the race to use their heads in the early stages, to go a sensible gallop and not to crowd towards the rails.

Happily—and doubtless partly because of his words—Merryman's National passed off without a single serious accident. But the senior National Hunt steward, Wing Commander Peter Vaux (himself an experienced amateur rider), was wisely not content. In the next twelve months he introduced two vital changes, partly to combat the charges of unfairness and partly in an attempt to bring the top-class 'chasers back to Aintree.

First and most important the great fences, hitherto built almost perpendicular, were considerably sloped on the take-off side. Tending as it did to prevent horses getting too close, this new method of construction gave them a vital extra yard or so in which to achieve the necessary height. This change was immediately successful and, though robbing the National of its old heroic, 'Survival of the fittest' character, has made it ever since an infinitely more spectacular, competitive and, in my opinion, more exciting race.

Secondly the permissible top weight was, in 1961, reduced from 12 st 7 lbs to 12 st. Though abandoned briefly since, this admirable rule is now again in force and, as I write, looks like attracting Mill House, though not Arkle, to Aintree in 1966.

The 1961 race, won by Bobby Beasley on Mr C. Vaughan's Nicolaus Silver (trained, like E.S.B., by Fred Rimell) had two other claims to special notice. To the prize money given by Messrs Topham and, since 1958, by the Irish Hospitals' Sweepstake, a further £5,000 was added by Messrs Schweppes, so that Nicolaus Silver earned for his lucky owner a record £20,000. Also, for the first—and so far the only—time there were in 1961 two challengers from behind the Iron Curtain. Carrying the automatic top-weight of 12 st and 'trained' for the race—on a snow-bound trotting track in Moscow, neither of the two Russians, Reljef and Grifel completed the course, though Grifel, remounted after falling at Becher's, got as far as the water before his rider finally called it a day. The Communist equivalent of our National is a gruelling contest in Czechoslovakia in which, apparently, it is quite customary for the winner to be remounted more than once. Peter Bromley of the B.B.C. and I, visiting the Russians before they came over, tried to explain that this was not the case at Aintree—but until taught by painful experience I don't think the jockeys had much idea of what they were in for.

As befits the last horse ever to win round Aintree in its old form, Merryman II was a powerful handsome ex-hunter from the border country and, apart from one blunder at Becher's second time round, he jumped brilliantly throughout. Gerry Scott who rode him is a popular and extremely competent northern jockey but has, since Merryman's triumph, been plagued almost constantly by injuries, breaking a leg three times in as many years.

He was for instance out of action next year when Merryman, ridden by Derek Ancil, made a gallant second attempt, this time with 11 st 12 lbs. Up in front rather sooner than his jockey wished with such a burden he hung on to Nicolaus Silver until the last fence but there, anchored by the weight, could do no more.

The winner, an exceptionally handsome grey, went on to win the Grand Sefton with 11 st 10 lbs on his back, got round in both the next two Nationals and, so far as I know, only fell once (while schooling) all his life. After winning the National he was pulled out again in the Whitbread Gold Cup and though no match for Pas Seul, then at the height of his powers, ran a wonderful race to be second.

Bobby Beasley who rode Nicolaus Silver so stylishly had already won a Gold Cup on Roddy Owen and a Champion Hurdle on Another Flash. If ever a man was bred to ride it is he.

His grandfather Harry rode in thirteen Nationals, was second in three and won on Come Away in 1891. He rode a winner at Punchestown when sixty-eight years old and his brother Tom, Bobby's great-uncle, won the National three times. As good an all-rounder as any man now riding, Bobby Beasley is married to a daughter of Arthur Thompson, who won on Sheila's Cottage and Teal; so on breeding alone there must be an odds-on chance that this wonderful family record will continue into the next generation.

Fred Rimell, Nicolaus Silver's trainer, had earlier won with E.S.B. and, with three Grand Seftons also to his credit, has a better recent record at Aintree than any other trainer. Four times champion jockey (he tied with Frenchie Nicholson in the first short post-war season), he took over his father's stables soon after the war and headed the trainers' list in Nicolaus Silver's year.

Season after season, Rimell turns out a high proportion of hard, fit, well-schooled winners and Terry Biddlecombe, his stable jockey for the past two years owes two championships as much to horses trained by Rimell as to his own very considerable skill.

The 1962 Grand National was run over exceptionally heavy ground and no one will ever know how much the victory of Mr N. Cohen's Kilmore was due to Fred Winter's tactical genius. Feeling from the start that, in such conditions, the leaders would cut each other's throats, Winter allowed Kilmore to creep quietly round behind and it wasn't until the second Canal Turn that, seldom straying far from the inside rail, he asked the little ex-Irish horse to race in earnest.

There, as always since the fences were modified, at least half a dozen horses were left with a chance among them; three already famous Aintree names, Wyndburgh, Mr What and Nicolaus Silver. None of these, however, could match the reserves of strength Kilmore and his rider had so carefully hoarded and up the run-in Winter drove him steadily further ahead.

This triumph, gained as it was on a horse trained by Ryan Price to whom he owed so much, gave Fred Winter more pleasure than any other in his long career. Dismounting that day, tired but supremely happy, he can hardly have dreamt that, only three years later, he would be back in the same historic unsaddling enclosure, not as a jockey but as the trainer of Jay Trump.

All the first three to finish in 1962 were twelve-year-olds. Wyndburgh beaten ten lengths in the end was second with Mr What an almost equally gallant third. His devoted owner, Miss R. P. Wilkinson, announced immediately that Wyndburgh would be retired. Three times second and once fourth in the National, a winner of the Grand Sefton and a luckless second in the same race, he deserves to be remembered as one of the select few who have thoroughly mastered Aintree and who despite many hard, unavailing struggles there, always came back, willing as ever to try again.

Only four more Nationals remain and the next one, 1963, is a bitter-sweet memory for the writer.

Half-way up the run-in, with Carrickbeg still strong beneath me, the dream of a lifetime seemed to be coming true. Only seven years old, Gay Kindersley's gallant horse had jumped superbly from first to last and, but for a momentary check when Out and About fell in front of him five fences from home, might just have seen it through. But it wasn't to be. Fifty yards from the line Carrickbeg faltered—and had, alas, no Fred Winter to hold him together. Pat Buckley, who only moments earlier had called out, 'Go on John, you'll win,' drove Ayala past us and that dreadful staring flat run-in had claimed another victim. But at least I know a little how it feels to win a National—enough to know that, if humanly possible, an experience as unforgettable as this must be kept alive for future generations.

Ayala, owned by the well-known ladies' barber Mr P. B. Raymond and trained by Keith Piggott, father of Lester and himself a top-class jumping jockey in his day, has never won another race; indeed has only finished twice in the nine times he has run. But that's the National—a law unto itself, a race the result of which can never be predicted.

Who, for instance, could have foreseen that in 1964 Team Spirit, a twelve-year-old running in his fifth Grand National, would succeed where he had already four times failed? A small bay horse who, until he won the 1963 Grand Sefton, had always seemed to treat the big fences with a trifle too much caution, Team Spirit was ridden, as in all his previous attempts by Willie Robinson, and any other jockey less familiar with his habits might excusably have given up hope long before the end.

For reluctant as always to loose himself completely while there were fences to be jumped, Team Spirit came to the last still well behind the leaders Purple Silk and Peacetown. Hard at work already for more than a mile Robinson sat down to ride with the strength and style that had earned him second place in an Epsom Derby—but although Team Spirit answered bravely it seemed, until the final hundred yards, that the leeway would be too great. But Purple Silk, unlike his rival, was missing the spur of a fence ahead. Johnny Kenneally did all he could, but Team Spirit simply would not be denied and, as Purple Silk's stamina ran out close home, forged past to win by half a length.

If for the winner this was the end of a long and patient wait, his trainer Fulke Walwyn who rode Reynoldstown in 1936 had waited even longer. At the summit of his profession ever since the war Walwyn had saddled the winners of almost every other National Hunt prize of any real importance but, though he was second twice with Legal Joy and Mont Tremblant, the National itself had always eluded him.

Now that honour too came back to Saxon House in Lambourn

and, for the fifth time Walwyn was leading trainer under National Hunt rules. Some of his many other triumphs will be described elsewhere but this is as good a moment as any to say that, during the post-war period, no other English trainer can claim a finer record of success in the hard and often heartbreaking task of preparing and schooling top-class 'chasers and hurdlers.

Team Spirit was owned by three Americans, Mr R. B. Woodward, Mr J. K. Goodman and Mr G. North. And, in 1965 the National prize again went across the Atlantic—won for the first time by an American horse ridden by an American jockey.

More than one winner of America's greatest timber race, the Maryland Hunt Cup, had tried and failed at Aintree but, beaten only twice in his five preparatory English races, Mrs M. Stephenson's Jay Trump, a handsome superbly balanced bay, soon showed that he had better credentials than any of his predecessors. Nevertheless it seemed to many a grave disadvantage that his rider Mr Tommy Crompton Smith had not only never ridden round Aintree but had (understandably determined not to let injury interrupt his plans) only ridden five times in England altogether.

No fear was ever more groundless. Riding a race that even his guide and mentor Fred Winter could not have bettered, Mr Smith took Jay Trump the shortest way throughout and brought him to the last fence still on the bit and full of running. Landing just ahead of the red hot favourite Freddie he had snatched a clear lead halfway up the run-in, but then as Mr Smith hit Jay Trump twice the horse's tail went round in protest and, for a moment his stride began to shorten. For fifty yards, with Freddie gaining fast, it looked like the last two years all over again. But Mr Smith had realized his error in the nick of time. Putting down the whip he balanced Jay Trump, rode him out with his hands and Freddie, conceding 5 lbs, could do no more.

So, after a heroic attempt at the Grand Steeplechase de Paris, in which they led over the last fence and finished third, Jay Trump and his skilful, utterly dedicated rider went back to America, their mission gloriously accomplished.

Freddie again started favourite for the 1966 Grand National, but again found one too good. Mr Stuart Levy's Anglo, ridden by Tim Norman, gave Fred Winter a second National in two seasons as a trainer and his unique achievement is a fitting end to the story.

In the last two years, probably because of doubts about its future, the race has attracted crowds of almost pre-war proportions. If after reading these pages you think it is not worth fighting for, then the writer not the story is to blame.

VII

Although the Grand National has served as a peg on which to hang much of this story it is no longer the only or even, many would say, the best test of a steeplechaser's merit. Since the war the class of horses put to jumping has risen steadily and the fast chaser, capable of staying up to three and a half miles on a Park course, has earned more and more of the limelight without in many cases ever running at Aintree.

In keeping with this change, the National Hunt meeting in general and the Cheltenham Gold Cup in particular have progressively ousted Aintree and the National from their place as the central climax of the jumping season.

Until the coming of Arkle, Cottage Rake had been the only horse since the war to win more than one Gold Cup but several came desperately close to doing so and of these the best was, in this observer's opinion, Mr John Rogerson's Pas Seul.

Running in his first Gold Cup in 1959, Pas Seul, then only six years old, had already built up a reputation for brilliance marred by jumping which varied from the superlative to the abysmal. He had fallen in his last race before the Gold Cup and blundered his chance away the time before that so it was not surprising that, despite the last-minute withdrawal of the ante-post favourite Saffron Tartan, he started a relative outsider.

But Pas Seul *was* a brilliant horse and, beautifully ridden by Bill Rees, a nephew of the great F. B. Rees, he proved it that day at Cheltenham. Storming past Linwell and Lochroe between the last two fences he came to the last full of running, a certain winner bar a fall. But fall he did and, in the fracas that followed both Linwell and Lochroe were badly hampered. Owned by one fine amateur and named after another, Lord Fingall's Roddy Owen, shot through unimpeded to beat Linwell by three lengths but, good horse though he was, must be considered one of the luckiest ever Gold Cup winners.

In every one of his races before the next Gold Cup Pas Seul either blundered fatally or fell. But on the great day itself his old weakness was, at long last, overcome. With, as it seemed, the whole world holding its breath, he jumped the last fence cleanly and, though furiously challenged up the hill by Lochroe held on to beat him by a length. Six weeks later Pas Seul failed narrowly and heroically to give Plummer's Plain two stone in the Whitbread Gold Cup.

Although he never won at Cheltenham again, it was the next

Halloween with Fred Winter up jumping the last fence at Kempton to
win in the 1954 King George VI Chase from Galloway Braes

Becher's Brook, 1956. LEFT TO RIGHT: Devon Loch (R. Francis), E.S.B. (D. V. Dick)—the winner, and Sundew (F. Winter), who was to win in 1957

season that in two sensational races his greatness was finally established beyond all doubt. First time out, over two-miles at Hurst Park, giving weight to some high-class specialist two-milers including Quick Approach and Blue Dolphin, Pas Seul (who had in the meanwhile been hobdayed) was understandably not much fancied. Ridden now by Dave Dick because Rees had become first jockey to Peter Cazalet, he proceeded to put up one of the most remarkable performances seen in England since the war, winning on a tight rein, having gained at least three lengths with an unbelievable leap at the last fence.

Four months later at Sandown over a distance almost double that of the Hurst Park race Pas Seul reached the peak of his fame in the 1961 Whitbread Gold Cup. Always going well he was knocked sideways by a falling horse at the fence after the water, lost half a dozen lengths and yet, almost literally, pulled his way back to the front. Giving weight all round (21 lbs to the Grand National winner Nicolaus Silver and 4 lbs to Mandarin whom he beat by nearly twenty lengths) he became, until Mill House and Arkle, the first horse ever to defy top weight in one of the two great sponsored chases and he did it, what's more, with ease.

Between these two great victories Pas Seul had been beaten by Saffron Tartan in the Cheltenham Gold Cup—run on fast ground that suited his rival far better than him. This, Fred Winter's first Gold Cup (he had already been placed in six), was a wonderful race fought to the last gasp by two supremely gallant horses— three, really, for Mandarin was third.

Originally trained by Vincent O'Brien and thought by him a world beater, Saffron Tartan was a massive old-fashioned type of 'chaser with speed very rare in a horse of his size. He was, however, beset by physical troubles of various kinds—first in his wind then in his legs—and it was a wonderful piece of training by Don Butchers, not only to win with him the 1960 King George VI Chase but, three months later, to bring him to Cheltenham at, or very near, his best.

Saffron Tartan now only barely stayed the Gold Cup distance and Winter made superb tactical use of his speed and brilliant jumping. Setting the big horse alight down the hill he jumped the second last three lengths ahead of Pas Seul but then, going to the last, felt Saffron Tartan 'dying' under him. Pas Seul was almost equally exhausted however and, though he gained slowly but surely up the run-in, Saffron Tartan, driven as only Fred Winter could drive, held on by a length. Owned in partnership by Col. Guy Westmacott, his son Ian and Lord Cottenham, the winner,

15

who finished third in the 1960 Champion Hurdle, might, but for his various infirmities, have reached all the heights Vincent O'Brien originally predicted for him. He was in any case a brilliant 'chaser but not, in my opinion, despite this result, quite the equal of Pas Seul at his best.

That best, however, was never to be achieved again, for Pas Seul broke down in the 1962 Whitbread won by Frenchman's Cove and, although he recovered to run, at the age of eleven, in the 1964 Grand National, was only a shadow of his former self. Trained throughout his career by Bob Turnell he was by Erin's Pride out of a mare called Pas de Quatre—and by her there hangs a strange romantic tale.

Pas de Quatre was bought from Fred Darling in the early years of the war by Mr Harry Frank, a farmer and well known horse-dealer living in the Wiltshire village of Crudwell. Half a mile up the road from his farm, Crudwell himself, the winner of fifty races, was born. Bob Turnell, a lifelong friend of the Franks, hunted Pas de Quatre while on leave from the army and found her one of the boldest mares he had ever ridden.

Retired to stud after the war (she only ran a few times) Pas de Quatre's first offspring of note was a big colt by Gay Light whom she foaled standing up in a field—leaving on her son's eye a scar which he carried all his days. Nine years later, in 1955, now named Gay Donald, owned by Mr P. J. Burt and trained by Jim Ford, he pulled off one of the biggest surprises in Gold Cup history, storming clear after three fences and winning by ten lengths from Halloween. Gay Donald was widely held at the time to have been a flukish winner but threw that slander back in its authors' teeth when, nine days later, he gave Mont Tremblant weight and a sound beating at Sandown.

Pas de Quatre had in the meanwhile become an extremely shy breeder. In 1952 she was certified *not* in foal and Mr Burt's father asked Harry Frank if he could lend her to a girl who wanted to ride to point to points and hunter trials. Pas de Quatre took part in both but then Mr Burt senior died and the mare came back to Mr Frank. Seeing his old friend one day at Crudwell Bob Turnell offered to try and get her in foal once more—and Pas de Quatre was actually covered twice by Royal Tara at the Lambourn Stud. There, a few days later, to the surprise of all concerned, she calmly produced a foal—who had already accompanied her round in two point to points and several hunter trials. His name, of course, was Pas Seul; and if pre-natal influence was all it is cracked up to be his career would doubtless have been even more illustrious.

Since he took out a trainer's licence in 1954 Bob Turnell has built up, at Ogbourne, one of the best and most successful stables in the land—and few have worked longer or harder for their reward. The son of a famous nagsman and dealer in the Beaufort country Turnell first rode (on the flat) in 1927 and, from 1928 to the beginning of the war, served a long and hazardous apprenticeship under National Hunt rules, mostly on moderate, if not downright dangerous horses. In all that time he rode less than twenty winners and, coming out of the army at the age of thirty-one, his future can have looked by no means certain.

But now at last the luck began to turn. Riding three winners in one day at Fontwell, Turnell was spotted and engaged as first jockey by Mr John Rogerson whose horses were then trained by Bruce Hobbs. Two years later, now firmly established, he was retained by Ivor Anthony—a tremendous compliment to a man of thirty-five in a trade where youth is normally at a premium.

A strong and fearless horseman, Bob Turnell, who came so close to winning the 1950 National on Cloncarrig, fought a constant battle with his weight, and despite arduous wasting (which gets harder with age) went on riding till he was forty-two. He still schools many of his own horses and is never happier than when out hunting with the Beaufort—often nowadays on Pas Seul.

Unlike many jockeys turned trainer, this one has the knack of passing on his knowledge. When Bill Rees was still comparatively unknown Turnell engaged him to take his own place as stable jockey and has since produced, from scratch so to speak, those two fine young riders Jeff King and Johnny Haine. Now Andrew Turnell is carrying on the family tradition and his brilliant first season as a jumping jockey contrasted ironically with his father's slow and painful climb to the top.

It was hard, in Saffron Tartan's Gold Cup, to have eyes for any but the leading pair. Those who glanced back, however, saw a small familiar shape hurtling down the hill—and up it—to finish only three lengths behind Pas Seul, gaining with every stride. A little earlier they had seen Mandarin—for it was he—make two disastrous errors and, if they concluded that, but for these he would almost certainly have won, they were almost certainly right.

The climax of Mandarin's career has been described, but long before that unforgettable day in Paris he had in eight hard seasons and fifty races become, more than any other 'chaser of his day, the nonpareil of courage and toughness. Coming from France as a three-year-old—one of the fattest Fulke Walwyn had ever seen—he won a couple of hurdle races in his first two seasons, but used in those days to treat the obstacles with a lack of respect which, though it seldom bothered him, was both uncomfortable and frightening for his riders. To almost everyone's surprise a highly successful season followed as a novice 'chaser and in 1957 at Cheltenham Mandarin won the first Hennessy Gold Cup sponsored by his owner's family firm.

Getting 16 lbs from Linwell he seemed, that day, no more than a highly promising six-year-old, but shot to the top of the tree a month later by giving Lochroe 7 lbs and a beating in the King George VI Chase. This was the first real example of the dogged courage which, more than any other quality, enabled Mandarin, wiry and insignificant-looking as he always was, to overcome far bigger, more handsome horses. Gerry Madden, the little Irishman who rode him for most of the first half of his career, tells how, six fences out at Kempton, he all but gave up hope. But instead he kept on riding and Mandarin kept on struggling. Lochroe made one error and that was all his relentless rival needed.

Mandarin started favourite for the 1958 Gold Cup and should, almost certainly, have won it. But he blundered horribly at the thirteenth fence and even Gerry Madden, used as he was to the little horse's antics could not keep his seat. Linwell, taking off a length or so behind, fell at the same fence and the brave and beautiful northern mare Kerstin went on to win from Polar Flight.

Owned by Mr G. H. Moore, Kerstin is so far the only one of her sex to win a Cheltenham Gold Cup. And although she was probably lucky to do so no luck was ever better deserved. Trained throughout her career by Verley Bewicke in Northumberland, Kerstin had to make repeated and arduous journeys for all her major races. No one can tell how much they cost her and even so she won one Hennessy Gold Cup, was a desperately unlucky second in another, finished third in a Whitbread and won twelve races in all. She was, without much doubt, the best mare to run over fences since the war.

Mandarin had already been beaten narrowly by Much Obliged in the 1957 Whitbread Gold Cup and in 1958 he was second again, beaten fair and square this time by his stable companion Taxidermist.

Only two years before Taxidermist, owned jointly by Mrs Peter Hastings and Mrs Fulke Walwyn, had won a humble selling hurdle at Newbury, and, when bidding at the subsequent auction reached 160 gns, Ivor Anthony, standing beside the four-year-old's owners, advised them to let him go. Some sixth sense prompted them to have one more bid—and a tenner has seldom been

Dick Francis and Devon Loch walking back at Aintree, 1956

Martin Molony (left) and Fred Winter out hunting in Ireland with the Black and Tans. *Photograph by courtesy of Frank H. Meads*

better spent. Though plagued latterly by various ailments, Taxidermist won over £13,000 and 13 races and, incidentally, gave
the writer two of the happiest, least forgettable moments of his
life.

One of these came in the Whitbread referred to above and the
other in the 1958 Hennessy Gold Cup when, landing fifth over the
last fence, Taxidermist produced the explosive burst of speed for
which, at his best, he was famous and got up to beat poor Kerstin
by the length of a cigarette end.

I shall always believe that, but for putting his foot in a mud-hole
and falling, Taxidermist might have won the Gold Cup that
season. And if anyone considers this wishful thinking I would like
to point out that, a month earlier, he had four lengths to spare
over Linwell who, though baulked by the fallen Pas Seul, finished
second to Roddy Owen at Cheltenham.

Two of Mandarin's attempts on the Gold Cup have been described. With a little more luck he might have won them both but,
before the Fates finally relented his courage was put to different,
still more searching tests. In the 1958 King George VI Chase won
by Lochroe, Mandarin, making one of those hair-raising acrobatic
recoveries, fractured his fibula four inches below the stifle.

Recovered, after only a few months' rest, and a warm-up over
hurdles, he ran for the third time in the Whitbread Gold Cup and
for the third time finished second. There is a special reason for
recalling this race for Mr J. U. Baillie's Done Up, Mandarin's
conqueror by a short head in one of the finest finishes ever seen at
Sandown, was ridden by Harry Sprague. Principally a hurdle race
jockey, Sprague was called on at the last moment by Done Up's
trainer, Ryan Price—firstly because Fred Winter was injured and
secondly because Done Up, one of the laziest horses ever to look
through a bridle, needed a jockey of abnormal strength.

The implied compliment was richly deserved, for Sprague,
though a veteran by this time (Done Up was the last horse he ever
rode), had long been famous for his dynamic finishing power.
Small and short legged with a flourish reminiscent of Sir Gordon
Richards, he won two Imperial Cups, both on High Point trained
by Ginger Dennistoun, and a Champion Hurdle on Doorknocker
for Mr Clifford Nicholson. Fred Winter says that the sight he
least welcomed in his riding days was that of Harry Sprague
beside him two flights from home in a hurdle race—and I'm not
surprised to hear it.

It can be said without fear of contradiction that few other men
would have got Done Up home in front that day at Sandown and

returning to scale Sprague was actually physically sick with the strain of his exertions.

Mandarin's season was not over for, going back to the land of his birth he ran in the Grand Steeplechase de Paris two months later and, having lost at least ten lengths through hesitating at an unfamiliar post and rails with water on the landing side, finished a close, gallant and infinitely unlucky second. That race left its mark on even his iron physique and although he struggled home to beat Pointsman in the 1959 King George VI Chase he had then to be fired for slight but definite leg trouble.

Worse was to come, for running next season in the Rhymney Breweries Chase at Chepstow Mandarin fell, for the first and only time in his life. He never did anything by halves and it was a crashing earthquake of a fall which, for a while, left him a shadow of himself. It may also have partly caused those two disastrous errors which, arguably, cost him Saffron Tartan's Gold Cup— but these were to be the last of the many setbacks in his epic story. The rest was triumph all the way.

Fred Winter had first ridden Mandarin back in 1955 over hurdles, and won on him. Now Fulke Walwyn secured second claim on the great jockey's services—but Winter was hurt in November 1961 and Willie Robinson rode Mandarin when, at Newbury, he won his second Hennessy Gold Cup. Taxidermist was third in that race, flying from the last as usual, and so for the second time the two old friends walked into an unsaddling enclosure together. They had spent many happy weeks turned out in the same field at Lambourn and met once more at Kempton on Boxing Day in 1965, parading before Arkle's King George VI Chase. But now their paths diverged and Mandarin's led to glory.

In the 1962 Gold Cup, ridden by Fred Winter this time, he was opposed by Pas Seul and, more seriously as it turned out, by the great Irish horse Fortria, winner of two National Hunt Champion two-mile chases and, even more to the point, of an Irish Grand National under twelve stone in brilliantly fast time. Ridden for speed by Pat Taaffe Fortria pounced on Mandarin at the second last and, against any other horse, would have looked a certain winner. But now, eleven years old, battered by fate, hard races and injury, Mandarin had stared defeat in the face too often to be daunted. And for the first time in a Gold Cup he was ridden by a jockey whose strength matched his courage all the way.

Together, gritting their teeth, he and Fred Winter hurled themselves at the last, wore down Fortria up the hill and won by a length a Gold Cup as moving as any in all the history of Cheltenham.

When Mandarin retired, he was the winner of £26,779 and 250,000 N.F.: more, until Arkle, than any horse in National Hunt history. As I write he is still alive and as well as ever, acting, when his exuberance permits, as Fulke Walwyn's hack. I make no apology for telling his story at such length for it contains all that is best in jumping. There have been bigger, better, faster 'chasers than Mandarin, but none who more fully deserved the title Napoleon gave Marshal Ney: 'the bravest of the brave'.

His story is also that of a great trainer and a great stable for to bring a horse of even Mandarin's toughness back after so many trials and tribulations was perhaps the finest feat in even Fulke Walwyn's long career. Two days before the Gold Cup described above he had won the Champion Hurdle with Sir Thomas Ainsworth's Anzio, in 1963 Mill House gave him his third Gold Cup, in 1964 Team Spirit won the National and in 1965 Kirriemuir the Champion Hurdle again.

Apart from his own skill, both inborn and acquired through long experience, Walwyn's success like that of most great trainers is the result of teamwork. Joe Lammin, his head lad and Darkie Leatham who travels his horses have both been at Saxon House for over twenty years. And this is perhaps the moment to pay tribute to them and others like them: to Jim Fairgrieves and Bill Braddon, Peter Cazalet's faithful servants at Fairlawne; Ron Peachey and Jack Kidd with Fred Rimell at Kinnersley; Snowy Davies with Ryan Price; and many more no less conscientious, skilful and hard-working. It is these men, the head lads, travelling head lads and ordinary stable-lads on whom, in the last analysis, all racing heavily depends. Their names seldom reach the headlines but, working long hours, riding out in all weathers they go on doing their hard, often dangerous job. Without them none of the events described in this book could have taken place.

Of the post-war Gold Cup winners not already mentioned Red Rower in 1945 earned only a paltry £340 for his owner and trainer Lord Stalbridge to whose lifelong support of National Hunt racing Roger Mortimer has paid tribute. Another great supporter and pillar of the National Hunt Committee, Lord Grimthorpe, won in 1947 with Fortina—the only entire horse to win since the war and also the only one to be ridden by an amateur. Trained by Hector Christie (whose head lad Charlie Mallon held the licence for Ivor Herbert when Linwell won ten years later), Fortina was a brilliant six-year-old and, ridden by Mr Dick Black, won in a canter by ten lengths from Miss Paget's Happy Home; far more easily than Cottage Rake beat the same horse the next year. Though never so good again, Fortina made a tremendous name for himself as a sire of jumpers throughout the post-war period. His best son was probably Fortria, second to Mandarin in 1962 and the outstanding Irish 'chaser of his day.

Mr A. Strange's Four Ten, an outsider when he won in 1954, was a big bold ex-point to point horse who, ridden by Tommy Cusack, outstayed Mariner's Log decisively after these two had jumped the last in line abreast. He never accomplished much of great note thereafter but was third the next year to Gay Donald and Halloween. John Roberts who trained Four Ten at Cheltenham has not, since then, had the luck to handle a horse of comparable ability but soldiers cheerfully on, doing his best with moderate animals, deservedly popular with all who know him. Tommy Cusack, an exceptionally strong determined rider was forced to give up by repeated injuries but is doing well as a partner in one of the leading horse-box companies.

Mr J. Davey's Limber Hill started his career, like Four Ten and so many other good 'chasers, out hunting and in point to points. A freak of breeding (his sire Bassam, once owned by Lord Mildmay, never got another winner), he was the outstanding performer of the season 1955-6 winning, besides the Gold Cup, the Emblem Chase at Manchester and the King George VI at Kempton (in which, however, as we shall see, he was probably lucky to beat Galloway Braes).

Ridden in all these races by Jimmy Power, of Freebooter fame, Limber Hill was trained by the late Bill Dutton who, as an amateur, won the National on Tipperary Tim. Dutton also had in his yard at that time Pappa Fourway, perhaps the greatest sprinter seen in England since the war, and the story goes that Limber Hill, a massive broad-beamed gelding well up to carrying fifteen stone out hunting, used to match strides with his distinguished stable companion in their work at home.

Mr David Brown's Linwell has been mentioned already several times. Trained by Ivor Herbert (who could not hold a licence owing to his career as a journalist) he beat Kerstin fair and square in 1957 and would presumably have done so again in 1958 had he not fallen—perhaps distracted by Mandarin's antics at the same fence. And since, in 1959, Linwell was badly hampered by Pas Seul (though not quite so badly as Lochroe) he deserves to be remembered, with Pas Seul and Mandarin, as one of those who might with a bit more luck have won three Gold Cups instead of only one.

Retired in 1961 Linwell had won twenty races in seven seasons including a Mildmay Memorial at Sandown. A gallant and consistent stayer he has, I'm afraid, been done scant justice here—but this is a play with so many stars that, if all were treated equally, the book would never end.

For the Grand National and Gold Cup are not everything and among those who won neither there are many well-loved names. At the risk of offending those whose favourites are left out, four may, perhaps arbitrarily, be chosen: Halloween, Galloway Braes, Lochroe and Crudwell.

There have been many fine hunter-chasers since the war—The Callant, Colledge Master, Baulking Green, Freddie and many more—but of them all only one successfully crossed the yawning gap which, in a normal year, separates the hunter from the top-class three mile 'chaser. His name was Halloween and, apart from his thirty-six races, seventeen victories and seven seasons of cheerful service he will always be remembered as the horse only two men could ride.

The first of those two was Captain R. B. Smalley of the Royal Marines who bought Halloween from his breeder Mr F. E. Woodman, hunted him, rode him in point to points and, in 1951, won on him five hunter chases in five starts culminating with the Foxhunters' at Cheltenham.

Trained then and thereafter by Bill Wightman, Halloween was bought before the next season by the Contessa di Sant Elia. He was ridden in his first two races by professionals, Dick Francis and D. Dartnall, and promptly demonstrated his dislike for their methods by falling on both occasions.

Captain Smalley was then recalled to the colours and, reunited with his old friend Halloween, won two amateur chases at Newbury in style. But the captain never claimed to be a top-class jockey and, looking round for a suitable replacement, Wightman offered the ride to Fred Winter, then rising comet-like towards the top. 'I asked Dick Smalley what he did on the horse,' Fred recalls, 'and he said, "Well, nothing". So I did nothing too—and it worked.' It worked so well in fact that, with good horses like Crudwell behind him, Halloween won the four-mile Grand National trial at Hurst Park in a hack canter. The understanding he and Fred Winter struck up that day carried them to victory next season in the King George VI Chase when, still only seven years old, Halloween wore down Mont Tremblant in a memorable struggle from the last. It kept them invincible, in fact, until in the Gold Cup itself Knock Hard's blistering speed held Halloween in second place.

That was the first of four successive Gold Cups in which Halloween was placed and Fred Winter rode him in all but one of them. For some reason, although he won the Foxhunters' and other races on the course, the little horse never really shone round Cheltenham. Probably he did not like the downhill gallop to the second last—for again and again he lost ground there only to make it up too late.

The season after Halloween's first King George VI, Fred Winter broke his leg and, whatever other factors may have been involved, it is a historical fact that, in eight races, ridden by four different top-class jockeys, Halloween only won once—beating the fourteen-year-old Cottage Rake in a minor event at Wincanton. It is hard to resist the conclusion that he *was* a one, or rather a two-man horse. And sure enough, with Winter fit again next season, the old firm was back in business.

Lady Orde's Galloway Braes was the same age as Halloween and their paths had already crossed several times. A bold and headstrong front-runner Galloway Braes used to treat his fences with hair-raising lack of respect. He galloped through rather than over them and few more spectacular sights have been seen on an English racecourse since the war than this big raking dark brown horse in full cry round Kempton or Hurst Park.

He fell in the 1952 King George won by Halloween but his turn came next year and, making almost all the running, he set up a record for the track which stood until Frenchman's Cove broke it in 1964.

Halloween (plus Fred Winter) was however to take his revenge in 1954 when receiving 7 lbs he caught Galloway Braes between the last two fences, brushed him aside and stormed away to win by six lengths. Two months later, getting only one pound over the same course and distance he confirmed that superiority, wearing his old rival down a mere fifty yards from the line.

Poor Galloway Braes was never to win another King George, but he should have done so and, ironically enough, it was Fred Winter's fault that he didn't. For in 1955, with Halloween a non-runner Fred rode the old horse in place of his usual jockey Bert Morrow and, brilliant as ever, Galloway Braes landed over the last with a clear lead and the race at his mercy. For what followed Fred Winter has never forgiven himself and it is only because he wishes it that I record the facts as he tells them. Halfway up the run-in he looked over his left shoulder, saw no danger and dropped his hands. But Jimmy Power and Limber Hill were challenging on the other side and, before Galloway Braes could get going again, they swept past to win by a neck.

Giving 4 lbs to the Gold Cup winner, Galloway Braes must have run one of his finest races that day and, in fact, was only to win one more. For the fences he had so often and so bravely scorned got him in the end. Falling next season in the King George, he fatally injured himself and had to be destroyed.

Trained all his life by Alec Kilpatrick, who in the same period had charge of another top-class 'chaser, Pointsman, Galloway Braes ran fifty-two times, won nineteen races and probably set more hearts afire than any jumper of his day. And before leaving him a special tribute is due also to Bert Morrow, the much battered but quite irrepressible little Irishman, who both on him and Pointsman survived so many head-on collisions, narrow shaves and earthquake blunders.

Halloween outlived his great contemporary. He is, in fact, still alive and full of beans as all who saw him at Kempton on Boxing Day 1965 (accompanied by the friend of his retirement, a twenty-nine-year-old mare who used to pull a milk-float) will testify. His record reads thirty-six races, seventeen victories and only seven times unplaced, and to him too the jumping crowds of the 'fifties owe an unpayable debt.

The other two horses of this memorable quarter had even longer, more extraordinary careers. Between them Lochroe and Crudwell ran in 169 races and won eighty-two. And although to that total Crudwell contributed fifty (only four horses in the history of the British turf have won more and none in the last 100 years), Lochroe took on more formidable rivals and was, on balance, probably the better horse.

Bought in Ireland by Peter Cazalet (he had won two 'Bumpers' there when trained by Willie O'Grady), Lochroe was by old-fashioned standards a light-framed flat-race type. He had, however, qualities far more important than mere size—superb, quicksilver jumping, great speed and, above all, an unconquerable heart. Owned by Lord Mildmay's sister Mrs Mildmay-White, he carried the famous light blue and white colours and was ridden many times by Lord Mildmay's godson, Mr Edward Cazalet who, until he turned his attention to the law, was in the top flight of post-war amateurs.

Like Halloween Lochroe was never quite at his best round Cheltenham, but he ran perhaps the finest of all his races there when beaten by only a length by Pas Seul in the 1960 Gold Cup. When twelve years old he had won the King George VI Chase in

1958, beating two Gold Cup winners Roddy Owen and Mandarin. That season in fact he went to Cheltenham unbeaten—and might easily have remained so but for the dreadful interference he suffered when Pas Seul fell.

Though plagued in his later years by foot trouble which may or may not have been a form of navicular, Lochroe went on racing until his fourteenth year. He was unplaced in only fourteen out of sixty-one races and this supremely consistent record is a glowing tribute to Peter Cazalet's skill. Although that skill has never yet been rewarded by a Grand National, a Gold Cup or a Champion Hurdle, Cazalet has turned out an unending stream of high-class winners in every season since the war. In 1964-5 he saddled a total of eighty-two—breaking the record held till then by Ryan Price.

On 9th January, 1958, in a three-mile chase at Hurst Park, one of his favourite courses, Lochroe was beaten the insulting distance of eight lengths by a horse two years his senior. No one thought it a disgrace for, enormously popular though Lochroe was, his conqueror had at least as many devoted admirers. Part of the charm of jumping is the way old friends keep reappearing and that day at Hurst Park Mrs D. M. Cooper's Crudwell was already halfway through his eighth season under National Hunt rules. Still then in his prime he served cheerfully on until, on 15th September at Wincanton, waiting as usual, till the end, he released his famous final burst for the last time. It was Crudwell's fiftieth victory and his elegant frame was as sound as on the day, fourteen years before, when a mare called Alexandrina dropped her foal not half a mile from the farm where Gay Donald and Pas Seul were to spend their childhood.

Between those two days the old horse had won seven races on the flat, four over hurdles and thirty-nine over fences. He had been ridden by Sir Gordon Richards, Lester Piggott, Bryan Marshall, Fred Winter, Bob Turnell, Dick Francis, Michael Scudamore, Atty Corbett and several more. He had beaten Linwell, Lochroe, Four Ten, Pointsman, Hatton's Grace and a whole form-book full of other good horses. Making history that day at Wincanton, he *was* a history in himself, and his record is never likely to be surpassed.

The weapons with which Crudwell had built it up were safe, if not brilliant jumping (he never took a risk if he could help it) and a power of acceleration from the last fence that few of his contemporaries could match. Often they beat him *before* the last—but if he stayed with them that far, nine times out of ten, it was all over.

Crudwell (W. Rees) and Lochroe (A. Freeman)—winners between them of 82 races. Hurst Park, 1958

Arkle's first victory over Mill House in the 1964 Cheltenham Gold Cup

Although, in his younger days, Crudwell won a Henry VIII
Chase and a Welsh Grand National he never really appreciated
the hurly burly of large fields and, superbly placed by his trainer
Frank Cundell, used to avoid them whenever possible.

Cundell, a top-class amateur before the war and a qualified vet,
has trained—and still trains—many good horses both on the flat
and under National Hunt rules. But in his beautifully managed
yard at Aston Tirrold nothing will ever take the place of Crudwell.

VIII

A few more threads remain to be gathered up. First of all the
hurdlers; and, among these, probably because of vastly increased
competition since the war, there have been few really dominant
personalities. The reign of Hatton's Grace has already been referred to. It divided those of Mr L. Abelson's National Spirit and
Mr Maurice Kingsley's Sir Ken, and no other horse since has
equalled the supremacy these three established each in turn.

In the second post-war season National Spirit proved himself an
outstanding novice and, in fact, from May 1946 to January 1949
(when he gave Frenchie Nicholson a particularly horrible fall at
Plumpton) he was only twice beaten over hurdles—both times
more by weight than the quality of his opponents. In his first
Championship, ridden by Danny Morgan, National Spirit was all
out to beat the French horse Le Paillon by a length, and it was
generally held that, had the latter's rider Alec Head (later to become Aly Khan's trainer in France) known Cheltenham a little
better, the result might have gone the other way. Nor was this
theory much weakened when Le Paillon went on to win the Prix
de l'Arc de Triomphe!

The next year, ridden this time by Ron Smyth, then in the
evening of a successful career as a jockey and now an equally
successful trainer, National Spirit won more easily from D.U.K.W.
But, unrecognized that day, there lurked behind him the insignificant figure of Hatton's Grace, well beaten in 1948 but soon to be
his Nemesis. Though only fourth in 1949 (when Hatton's Grace
won easily) National Spirit made two more gallant attempts to
regain his title. In 1950 he was in front, though probably tiring,
when he blundered horribly at the last, and in 1951 Hatton's
Grace had still not caught him when he fell at the same fateful
flight.

A big rangy chestnut who was trained at Epsom by Victor
Smyth, National Spirit, unlike most modern hurdlers won his
races not by speed but by stamina and superlative, effortless

jumping. Almost always in front a long way from home, he used to stand far back from his hurdles, flowing over them with unbroken stride, and more often than not getting priceless ground from his less agile rivals. He was in fact the sort of horse who could make a hurdle race as spectacular and exciting as any steeplechase—and I wish we had a few more like him now.

Tough and game as they come, National Spirit ran in every Champion Hurdle from 1947 to 1952, and in the meantime more than earned his keep during the summer by winning plenty of races on the flat. He is still alive and well at the age of twenty-four and a few years back a friend of mine saw the memorable sight of the late George Duller riding him a canter up six-mile hill at Epsom.

Both National Spirit and Hatton's Grace ran in the 1952 Championship; but now it was time for youth to be served and neither could hold a candle to the French-bred five-year-old, Sir Ken. Bought in France for Mr Kingsley by Willie Stephenson, Sir Ken had burst on the English scene at Liverpool the year before when he won the Lancashire Hurdle in a canter on the day of Nickel Coin's Grand National. From that moment to October 1953 he went through two seasons, sixteen races and two Champion Hurdles without a single defeat—a record of absolute domination which has not been equalled or even approached by a hurdler since.

And though no longer quite so invincible, Sir Ken won his third Champion Hurdle in 1954 with odds of 9–4 laid on him. He was, at his best (and it lasted a long, long time), the complete hurdler, able to take each race as it came, winning now by speed, now by grinding stamina—always by lightning, catlike jumping. He was ridden throughout by Tim Molony, one of the truly great partnerships of National Hunt history.

In the years that followed Sir Ken, another famous team, that of Ryan Price and Fred Winter, dominated the Champion Hurdle. They won it three times, in 1955 with Clair Soleil, in 1959 with Fare Time (both owned by Mr G. C. Judd) and in 1961 with Dr B. N. Pajgar's Eborneezer who was running for only the fifth time over hurdles. Of these three the best was probably Clair Soleil—a tremendous character who, when winning the Triumph Hurdle, his first race in England, tried to take a mouthful out of Tim Molony's leg as they passed the stands at Hurst Park!

Ryan Price's part in Fred Winter's story has been told. His rise to the top of the training profession since the war kept pace with that of his stable jockey—and was the well-deserved result of a lifetime spent with horses and an infinite capacity for hard work. A highly successful point to point rider before the war, Price served through it in the Commandos and retains a lot of the fearless, outspoken attitude to life that service suggests. Except for a brief period when he fell foul of the authorities, his stable has an unbroken record of success, much of it with horses bred and bought in France. And, having picked two champions, Fred Winter and Josh Gifford, before anyone else recognized their merit, Ryan Price can fairly claim to be a judge of men as well as horses.

Talking of men there is of course a whole host, both of jockeys and of trainers, whom it has not been possible to mention here. The story of jumping is not only the story of big stables and great jockeys. Its solid foundation lies as well in hundreds of small sporting yards, run either by permit holders or by trainers who eke out a precarious living doing the best they can with moderate animals. They and the men who ride their horses may never make the list of honour at each season's end but they, perhaps even more than their more famous colleagues, are in the game for the love of it. And without them National Hunt racing as we know it could not possibly go on.

There is, however, one name which has so far found no place on these pages but which no follower of jumping in the immediate post-war years would forgive me for omitting. It is that of Jack Dowdeswell, champion jockey in 1946-7 with fifty-eight winners and, when he hung up his boots in 1957, as much a byword for courage and physical endurance as Mandarin was later to become. Dowdeswell first rode on the flat in 1931 and was just getting going as a jumping jockey when the war intervened. He served throughout the desert and Italian campaigns in the Royal Horse Artillery and, demobbed when the first full post-war season was almost over, rode nineteen winners before the end of it. The next season he headed the list, mostly on horses trained by Major J. B. (Bay) Powell whose stable was at that time second only to Fulke Walwyn's in the number of winners it produced.

Short-legged, broad-shouldered and immensely strong, Jack Dowdeswell suffered more crashing falls and injuries than any rider of his day. In all he broke fifty-two different bones from his toes to his neck and in 1951, when he fell at Taunton, one of his arms was wrenched clean out of its socket and smashed apparently beyond repair. The Press wrote Dowdeswell off. 'He must be finished now,' they said; but, in eleven months, with the help of that great orthopaedic surgeon Bill Tucker (who with his skilful physiotherapists, notably Miss Jean Cooper, has done more for injured jockeys than any other man), Dowdeswell proved them wrong. Returning at Newton Abbot he rode a winner his first day back—and the reception he was given by the crowd meant more to him than any of his victories at Liverpool or Cheltenham.

As has been said, the standard of amateur riding since the war has probably never reached the peak of earlier days but apart from men like Dick Francis, Tim Brookshaw, Michael Scudamore, Stan Mellor and Terry Biddlecombe, who learnt their trade as amateurs, there have been several who, though they never turned professional, were very little if at all behind the leading men who did.

The best English amateur of the period (though he rode a lot in Ireland) was probably Mr Alan Lillingston who won the 1963 Champion Hurdle on Winning Fair; only the second 'bumper' to achieve that honour. Forced by injury to give up race-riding, Mr Lillingston now runs a successful stud-farm in Co Limerick and is still one of the best half-dozen men to hounds across that formidable country.

Bob McCreery, who rode his first winner back in 1949 and still rides successfully on the flat, was Mr Lillingston's equal in every respect save possibly the finish. No one who saw it will forget his feat at Kempton when, falling at the last on a little horse called Rose's Pact he jumped back aboard while his mount was still on the ground, got him going again—and won!

Danny Moralee and Bobby Brewis were (and the latter still is) top-class amateurs from the north and, until other interests claimed him Sir William Pigott-Brown looked like becoming the most successful owner-rider since Lord Mildmay.

But the only man ever to approach the place held by that great amateur in the racing public's heart has I believe been Mr Gay Kindersley, whose cheerful courage made light of many appalling injuries and who in 1965, despite repeated medical advice that one more bad fall might well be fatal, realized his lifelong ambition to ride in a Grand National. Mr Kindersley is now, I'm glad to say, a member of the National Hunt Committee, and the senior National Hunt steward in this centenary year, Major David Gibson, also rode many winners, including those of three Grand Military Gold Cups at Sandown.

Nor would any account of post-war amateurs be complete without a mention of that formidable Australian Mr Laurie Morgan who, as captain of the winning Olympic three-day event team, came to this country in 1957 and proceeded to carry all before him on his great hunter-chaser, Colledge Master.

And so to the present day—a present dominated by one man and one horse, Tom Dreaper and Anne, Duchess of Westminster's Arkle.

In 1963 when Mr W. H. Golling's Mill House won the Cheltenham Gold Cup as a six-year-old, ridden by Willie Robinson and trained by Fulke Walwyn, he was hailed—and justifiably so—as the best young 'chaser seen since Golden Miller. Two days earlier at the same National Hunt meeting Arkle had won the Broadway Chase by twenty lengths but when, in the next season's Hennessy Gold Cup, Mill House gave him 5 lbs and an eight lengths beating there seemed no good reason to alter that first assessment.

We know now of course that Arkle's defeat at Newbury was caused only by his slip at the final open ditch. He has only been beaten once since then (by weight over a distance short of his best) and has four times taken a terrible revenge on poor Mill House. He towers, at this moment, higher above his contemporaries than any horse in the history of jumping and the only living 'chaser conceivably worthy to be mentioned in the same breath is his stable-companion, Mrs T. G. Wilkinson's Flyingbolt.

Arkle's story is nothing like finished. Only nine years old—just reaching the prime of a 'chaser's life—he may, with reasonable luck, go on for several seasons yet—bringing grey hairs to handicappers, despair to rival owners and delight to the public that adores him.

I wrote earlier that three characters, Queen Elizabeth the Queen Mother, Lord Mildmay and Fred Winter have done more than anyone else for National Hunt racing in England since the war. To those three Arkle's name must now be added. It is a name famous not only in England and Ireland but all over the world wherever men care about horses—and indeed in many places where hitherto they didn't.

National Hunt racing is, above all, designed to test the ability of a horse to gallop and jump. And so it is fitting that the story of its first hundred years should end with the appearance of one who does both things better than they have ever done before. If the sport had achieved nothing else in all those years, to produce a phenomenon like Arkle would be justification enough. For he is the ideal in search of which so many have laboured so long and so hard. Whatever the future holds for him and for National Hunt racing, the days of his supremacy will always be remembered as a golden age.

16

NATIONAL HUNT COMMITTEE
(Founded 1866)

FOUNDERS

VISCOUNT ANDOVER (afterwards Earl of Suffolk and Berkshire),
B. J. ANGELL, Esq., E. C. BURTON, Esq., and W. G. CRAVEN,
Esq.

LIST OF MEMBERS—PAST AND PRESENT
(Revised to 31st December, 1965)

Name, &c.	When Elected
His Royal Highness the Duke of York (afterwards King George VI)	May 14, 1934
His Royal Highness the Duke of Gloucester	May 14, 1934
His Royal Highness the Duke of Windsor	February 1, 1921
Abergavenny (Henry Gilbert Ralph), 3rd Marquess of	October 9, 1905
Abergavenny (Guy Temple Montacute Larnach-Nevill), 4th Marquess of	October 9, 1916
Abergavenny (John Henry Guy Nevill), 5th Marquess of, O.B.E.	December 14, 1942
Angell, Benjamin John	Original Member
Anglesey (Sir Henry William George), 3rd Marquess of	April 17, 1871
Anstruther-Gray, Major Sir William John, Bt., P.C., M.C.	July 19, 1948
Astley, Sir John Dugdale, Bt.	December 31, 1870
Aylesford (Heneage), 7th Earl of	October 25, 1872
Baird, Brig.-Gen. Edward William David, C.B.E.	October 10, 1892
Barclay, Major Hedworth Trelawny	December 14, 1885
Bass, Sir William Arthur Hamar, Bt.	July 16, 1923
Bassett, Ralph Thurstan	October 12, 1896
Beaufort (Sir Henry Charles FitzRoy), 8th Duke of, K.G.	Co-opted April 3, 1866
Bengough, Major Piers Henry George	March 1, 1965
Beresford, Lord Marcus Talbot de la Poer, C.V.O.	April 12, 1875
Beresford, Col. Lord William Leslie de la Poer, V.C., K.C.I.E.	December 11, 1880
Bibby, Frank	October 10, 1898
Bibby, Captain Frank Brian Frederic	December 9, 1918
Bicester (Vivian Hugh Smith), 1st Baron	July 16, 1928
Bicester (Randal Hugh Vivian Smith), 2nd Baron	July 21, 1958
Bingham, Major-Gen. the Hon. Sir Cecil Edward, K.C.M.G., C.B., G.C.V.O.	October 10, 1921
Blacker, Major-General Cecil Hugh, O.B.E., M.C.	December 13, 1954
Brabazon, Major-Gen. Sir John Palmer, K.C.B., C.V.O.	May 8, 1905
Brassey, Major Harold Ernest	October 8, 1900
Bulkeley, Col. Charles Rivers, C.B.	December 8, 1884

243

Bullough, Sir George, Bt.	December 14, 1914
Bulteel, John Crocker, D.S.O., M.C.	July 16, 1923
Bulteel, John George	May 12, 1902
Burton, Edmund Charles {	Co-opted Dec. 14, 1867
Byrne, Major-Gen. Thomas Edmond	April 12, 1875
Cadogan (William Gerald Charles Cadogan), 7t Earl, M.C. }	July 17, 1939
Calthorpe (Sir Frederick Henry William), 5th Baron	November 25, 1868
Cambaceres, Comte Delaire de	May 10, 1920
Campbell, Gen. Sir David Graham Muschet, K.C.B.	July 16, 1928
Carew, Charles Hallowell Hallowell-	Original Member
Carington (Rupert Clement George), 4th Baron Carrington, C.V.O., D.S.O. }	July 11, 1881
Case-Walker, Thomas Edward	June 17, 1871
Champion de Crespigny, Brig.-Gen. Sir Claude Raul, Bt., C.B., C.M.G., D.S.O. }	October 10, 1921
Chaplin (Henry), 1st Viscount	Original Member
Chetwynd, Sir George, Bt.	December 16, 1872
Cholmondeley (George Henry Hugh), 4th Marquess of }	December 19, 1889
Christie-Miller, Major Edward Goff	December 14, 1914
Clermont-Tonnerre, Comte Robert de	May 12, 1913
Collis, Lieut.-Col. Robert Henry, D.S.O.	October 9, 1905
Combe, Major-General John Frederick Boyce, C.B., D.S.O. }	July 15, 1946
Cooper, Capt. William Henry	January 3, 1870
Cotes, Lieut.-Col. Charles James	October 9, 1911
Cottenham (John Digby Thomas Pepys), 7th Earl of	October 11, 1954
Courage, Commander Archibald Vesey	July 16, 1934
Coventry (George William), 9th Earl of, P.C.	Original Member
Coventry, Capt. the Hon. Charles John, C.B.	October 8, 1900
Coventry, Capt. Henry Amelius Beauclerk	Original Member
Cowley (Henry Arthur Mornington), 3rd Earl	December 9, 1895
Craven (William George Robert), 4th Earl of	June 21, 1873
Craven, William George	Original Member
Curtis, Sir William Michael, Bt.	December 9, 1901
Denman (Sir Thomas), 3rd Baron, P.C., G.C.M.G., K.C.V.O. }	July 19, 1920
Derby (Sir Edward George Villiers Stanley), 17th Earl of, K.G., P.C., G.C.B., G.C.V.O. }	July 20, 1936
de Trafford, Sir Humphrey Edmund, Bt., M.C.	December 9, 1929
de Tuyll, Baron Francis Charles Owen, M.B.E.	December 8, 1919
Douglas-Pennant, Lieut.-Col. Frank (Succeeded as 5th Baron Penrhyn, June 26, 1949) }	May 10, 1915
Drogheda (Henry Francis Seymour), 3rd and last Marquess of, K.P. }	July 13, 1885
Du Bos, Auguste	December 9, 1912
Dudley (William Humble), 2nd Earl of, P.C., G.C.B., G.C.M.G., G.C.V.O. }	October 8, 1900
Dufosee, Henry William	March 4, 1963
Eden, Sir William, Bt.	December 9, 1889
Egerton, Charles Augustus	December 9, 1889
Egerton, Commander Hugh Sydney, D.S.C.	October 13, 1952
Enniskillen (Sir Lowry Egerton), 4th Earl of, K.P.	October 13, 1890

Essex (George Devereux de Vere), 7th Earl of	October 9, 1905
Feilden, Major-General Sir Randle Guy, K.C.V.O., C.B., C.B.E.	October 11, 1954
Fetherstonhaugh, Major Frederick Howard Wingfield	December 14, 1914
Filmer, Sir Robert Marcus, Bt.	October 14, 1907
Fisher-Childe, Col. Ralph Bromfield Willington, C.B.	December 9, 1912
Fitzhardinge (Francis William Fitzhardinge), 2nd Baron	January 2, 1884
Fitzwilliam, The Hon. William John Wentworth	December 12, 1887
Forestier-Walker, Lieut.-Col. Roland Stuart, D.S.O.	December 14, 1914
Forsyth-Forrest, Capt. Philip Maurice	October 12, 1953
Foster, Capt. James	May 13, 1907
Foster, Major John Bentley	July 20, 1931
Furlong, Major Noel Charles Bell	October 13, 1952
Garratt, Lieut.-Col. John Arthur Thomas	July 9, 1883
Gheest, Maurice de	October 13, 1919
Gibson, Major William David	October 12, 1959
Gilliat, Lt.-Col. Sir Martin John, K.C.V.O., M.B.E., D.L.	October 12, 1964
Gillois, Col. A. M.	October 13, 1919
Gordon, Major John Maxwell	December 10, 1906
Gordon-Smith, Sir Allan Gordon, K.B.E.	October 10, 1949
Gosling, Edward Lambert	July 15, 1946
Gosling, Capt. Henry Miles	March 1, 1965
Gowrie (Brig.-Gen. the Hon. Sir Alexander Gore Arkwright Hore-Ruthven), 1st Earl, V.C., P.C., G.C.M.G., C.B., D.S.O.	December 12, 1921
Gresson, William Jardine	May 13, 1929
Grimthorpe (Sir Ralph William Ernest Beckett), 3rd Baron, T.D.	July 19, 1926
Haddington (George Baillie-Hamilton), 12th Earl of, K.T., M.C., T.D.	July 18, 1932
Halifax (Charles Ingram Courtenay Wood), 2nd Earl of	October 9, 1950
Hamilton and Brandon (William Alexander Louis Stephen), 12th Duke of, K.T.	March 6, 1868
Hanmer, Sir (Griffin Wyndham) Edward, Bt.	December 11, 1933
Hardinge (Henry Charles), 3rd Viscount, C.B.	October 12, 1903
Harewood (Sir Henry George Charles Lascelles), 6th Earl of, K.G., G.C.V.O., D.S.O.	December 12, 1938
Harford, Lieut.-Col. Frederick Henry	June 17, 1871
Harrington (Charles Augustus), 8th Earl of	July 10, 1882
Hastings (Sir George Manners), 20th Baron	July 12, 1886
Hathorn, Lieut.-Col. John Fletcher	February 9, 1874
Helmsley (William Reginald Duncombe), Viscount	July 12, 1880
Henderson, Charles William Chipchase	December 11, 1905
Henderson, John Ronald, M.B.E.	July 19, 1965
Heneage, Edward (1st Baron Heneage)	December 31, 1870
Herbert, William Reginald Joseph Fitz-Herbert	April 29, 1869
Hoare, Major Robert, M.C.	October 8, 1956
Holland-Martin, Edward	August 28, 1940
Hope-Johnstone, Capt. Wentworth William	October 9, 1893
Howard, The Hon. Cecil Molyneux	July 12, 1880

Name, &c.	When Elected
Hughes-Onslow, Major Arthur	October 12, 1908
Hungerford, Henry Vane Forester Holdich	April 17, 1882
Huntington, Major Arthur William, D.S.O.	July 21, 1930
Ilchester (Edward Henry Charles James Fox-Strangways), 7th Earl of	July 15, 1946
Jarvis, George Eden	October 8, 1900
Jenkins, William Henry Phillips	July 9, 1883
Jersey (George Henry Robert Child-Villiers), 8th Earl of	December 11, 1905
Joel, Harry Joel	May 10, 1965
Johnstone, Sir Frederick John William, Bt.	Original Member
Johnstone, Lieut.-Col. George Charles Keppel	Co-opted Jan. 23, 1867
Johnstone, The Hon. Gilbert (Vanden Bempde)	December 10, 1906
Johnstone, John	July 21, 1924
Joicey (Lieut.-Col. Sir Hugh Edward), 3rd Baron, D.S.O.	December 13, 1948
Ker, Lord Charles John Innes-	January 5, 1872
Kindersley, Gay	July 16, 1962
King, Thomas Poole	May 10, 1915
Kinsky, Prince	May 14, 1906
Knox, Col. George Williams	November 25, 1868
La Rochefoucauld, Comte Jean de	May 10, 1915
Lascelles (Henry Ulick Lascelles), Viscount (5th Earl of Harewood)	December 1, 1873
Lawson, Col. Sir Peter Grant, Bt.	July 18, 1932
Leeds (Sir George Godolphin), 10th Duke of	April 10, 1887
Legard, Sir Charles, Bt.	November 25, 1868
Leigh (Rupert William Dudley), 4th Baron	February 25, 1952
Leigh, John Gerard	December 15, 1873
Leverhulme (Sir Philip William Bryce Lever), 3rd Viscount, T.D.	October 9, 1961
Leveson-Gower, Major Granville Charles Gresham	July 19, 1938
Lewis, Brigadier James Charles Windsor, D.S.O., M.C.	February 25, 1952
Lindsay, Lieut.-Col. Henry Edzell Morgan	October 12, 1903
Little, Capt. James Lockhart	Original Member
Llewellyn, Lieut.-Col. Henry Morton, C.B.E.	July 15, 1946
Lloyd, Sir Marteine Owen Mowbray, Bt.	May 12, 1902
Londesborough (Hugo William Cecil), 4th Earl of	December 13, 1920
Londonderry (Sir Charles Stewart), 6th Marquess of, K.G.	July 14, 1879
Lonsdale (Sir Hugh Cecil Lowther), 5th Earl of, K.G., G.C.V.O.	December 13, 1915
Lumsden, Lieut.-General Herbert, D.S.O., M.C.	July 19, 1937
McCalmont, Col. Harry Leslie Blundell, C.B.	October 9, 1899
McCreery, General Sir Richard (Loudon), G.C.B., K.B.E., D.S.O., M.C.	December 11, 1944
Machell, Capt. James Octavus	April 10, 1876
McKie, Lieut.-Col. John, D.S.O.	October 9, 1899
Mainwaring, Charles Francis Kynaston	May 8, 1905
Manners (John Thomas), 3rd Baron	July 10, 1882
Marshall, Major Anthony Charles	May 10, 1948
Marshall, John Anthony	May 11, 1959
Meux, Admiral of the Fleet the Hon. Sir Hedworth, G.C.B., K.C.V.O.	July 19, 1920

Middleton, Capt. William George	July 8, 1878
Mildmay of Flete (Francis Bingham Mildmay), 1st Baron, P.C.	} July 19, 1937
Mildmay of Flete (Anthony Bingham), 2nd Baron	December 14, 1942
Miller, Major James Christopher Vernon	May 13, 1957
Minto (Sir Gilbert John), 4th Earl of, G.C.M.G.	July 1, 1871
Montrose (Sir Douglas Beresford Malise Ronald), 5th Duke of, K.T.	} April 8, 1878
Morgan, Col. the Hon. Frederic Courtenay	April 10, 1866
Moseley, Lieut.-Col. Roger Bright	December 13, 1948
Murat, Prince, G.C.V.O.	May 12, 1913
Murland, William	May 13, 1901
Neuflize, Baron de	May 12, 1913
Newton, Charles Stancliffe	June 17, 1895
Noble, Brigadier Frederick Babington Bridgeman, O.B.E.	} December 13, 1965
Norfolk (Bernard Marmaduke Fitzalan-Howard), 16th Duke of, E.M., K.G., P.C., G.C.V.O.	} July 18, 1938
Normanton (Edward John Sidney Christian Welbore Ellis Agar), 5th Earl of	} May 9, 1960
Norrie (Lieut.-General Sir Charles Willoughby Moke), 1st Baron, G.C.M.G., G.C.V.O., C.B., D.S.O., M.C.	} July 19, 1937
Orr-Ewing, Major James Alexander	December 9, 1889
Owen, Hugh Darby Annesley	March 23, 1877
Owen, Morris Williams Lloyd	December 10, 1906
Paget, Lord Berkeley Charles Sidney	February 9, 1874
Paget, Edward Catesby	July 20, 1936
Paget, Sir (George) Ernest, Bt.	July 12, 1880
Part, Lieut.-Col. Sir Dealtry Charles, O.B.E.	December 9, 1946
Payne, George	Original Member
Payne-Gallwey, Lieut.-Col. Peter, D.S.O.	December 11, 1944
Paynter, Brig.-Gen. Sir George Camborne Beauclerk, K.C.V.O., C.M.G., D.S.O.	} October 9, 1911
Peacock, Major Hugh Myddleton	October 10, 1955
Penrhyn (George Sholto Gordon), 2nd Baron	{ Co-opted December 14, 1867
Penrhyn (Edward Sholto), 3rd Baron	December 13, 1926
Penrhyn (Hugh Napier Douglas-Pennant), 4th Baron	} July 17, 1933
Phillips, The Hon. James Perrott, T.D.	July 21, 1958
Phillips, Lieut.-Col. John Frederick Lort	December 12, 1898
Platt, Eric James Walter	December 14, 1914
Pole, Colonel Sir John Gawen Carew, Bt., D.S.O., T.D.	December 11, 1950
Poulett (William Henry), 6th Earl	Original Member
Queenborough (Almeric Hugh Paget), 1st Baron, G.B.E.	} July 21, 1927
Queensberry (Sir John Sholto), 8th Marquess of	April 27, 1872
Rank, James Voase	July 16, 1951
Rankin, Brig.-Gen. Charles Herbert, C.B., C.M.G., D.S.O.	} October 13, 1919
Rendlesham (Frederick William Brook), 5th Baron	October 13, 1890
Richardson, John Maunsell	May 4, 1874
Rogerson, John	December 12, 1949
Rose, Sir Charles Day, Bt.	October 19, 1892

Rosebery (Sir Albert Edward Harry Meyer Archibald Primrose), 6th Earl of, K.T., P.C., D.S.O., M.C.	December 10, 1934
Rossmore (Henry Cairns), 4th Baron	December 1, 1873
Rossmore (Derrick Warner William), 5th Baron	July 14, 1884
Rushout, Sir Charles FitzGerald, Bt.	December 1, 1873
St. Davids (Sir John Wynford), 1st Viscount, P.C.	December 11, 1905
Sassoon, Capt. Reginald Ellice	July 18, 1932
Sefton (Sir Osbert Cecil), 6th Earl of, G.C.V.O.	October 12, 1903
Sefton (Sir Hugh William Osbert Molyneux), 7th Earl of	May 11, 1936
Shrewsbury and Waterford (John Geo. Chas. Hy. Alton Alex. Chetwynd Chetwynd-Talbot), 21st Earl of	October 10, 1955
Smith, Gerald Dudley	December 14, 1914
Speed, Brigadier Elmer John Leyland, M.C.	December 9, 1946
Stalbridge (Hugh Grosvenor), 2nd Baron, M.C.	July 19, 1926
Stamford and Warrington (George Harry), 7th Earl of	November 25, 1868
Stanley (Edward Montague Cavendish), Lord	December 8, 1919
Stanley, Brig.-Gen. the Hon. Ferdinand Charles, C.M.G., D.S.O.	October 8, 1900
Stirling, Major Gilbert Chalmers	April 21, 1875
Straker, Major Ian Allgood	July 19, 1920
Straker, John Joicey, M.C.	October 12, 1953
Suffield (Sir Charles), 5th Baron	June 1, 1868
Suffolk and Berkshire (Henry Charles), 18th Earl of	Co-opted April 3, 1866
Suffolk and Berkshire (Henry Molyneux Paget), 19th Earl of	October 8, 1906
Sumner, Arthur Holme	Original Member
Sumner, John Richard Hugh, C.B.E.	December 12, 1955
Tempest, Capt. Arthur Cecil	January 3, 1870
Thomas, Hugh Lloyd, C.V.O., C.M.G.	December 10, 1934
Thompson, Colonel Reginald, D.S.O., T.D.	July 15, 1946
Thomson, Colonel John, T.D.	October 11, 1965
Throckmorton, Sir (Nicholas) William George, Bt.	November 5, 1868
Tomkinson, Brigadier Henry Archdale, D.S.O.	May 11, 1936
Tredegar (Sir Godfrey Charles), 1st Viscount	April 10, 1866
Vaux, Wing Commander Peter Douglas Ord	October 12, 1953
Vyner, Henry Frederick Clare	April 12, 1875
Walker, Sir Peter Carlaw, Bt.	December 9, 1901
Ward, Capt. the Hon. Reginald, D.S.O.	December 8, 1902
Westmacott, Colonel Guy Randolph, D.S.O.	July 15, 1946
Westminster (Sir Hugh Richard Arthur Grosvenor), 2nd Duke of, G.C.V.O., D.S.O.	December 9, 1901
Westmorland (Francis William Henry), 12th Earl of, C.B.	Original Member
Westmorland (Vere Anthony Francis St. Clair Fane), 14th Earl of	July 18, 1932
Weyland, Capt. Mark	July 18, 1927
Whichcote, Sir Thomas, Bt.	December 31, 1870
Whitbread, William Henry	July 16, 1956
White, Col. the Hon. Charles William	December 16, 1872
White, Capt. the Hon. Luke (3rd Baron Annaly), C.B.	December 11, 1882
Whitney, John Hay	July 15, 1957

Wickham, Major George Lamplugh	December 11, 1893
Wigan, Major Derek	December 14, 1964
Wilkins, Richard Sinclair	July 19, 1965
Williams, Charles Crofts Llewellyn, M.C.	July 19, 1938
Williams, Owen John	October 8, 1900
Willoughby de Broke (Henry), 18th Baron	May 4, 1874
Willoughby de Broke (John Henry Peyto Verney), 20th Baron, M.C., A.F.C.	December 9, 1940
Wilson-Todd, Sir William Pierrepont, Bt.	December 13, 1915
Wilton (Arthur Edward Holland), 3rd Earl of	Original Member
Withington, Frederick Edward, G.B.E.	May 11, 1931
Wolverton (George Grenfell), 2nd Baron	January 2, 1884
Wyndham, Colonel the Hon. Everard Humphrey, M.C.	December 9, 1918
Yarborough (Charles), 3rd Earl of	December 31, 1870
Yarborough (Charles Alfred Worsley), 4th Earl of	December 8, 1884
Yardley, Lieut.-Col. John Watkins, C.M.G., D.S.O.	December 9, 1912

		Owner	Trainer	Rider	S.P.
1837	The Duke	Mr Sirdefield	—	Potts	—
1838	Sir Henry	Mr Thompson	—	T. Oliver	—
1839	Lottery, a-12-0	Mr Elmore	—	J. Mason	5–1
1840	Jerry, a-12-0	Mr Elmore	—	B. Bretherton	12–1
1841	Charity, a-12-0	Lord Craven	—	Powell	14–1
1842	Gay Lad, a-12-0	Mr Elmore	—	T. Oliver	7–1
1843	Vanguard, a-11-10	Lord Chesterfield	—	T. Oliver	12–1
1844	Discount, a-10-12	Mr Quartermaine	—	Crickmere	5–1
1845	Cureall, a-11-5	Mr Crawford	—	Loft	—
1846	Pioneer, 6-11-12	Mr Adams	—	Taylor	—
1847	Matthew, a-10-6	Mr Courtney	—	D. Wynne	10–11
1848	Chandler, a-11-12	Capt. Little	—	Capt. Little	12–1
1849	Peter Simple, a-11-0	J. Mason	—	T. Cunning- ham	20–1
1850	Abd el Kader, a-9-12	Mr Osborne	—	C. Green	—
1851	Abd el Kader, a-10-4	Mr Osborne	—	T. Abbott	7–1
1852	Miss Mowbray, a-10-4	T. Mason	—	Mr. A. Good- man	—
1853	Peter Simple, a-10-10	Capt. Little	—	T. Oliver	9–1
1854	Bourton, a-11-12	Mr Moseley	—	Tasker	4–1
1855	Wanderer, a-9-8	Mr Dennis	—	J. Handon	25–1
1856	Free Trader, a-9-6	W. Barnett	—	G. Stevens	25–1
1857	Emigrant, a-9-10	G. Hodgman	—	C. Boyce	10–1
1858	Little Charlie, a-10-7	C. Capel	—	W. Archer	100–6
1859	Half Caste, 6-9-7	Mr Willoughby	—	C. Green	7–1
1860	Anatis, a-9-10	C. Capel	—	Mr Thomas	7–2
1861	Jealousy, a-9-12	J. Bennett	—	J. Kendall	5–1
1862	Huntsman, a-11-0	Vicomte de Namurs	—	H. Lamplugh	3–1
1863	Emblem, a-10-10	Lord Coventry	—	G. Stevens	4–1
1864	Emblematic, 6-10-6	Lord Coventry	—	G. Stevens	10–1
1865	Alcibiade, 5-11-4	B. Angell	—	Capt. Coventry	100–7
1866	Salamander, a-10-7	Mr Studd	—	Mr A. Good- man	40–1
1867	Cortolvin, a-11-13	Duke of Hamilton	—	J. Page	100–6
1868	The Lamb, 6-10-7	Lord Poulett	—	Mr Edwards	10–1
1869	The Colonel, 6-10-7	Mr Weyman	—	G. Stevens	13–1
1870	The Colonel, 7-11-12	M. Evans	—	G. Stevens	4–1
1871	The Lamb, 9-11-4	Lord Poulett	—	Mr Thomas	5–1
1872	Casse Tete, a-10-0	E. Brayley	—	J. Page	20–1
1873	Disturbance, 6-11-11	Capt. Machell	—	Mr J. Richard- son	20–1
1874	Reugny, 6-10-12	Capt. Machell	—	Mr J. Richard- son	5–1
1875	Pathfinder, a-10-11	H. Bird	—	Mr Thomas	100–6
1876	Regal, 5-11-3	Capt. Machell	—	J. Cannon	25–1
1877	Austerlitz, 5-10-8	F. Hobson	—	Mr E. Hobson	15–1
1878	Shifnal, a-10-12	J. Nightingall	—	J. Jones	7–1
1879	Liberator, a-11-4	G. Moore	—	Mr G. Moore	5–1
1880	Empress, 5-10-7	P. Ducrot	—	Mr T. Beasley	8–1
1881	Woodbrook, 7-11-3	Capt. Kirkwood	—	Mr T. Beasley	6–1
1882	Seaman, 6-11-6	Lord Manners	—	Lord Manners	10–1

		Owner	Trainer	Rider	S.P.
1883	Zoedone, 6-11-0	Count C. Kinsky	—	Count C. Kinsky	100–8
1884	Voluptuary, 6-10-5	H. Boyd	T. Wilson	Mr E. Wilson	10–1
1885	Roquefort, 6-11-0	A. Cooper	Swatton	Mr E. Wilson	100–30
1886	Old Joe, 7-10-9	A. Douglas	—	T. Skelton	25–1
1887	Gamecock, 8-11-0	E. Jay	Jordan	W. Daniells	20–1
1888	Playfair, 7-10-7	E. Baird	—	Mawson	40–1
1889	Frigate, 11-11-5	M. Maher	—	Mr. T. Beasley	8–1
1890	Ilex, 6-10-5	G. Masterman	Nightingall	A. Nightingall	4–1
1891	Come Away, 7-11-12	W. Jameson	—	Mr H. Beasley	4–1
1892	Father O'Flynn, 7-10-5	G. Wilson	—	Capt. R. Owen	20–1
1893	Cloister, 9-12-7	C. Duff	Swatton	Dollery	9–2
1894	Why Not, 13-11-3	Capt. C. Fenwick	Collins	A. Nightingall	5–1
1895	Wild Man from Borneo, 7-10-1	J. Widger	Gatland	Mr J. Widger	10–1
1896	The Soarer, a-9-13	W. Walker	Collins	Mr D. Campbell	40–1
1897	Manifesto, 9-11-3	H. Dyas	McAuliffe	T. Kavanagh	6–1
1898	Drogheda, 6-10-12	G. Adams	E. Woods	J. Gourley	25–1
1899	Manifesto, 11-12-7	J. Bulteel	R. Collins	G. Williamson	5–1
1900	Ambush II, 6-11-3	Prince of Wales	A. Anthony	A. Anthony	4–1
1901	Grudon, 11-10-0	B. Bletsoe	J. Holland	A. Nightingall	9–1
1902	Shannon Lass, 7-10-1	A. Gorham	Hackett	D. Read	20–1
1903	Drumcree, 9-11-3	J. Morrison	Sir C. Nugent	P. Woodland	13–2
1904	Moifaa, 8-10-7	S. Gollans	O. Hickey	A. Birch	25–1
1905	Kirkland, 9-11-5	F. Bibby	Thomas	F. Mason	6–1
1906	Ascetic's Silver, 9-10-9	Prince Hatzfeldt	A. Hastings	Mr A. Hastings	20–1
1907	Eremon, 7-10-1	S. Howard	T. Coulthwaite	A. Newey	8–1
1908	Rubio, 10-10-5	Maj. F. D-Pennant	W. Costello	H. Bletsoe	66–1
1909	Lutteur III, 5-10-11	J. Hennessy	H. Escott	G. Parfrement	100–9
1910	Jenkinstown, 9-10-5	S. Howard	T. Coulthwaite	R. Chadwick	100–8
1911	Glenside, 9-10-3	F. Bibby	Capt. Collis	Mr J. Anthony	20–1
1912	Jerry M, 9-12-7	Sir C. A-Smith	R. Gore	E. Piggott	4–1
1913	Covercoat, 7-11-6	Sir C. A-Smith	R. Gore	P. Woodland	100–9
1914	Sunloch, 8-9-7	T. Tyler	T. Tyler	W. Smith	100–6
1915	Ally Sloper, 6-10-5	Lady Nelson	A. Hastings	Mr J. Anthony	100–8
1916	Vermouth, 6-11-10	P. Heybourn	J. Bell	J. Reardon	100–8
1917	Ballymacad, 10-9-12	Sir G. Bullough	A. Hastings	E. Driscoll	100–9
1918	Poethlyn, 8-11-6	Mrs H. Peel	A. Escott	E. Piggott	5–1
1919	Poethlyn, 9-12-7	Mrs H. Peel	A. Escott	E. Piggott	11–4
1920	Troytown, 7-11-9	Maj. T. Gerrard	A. Anthony	Mr J. Anthony	6–1
1921	Shaun Spadah, 10-11-7	M. McAlpine	G. Poole	F. Rees	100–9
1922	Music Hall, 9-11-8	H. Kershaw	O. Anthony	L. Rees	100–9
1923	Sergeant Murphy, 13-11-3	S. Sandford	G. Blackwell	Capt. G. Bennett	100–6
1924	Master Robert, 11-10-5	Lord Airlie	A. Hastings	R. Trudgill	25–1
1925	Double Chance 9-10-9	D. Goold	F. Archer	Maj. J. Wilson	100–9
1926	Jack Horner, 9-10-5	A. Schwartz	H. Leader	W. Watkinson	25–1
1927	Sprig, 10-12-4	Mrs M. Partridge	T. R. Leader	T. E. Leader	8–1

	Owner	Trainer	Rider	S.P.
1928 Tipperary Tim, 10-10-0	H. Kenyon	J. Dodd	Mr W. Dutton	100–1
1929 Gregalach, 7-11-4	Mrs M. Gemmall	T. R. Leader	R. Everett	100–1
1930 Shaun Goilin, 10-11-7	W. Midwood	F. Hartigan	T. Cullinan	100–8
1931 Grakle, 9-11-7	C. Taylor	T. Coulthwaite	R. Lyall	100–6
1932 Forbra, 7-10-7	W. Parsonage	T. Rimell	J. Hamey	50–1
1933 Kellsboro' Jack, 7-11-9	Mrs F. Clark	I. Anthony	D. Williams	25–1
1934 Golden Miller, 7-12-2	Miss D. Paget	A. B. Briscoe	G. Wilson	8–1
1935 Reynoldstown, 7-11-4	Maj. N. Furlong	N. Furlong	Mr F. Furlong	22–1
1936 Reynoldstown, 9-12-2	Maj. N. Furlong	N. Furlong	Mr. F. Walwyn	10–1
1937 Royal Mail, 8-11-13	H. L. Thomas	I. Anthony	E. Williams	100–6
1938 Battleship, 11-11-6	Mrs M. Scott	R. Hobbs	B. Hobbs	40–1
1939 Workman, 9-10-6	Sir A. Maguire	J. Ruttle	T. Hyde	100–8
1940 Bogskar, 7-10-4	Lord Stalbridge	Lord Stalbridge	M. Jones	25–1
1946 Lovely Cottage, 9-10-8	J. Morant	T. Rayson	Capt. R. Petre	25–1
1947 Caughoo, 8-10-0	J. McDowell	H. McDowell	E. Dempsey	100–1
1948 Sheila's Cottage, 9-10-7	J. Proctor	N. Crump	A. Thompson	50–1
1949 Russian Hero, 9-10-8	W. Williamson	G. Owen	L. McMorrow	66–1
1950 Freebooter, 9-11-11	Mrs L. Brother-ton	R. Renton	J. Power	10–1
1951 Nickel Coin, 9-10-1	J. Royle	J. O'Donoghue	J. Bullock	40–1
1952 Teal, 10-10-12	H. Lane	N. Crump	A. Thompson	100–7
1953 Early Mist, 8-11-2	J. Griffin	V. O'Brien	B. Marshall	20–1
1954 Royal Tan, 10-11-7	J. Griffin	V. O'Brien	B. Marshall	8–1
1955 Quare Times, 9-11-0	Mrs W. Wel-man	V. O'Brien	P. Taaffe	100–9
1956 E.S.B., 10-11-3	Mrs L. Carver	F. Rimell	D. Dick	100–7
1957 Sundew, 11-11-7	Mrs G. Kohn	F. Hudson	F. Winter	20–1
1958 Mr What, 8-10-6	D. Coughlan	T. Taaffe	A. Freeman	18–1
1959 Oxo, 8-10-13	J. Bigg	W. Stephenson	M. Scudamore	8–1
1960 Merryman II, 9-10-12	Miss W. Wallace	N. Crump	G. Scott	13–2
1961 Nicolaus Silver, 9-10-1	C. Vaughan	F. Rimell	H. Beasley	28–1
1962 Kilmore, 12-10-4	N. Cohen	R. Price	F. Winter	28–1
1963 Ayala, 9-10-0	P. Raymond	K. Piggott	P. Buckley	66–1
1964 Team Spirit, 12-10-3	J. Goodman	F. Walwyn	W. Robinson	18–1
1965 Jay Trump, 8-11-5	Mrs M. Stephen-son	F. Winter	Mr C. Smith	100–6
1966 Anglo, 8-10-0	S. Levy	F. Winter	T. Norman	50–1

CHELTENHAM GOLD CUP

	Owner	Trainer	Rider	S.P.
1924 Red Splash, 5-11-5	Maj. E. H. Wyndham	F. E. Withing-ton	F. Rees	5–1
1925 Ballinode, a-12-0	J. Bentley	F. Morgan	T. Leader	3–1
1926 Koko, a-12-0	F. Barbour	J. Bickley	J. Hamey	10–1
1927 Thrown In, a-12-0	Lord Stalbridge	Owner	Mr. H. Grosvenor	10–1

		Owner	Trainer	Rider	S.P.
1928	Patron Saint, 5-11-5	F. Keen	H. Harrison	F. Rees	7-2
1929	Easter Hero, a-12-0	J. Whitney	J. Anthony	F. Rees	7-4
1930	Easter Hero, 10-12-0	J. Whitney	J. Anthony	T. Cullinan	8-11
1932	Golden Miller, 5-11-5	Miss D. Paget	A. B. Briscoe	T. Leader	13-2
1933	Golden Miller, 6-12-0	Miss D. Paget	A. B. Briscoe	W. Stott	4-7
1934	Golden Miller, 7-12-0	Miss D. Paget	A. B. Briscoe	G. Wilson	6-5
1935	Golden Miller, 8-12-0	Miss D. Paget	A. B. Briscoe	G. Wilson	1-2
1936	Golden Miller, 9-12-0	Miss D. Paget	O. Anthony	E. Williams	21-20
1938	Morse Code, 9-12-0	Lt.-Col. D. Part	I. Anthony	D. Morgan	13-2
1939	Brendan's Cottage, 9-12-0	Mrs A. S-Bingham	G. Beeby	G. Owen	8-1
1940	Roman Hackle, 7-12-0	Miss D. Paget	O. Anthony	E. Williams	Evens
1941	Poet Prince, 9-12-0	D. Sherbrooke	I. Anthony	R. Burford	7-2
1942	Medoc II, 8-12-0	Lord Sefton	R. Hobbs	H. Nicholson	9-2
1945	Red Rower, 11-12-0	Lord Stalbridge	Lord Stalbridge	D. Jones	11-4
1946	Prince Regent, 11-12-0	J. Rank	T. Dreaper	T. Hyde	4-7
1947	Fortina, 6-12-0	Lord Grimthorpe	H. Christie	Mr R. Black	8-1
1948	Cottage Rake, 9-12-0	F. Vickerman	V. O'Brien	A. Brabazon	10-1
1949	Cottage Rake, 10-12-0	F. Vickerman	V. O'Brien	A. Brabazon	4-6
1950	Cottage Rake, 11-12-0	F. Vickerman	V. O'Brien	A. Brabazon	5-6
1951	Silver Fame, 12-12-0	Lord Bicester	G. Beeby	M. Molony	6-4
1952	Mont Tremblant, 6-12-0	Miss D. Paget	F. Walwyn	D. Dick	8-1
1953	Knock Hard, 9-12-0	Mrs. M. Keogh	V. O'Brien	T. Molony	11-2
1954	Four Ten, 8-12-0	A. Strange	J. Roberts	T. Cusack	100-6
1955	Gay Donald, 9-12-0	P. Burt	J. Ford	A. Grantham	33-1
1956	Limber Hill 9-12-0	J. Davey	W. Dutton	J. Power	11-8
1957	Linwell, 9-12-0	D. Brown	C. Mallon	M. Scudamore	100-9
1958	Kerstin, 8-12-0	G. Moore	C. Bewicke	S. Hayhurst	7-1
1959	Roddy Owen, 10-12-0	Lord Fingall	D. Morgan	H. Beasley	5-1
1960	Pas Seul, 7-12-0	J. Rogerson	R. Turnell	W. Rees	6-1
1961	Saffron Tartan, 10-12-0	Col. G. Westmacott	D. Butchers	F. Winter	2-1
1962	Mandarin, 11-12-0	Mme K. Hennessy	F. Walwyn	F. Winter	7-2
1963	Mill House, 6-12-0	W. Gollings	F. Walwyn	W. Robinson	7-2
1964	Arkle, 7-12-0	Duchess of Westminster	T. Dreaper	P. Taaffe	7-4
1965	Arkle, 8-12-0	Duchess of Westminster	T. Dreaper	P. Taaffe	30-100
1966	Arkle, 9-12-0	Duchess of Westminster	T. Dreaper	P. Taaffe	9-100

		Owner	Trainer	Rider	S.P.
1927	Blaris, 6-12-0	Mrs H. Hollins	W. Payne	G. Duller	11–10
1928	Brown Jack, 4-11-0	Maj. H. Wernher	I. Anthony	L. Rees	4–1
1929	Royal Falcon, 6-12-0	Mrs W. Bulkeley	R. Gore	F. Rees	11–2
1930	Brown Tony, 4-11-0	Mrs J. de Selincourt	J. Anthony	T. Cullinan	7–2
1932	Insurance, 5-11-10	Miss D. Paget	A. B. Briscoe	T. Leader	4–5
1933	Insurance, 6-12-0	Miss D. Paget	A. B. Briscoe	W. Stott	10–11
1934	Chenango, 7-12-0	G. Bostwick	I. Anthony	D. Morgan	4–9
1935	Lion Courage, 7-12-0	R. F-Carylon	F. Brown	G. Wilson	100–8
1936	Victor Norman, 5-11-10	Mrs M. Stephens	M. Blair	H. Nicholson	4–1
1937	Free Fare, 9-12-0	B. Warner	E. Gwilt	G. Pellerin	2–1
1938	Our Hope, 9-12-0	R. Gubbins	R. Gubbins	Capt. R. Harding	5–1
1939	African Sister, 7-12-0	H. Brueton	C. Piggott	K. Piggott	10–1
1940	Solford, 9-12-0	Miss D. Paget	O. Anthony	S. Magee	5–2
1941	Seneca, 4-11-0	Sir M. McAlpine	V. Smyth	R. Smyth	7–1
1942	Forestation, 4-11-0	V. Smyth	V. Smyth	R. Smyth	10–1
1945	Brains Trust, 5-11-10	F. Blakeway	G. Wilson	F. Rimell	9–2
1946	Distel, 5-11-10	Miss D. Paget	C. Rogers	R. O'Ryan	4–5
1947	National Spirit, 6-12-0	L. Abelson	V. Smyth	D. Morgan	7–1
1948	National Spirit, 7-12-0	L. Abelson	V. Smyth	R. Smyth	6–4
1949	Hatton's Grace, 9-12-0	Mrs M. Keogh	V. O'Brien	A. Brabazon	100–7
1950	Hatton's Grace, 10-12-0	Mrs M. Keogh	V. O'Brien	A. Brabazon	5–2
1951	Hatton's Grace, 11-12-0	Mrs M. Keogh	V. O'Brien	T. Molony	4–1
1952	Sir Ken, 5-11-12	M. Kingsley	W. Stephenson	T. Molony	3–1
1953	Sir Ken, 6-12-0	M. Kingsley	W. Stephenson	T. Molony	2–5
1954	Sir Ken, 7-12-0	M. Kingsley	W. Stephenson	T. Molony	4–9
1955	Clair Soleil, 6-12-0	G. Judd	R. Price	F. Winter	5–2
1956	Doorknocker, 8-12-0	C. Nicholson	W. Hall	H. Sprague	100–9
1957	Merry Deal, 7-12-0	A. Jones	A. Jones	G. Underwood	28–1
1958	Bandalore, 7-12-0	Mrs D. Wright	J. Wright	G. Slack	20–1
1959	Fare Time, 6-12-0	G. Judd	R. Price	F. Winter	13–2
1960	Another Flash, 6-12-0	J. Byrne	P. Sleator	H. Beasley	11–4
1961	Eborneezer, 6-12-0	Dr B. Pajgar	R. Price	F. Winter	4–1
1962	Anzio, 5-11-12	Sir T. Ainsworth	F. Walwyn	W. Robinson	11–2
1963	Winning Fair, 8-12-0	G. Spencer	G. Spencer	Mr A. Lillingston	100–9
1964	Magic Court, 6-12-0	J. McGhie	T. Robson	P. McCarron	100–6
1965	Kirriemuir, 5-11-12	Mrs D. Beddington	F. Walwyn	G. Robinson	50–1
1966	Salmon Spray, 8-12-0	Mrs J. Rogerson	R. Turnell	J. Haine	4–1

General Index

Index of Horses